PORTSMOUTH
On This Day & Miscellany

PORTSMOUTH
On This Day & Miscellany
Pompey Anecdotes, Legends, Stats & Facts

Roger Holmes

PORTSMOUTH
On This Day & Miscellany

All statistics, facts and figures are correct as of 1st September 2014

© Roger Holmes

Roger Holmes has asserted his rights in accordance with the Copyright, Designs and Patents Act 1988 to be identified as the author of this work.

Published By:
Pitch Publishing (Brighton) Ltd
A2 Yeoman Gate
Yeoman Way
Durrington
BN13 3QZ

Email: info@pitchpublishing.co.uk
Web: www.pitchpublishing.co.uk

First published 2014

A catalogue record for this book is available from the British Library.

10-digit ISBN: 1-9096267-9-1
10-digit ISBN: 978-19096267-9-9

Printed and bound in Great Britain by TJ International

FOREWORD BY ALAN KNIGHT

As an "adoptee" of Portsmouth Football Club at the age of 14, with a subsequent lengthy career as a professional footballer, there are quite a few stories I could relate about our national game in general, and, more specifically, about the elation and despair that overcomes in equal measure those of us defined frequently as the "Pompey faithful". However, my memory bank could never compete with the likes of Roger Holmes, an archetypical member of that special breed of Pompey buffs, whose lifetime fascination with the affairs and fluctuating fortunes of our city's football club is laid bare with the publication of this intriguing collection of diverse anecdotes, mingled with sundry facts and figures. In my current role as club ambassador, I have become increasingly aware of the wide level of interest our citizens continue to show in the destiny of their football club, and their intense commitment to it. I am sure that when flicking through the pages of this singularly Pompey blue book, many items will flag up "I was there" moments among those readers of a certain age. Those from a younger generation may take a leisurely ramble back through this entertaining 116 years of footballing miscellany and conclude that Portsmouth Football Club has always been a sum of its parts - and continues to be so to this day. For those of us who have a passion, whether lifelong or budding, for the star and crescent that defines not only our city, but also our football club, this little volume will be an unfailing bookshelf companion to fill those moments of leisure, and perhaps highlight some hitherto unknown fact. I congratulate Roger on his dedicated compilation, and I am sure that it will give pleasure not only to the faithful, but also to the, as yet, uncommitted. By the way, did you know that there were two A.E. Knights? Now there's a funny thing!

Alan Knight
Ambassador, Portsmouth Football Club

ABOUT THE AUTHOR

Roger Holmes was first taken to Fratton Park by his father and two grandfathers at the age of five in 1965 and has hardly missed a home match since. Isle of Wight born and bred, Roger has previously written three books on Portsmouth Football Club and currently contributes to the Pompey matchday programme while also serving on the committee of the Portsmouth Former Players Association.

ACKNOWLEDGEMENTS

Firstly I would like to thank Pitch Publishing for approaching me with the idea of updating and amalgamating two of my previous books *On This Day* and *Pompey Miscellany*. I also want to thank Alan Knight for writing the foreword to this book and Pat Neil for his constant help and encouragement.

INTRODUCTION

When my doting father and grandfathers – Isle of Wight born all three – ferried me across the Solent on an early autumn Saturday in 1965 to Fratton Park, I was blissfully unaware of the seminal impact this day trip would have on my life. Though having barely mastered the abacus during my first few months in my Sandown Infants' School, I was clearly bewitched by the size of Pompey's 4-1 victory over Carlisle United that day, and by the time I was eight, the magical clicking of the Fratton Park turnstiles had begun to herald yet another intoxicating matchday visit. Even at this tender age I was not only beginning to learn the truth of what it means to be a committed fan, with its mandatory extremes of elation and utter despair, but also, Kiplingesque-like, to treat these two imposters just the same!

Small wonder then that with copies of the *Football Mail* and match programmes permanently within arm's reach in the house, along with a cat called Scoular, I was drawn into a world in which I would harvest any snippet of information concerning the life and times of Portsmouth FC. With a budding career in feverish scrapbook keeping already on stream, and aided and abetted by my elders' winsome recollections from times of yore, my stockpile of information and knowledge in my own wonderland just "growed and growed".

With the arrival of adulthood and the completion of my anorak apprenticeship, the time had come to put my collection to good use, and so my obsessively alphabeticised (naturally!) player index morphed into my first book, *Pompey Players*, published in 2001, followed by *The Pompey Miscellany*, a handbook of club trivia, five years later. However, such was the allure of the material left simmering in my hoard that I coaxed myself into going once again to market to set out my stall in this calendar-driven collation recalling day to day episodes, events and affairs which, throughout the ages have combined to create the romance that is Pompey. I take great comfort in the knowledge that there are others out there similarly afflicted, and I know that they will treat this booklet sympathetically! I hope, in addition, that this bundle of facts, figures and deeds, comings and goings, will inform the devotee, inspire the non-committed, and above all, amuse and entertain all comers.

Roger Holmes

DEDICATION

To my sister Linda –
the bravest person I know
and my inspiration

PORTSMOUTH
On This Day & Miscellany

JANUARY

TUESDAY 1st JANUARY 1974

A second-half goal by Bobby Kellard was enough to earn Pompey victory over Cardiff City in a Second Division clash at Fratton Park – the first time New Year's Day was an official Bank Holiday. The attendance of 20,062 was the highest for a home league match all season. The three-day week meant the programme was a four-page effort costing 2p.

TUESDAY 1st JANUARY 1985

Fulham produced an amazing comeback to draw 4-4 at Fratton Park after Pompey had led 4-0 at half-time. Malcolm Waldron, Alan Biley (2) and Neil Webb were the Pompey goalscorers before the Cottagers hit back with strikes from Dean Coney, Leroy Rosenior and Gary Barnett to make the score 4-3. In the final minute, Noel Blake chopped down Cliff Carr in the box and Kevin Lock buried the penalty kick.

FRIDAY 1st JANUARY 1988

A penalty save by John Lukic denied Pompey victory over Arsenal at a soggy Fratton Park. With three minutes left he dived to his right to save Kevin Dillon's kick. Terry Connor had put Alan Ball's side ahead in the eigthth minute. Niall Quinn equalised for the Gunners in the 80th minute.

THURSDAY 1st JANUARY 2009

French midfielder Lassana Diarra completed a £20m move to Real Madrid. He joined Pompey from Arsenal twelve months earlier for a £5m fee, appearing in the club's FA Cup Final win over Cardiff City and scoring its first goal in a major European competition.

SATURDAY 2nd JANUARY 1954

Charlie Vaughan scored the only hat-trick of his Pompey career and Peter Harris notched his hundredth league goal in a 5-2 victory at home to Huddersfield Town in Division One. Jackie Henderson got the other.

MONDAY 2nd JANUARY 1978

Manager Jimmy Dickinson pleaded with fans before Pompey's Third Division home fixture with Bradford City to stop barracking Paul Gilchrist and the player responded by turning in his best performance in the club shirt. He also made the game safe for the Blues, scoring in the

88th minute after Dave Kemp and Steve Foster had netted for Pompey following Bernie Wright's opener for the Yorkshiremen.

SATURDAY 2ND JANUARY 1999

Pompey pulled off the shock of the FA Cup third round as Steve Claridge's 18th minute strike gave them victory over the Premiership's bottom club Nottingham Forest at the City Ground.

SATURDAY 2ND JANUARY 2010

A mass fans' demonstration was held outside Fratton Park's main entrance after Pompey were held to a 1-1 draw by Coventry City in the third round of the FA Cup. They were furious about the financial situation of their club as debts were mounting up, wages had not been paid on time for three of the last four months, there was a serious threat of administration (the club entered administration eight weeks later) and nobody was quite sure who the club owners were.

SATURDAY 3RD JANUARY 1959

Goalkeeper Norman Uprichard scored the winning goal for Pompey Reserves in their Football Combination fixture against Nottingham Forest at the City Ground. He was injured early in the game and, as this was before the days of substitutes, was replaced by Mike Barnard while he moved to the outside-right position. Meanwhile, at Fratton Park, the two senior sides met in Division One with Forest winning 1-0

MONDAY 3RD JANUARY 2000

Pompey's first match of the millennium ended in a 2-1 defeat against Norwich City at Carrow Road. Veteran Alan Knight solved a goalkeeping injury crisis to make his final appearance, nearly 22 years after his debut.

SATURDAY 3RD JANUARY 2004

Chairman Milan Mandaric witnessed his team win an FA Cup tie for the first time. Pompey had fallen at the first hurdle ever since Mandaric bought the club in 1999 but on this occasion Yakubu scored in the last minute to give Pompey a 2-1 win at Fratton Park over Second Division Blackpool in the third round.

SATURDAY 4th JANUARY 1930

Johnny Weddle grabbed the first hat-trick of his career as Pompey beat Burnley 7-1 in a First Division clash at Fratton Park. This was the first time Pompey had scored more than five goals in the top flight.

SATURDAY 4th JANUARY 1992

Pompey embarked on their best FA Cup run for 43 years – they reached the semi-final – with a 2-1 win over Alan Ball's Exeter City at St James' Park. Guy Whittingham opened the scoring for Pompey, Steve Moran equalised then Warren Aspinall hit a late winner.

SATURDAY 4th JANUARY 2003

Nine thousand Pompey fans travelled to Old Trafford and saw Pompey lose 4-1 to Manchester United in the FA Cup third round. After going 2-0 down to a Ruud van Nistelrooy penalty and David Beckham free-kick, Steve Stone pulled a goal back before half-time. A spirited second-half performance failed to bring an equaliser and United added two late goals – another van Nistelrooy penalty and a last minute strike by Paul Scholes.

SATURDAY 5th JANUARY 1929

Pompey defeated reigning League Champions Everton 3-0 thanks to goals by Jack Smith, Fred Forward and former Toffees' inside-left Bobby Irvine.

SATURDAY 5th JANUARY 1946

Jimmy Scoular made history by becoming the first player to play for two different clubs in the same FA Cup competition. He played in Pompey's 1-0 defeat away to Birmingham City in the third round first leg after he had appeared for Gosport Borough in a preliminary round. The only other player to later play for two different clubs was Stan Crowther who was allowed to represent Manchester United in the 1958 FA Cup Final following the Munich air disaster after he had earlier played for Aston Villa.

SATURDAY 5th JANUARY 1952

Pompey remained top of the First Division after beating Huddersfield Town 3-1 at Fratton Park in front of 30,048 but they had no easy journey against the league's wooden-spoonists. Harry Ferrier (penalty), Duggie Reid and Jackie Henderson were the Pompey goalscorers.

SATURDAY 6TH JANUARY 1951

Reigning First Division champions Pompey suffered an embarrassing defeat in the FA Cup third round – losing 2-0 to Luton Town at Kenilworth Road.

SATURDAY 6TH JANUARY 1962

A Tony Barton goal ten minutes from time earned Pompey a 1-0 victory away to Hull City. The win put them three points clear at the top of Division Three.

WEDNESDAY 6TH JANUARY 1988

"I didn't expect to have to go," said Mick Kennedy, after agreeing to move to Bradford City for £250,000 – the move was completed two days later. It was also announced that Gordon Taylor was to take Pompey to the Professional Footballers Association unless they paid money owed to two current squad members Ian Baird and Ian Stewart as well as former player Gary Stanley.

TUESDAY 6TH JANUARY 2009

Jermain Defoe completed a £16m move to Tottenham Hotspur. The striker, who had joined Pompey from Spurs a year earlier, asked for a transfer on New Year's Eve, blaming manager Tony Adams' preference for playing a 5-4-1 formation for his reason to want to leave.

SATURDAY 7TH JANUARY 1905

Roderick Walker became the first Pompey player to be sent off when he received his marching orders during Pompey's 2-1 defeat by Bristol Rovers in a Southern League Division One meeting at Fratton Park.

SATURDAY 7TH JANUARY 1933

On this morning, Pompey sent a telegram to Salisbury City of the Western League requesting that Jessie Weekes, who had previously been given a trial by the club, keep goal for them in a First Division fixture that afternoon against Sheffield United. Weekes made a hurried dash to Fratton Park and performed heroically as the Blades were beaten 1-0. It culminated in Weekes being signed on professionally with Pompey but he failed to make another first-team appearance.

SATURDAY 7TH JANUARY 1939

Pompey took their first step towards winning the FA Cup with a 4-0 victory at home to Lincoln City in the FA Cup third round.

SATURDAY 7TH JANUARY 1956

Pompey made history by playing a third round FA Cup-tie under floodlights. The match, against Grimsby Town, ended 3-1 in Pompey's favour and it was also the last game in which Len Phillips appeared for the Blues. Four other ties were played under lights that day – the first time the FA had permitted artificial lights at that stage of the competition. A few weeks later, Pompey were the first club to stage a league match under floodlights when Newcastle United came to Fratton Park and won 2-0.

SATURDAY 8TH JANUARY 1949

Pompey cruised into the FA Cup fourth round by beating Stockport County 7-0 at Fratton Park in front of 33,590. Peter Harris notched a hat-trick while Len Phillips and Ike Clarke scored two apiece. This is Pompey's biggest FA Cup victory bar their their first match in the competition when Ryde were beaten 10-0 in a qualifying round in 1899.

SATURDAY 8TH JANUARY 2005

Yakubu converted Patrik Berger's cross shortly after half-time to score the only goal as Pompey beat Gillingham 1-0 to go through to the FA Cup fourth round at Fratton Park before a crowd of 14,252.

SATURDAY 8TH JANUARY 2010

Pompey, the previous season's losing FA Cup finalists, were dumped out of the FA Cup by Brighton & Hove Albion at the first hurdle. The Seagulls inflicted a 3-1 defeat on the Blues who had Dave Kitson sent off and seven other players booked.

TUESDAY 9TH JANUARY 1980

A linesman's flag ruled out a last-minute goal by Jeff Hemmerman just as it looked like Fourth Division Pompey had beaten Middlesbrough from Division One before a crowd of 31,743 at Fratton Park. Terry Cochrane put Boro' ahead and Terry Brisley snapped up the equaliser. With four minutes left Jim Platt just managed to turn away a shot by David Gregory and then with only seconds remaining, Hemmerman turned in Alan Rogers' low cross – only for the linesman to silence the ecstatic Fratton crowd.

FRIDAY 9TH JANUARY 2004

Eyal Berkovic became the highest paid player in Pompey history when he left Manchester City to sign a two-and-a-half year contract on wages of £25,000 a week.

SATURDAY 10TH JANUARY 1976

A home win at last! Pompey defeated Carlisle United to earn their first home league victory of the season. A fan had promised to buy a leather coat for the scorer of the first goal in a home win as an incentive, so the coat went to Billy Eames who netted the only goal of the match.

SATURDAY 10TH JANUARY 1987

Mick Quinn scored both goals to give Pompey a 2-0 victory over Blackburn Rovers in the FA Cup third round. It was Pompey's 15th home win in a row.

SATURDAY 10TH JANUARY 1998

Pompey's biggest crowd of the season left the ground chanting for manager Terry Fenwick's head after seeing their team crash 3-0 to fellow strugglers Manchester City and leave them rooted at the bottom of the First Division. They also turned on their chairman with chants of, "Bye Bye Venables."

SATURDAY 10TH JANUARY 2004

Eyal Berkovic made his Pompey debut against Manchester City, 24 hours after leaving the City of Manchester Stadium. Yakubu scored twice in a 4-2 Pompey win and City goalkeeper David Seaman played his last senior match. He left the field early with a shoulder injury and announced his retirement two days later.

SATURDAY 11TH JANUARY 1964

After six matches without a win, Pompey demoralized a struggling Cardiff City at Fratton Park by sweeping to a 5-0 victory. Ron Saunders broke the deadlock with an early penalty then he, Albert McCann, John McClelland and Micky Lill added goals in the second half.

SATURDAY 11TH JANUARY 1975

A superb second-half display swept Pompey to their most sensational victory of the season against Sunderland at Fratton Park in front of 14,133. Sunderland had arrived as everybody's bet for promotion and had lived up to the tag in the first half when Pop Robson's goal was poor reward for their total control. But within five minutes of the resumption Ray Hiron equalised and Pompey added three more goals through Paul Went, Norman Piper and George Graham. Sunderland pulled a goal back through Vic Halom in the closing stages.

SATURDAY 11TH JANUARY 1986

Manager Alan Ball lashed his players – and the fans – after watching his side manage to draw 1-1 at home to Fulham. He said, "We were awful. That's the worst performance by a team I've sent out in my eighteen months here." Then Ball turned on the crowd. "They disappointed me almost more than my team. This crowd demands too much. If you're not two or three up after 15 or 20 minutes they're not satisfied."

SATURDAY 12TH JANUARY 1907

The FA Cup first round tie between Pompey and Manchester United attracted a crowd of 24,329 to Fratton Park, and the gate receipts of £1,101.10 shillings was the first to reach four figures. The match ended in a 2-2 draw and Pompey won the replay 2-1.

SATURDAY 12TH JANUARY 1974

Play was held up for 20 minutes because of floodlight failure during a goalless draw at home to Luton Town. Because of a power crisis, the club hired a generator but it broke down midway through the second half and the players left the field. The match was able to finish as Pompey chairman John Deacon gave the order to switch to the mains. Although this was technically a breach of the emergency lighting regulations, Mr Deacon emphasised that he ordered the "switch-over" in the interests of safety.

SATURDAY 12TH JANUARY 2008

Harry Redknapp pledged his future to Pompey after rejecting the chance to take over at Newcastle United. The Pompey boss said, "This is my club. It would be too big a wrench to leave here. This is where I belong."

SATURDAY 13TH JANUARY 1962

Third Division leaders Pompey played some of their best attacking football of the season at home to Queens Park Rangers but they were helped to a 4-1 victory by two penalties that were both converted by Allan Brown.

SATURDAY 13TH JANUARY 1973

An injury time goal by Bristol City's Bobby Gould robbed Pompey of victory in the FA Cup third round at Fratton Park after Norman Piper's free-kick had given Ron Tindall's men a 1-0 lead.

SATURDAY 13TH JANUARY 1996

Alan Knight made his 601st league appearance for Pompey in a 3-1 victory at home to Grimsby Town. This meant that Knight surpassed a goalkeeper's record appearance for one club, previously held by Chelsea's Peter Bonetti. Paul Walsh, Paul Wood and Jimmy Carter gave the Blues a 3-0 lead but Paul Groves denied Knight a clean sheet on his big day.

SATURDAY 13TH JANUARY 1998

Terry Fenwick lost his job as Pompey manager just 24 hours after Terry Venables announced he was leaving. Assistant manager Keith Waldon was put in charge. American tycoon Vince Wolanin promised to plough £90m into a new stadium if he was allowed to buy the club.

SATURDAY 14TH JANUARY 1950

Pompey came from behind to beat Everton at Goodison Park before a crowd of 50,421. The goalscorers were Len Phillips and Peter Harris. A missile was thrown at the referee by a home supporter during the game.

SATURDAY 14TH JANUARY 1989

Pompey were defeated 2-1 by Leicester City at Filbert Street in the last match under Alan Ball before he was sacked by Jim Gregory. The Blues were top of the Second Division on 26 November but by the end of their clash with Leicester they had dropped to thirteenth.

MONDAY 14TH JANUARY 2008

A plan by Portsmouth Football Club to build a 55-acre training ground at Titchfield that was to include eleven football pitches was rejected by Fareham Borough Planning Committee.

SATURDAY 15TH JANUARY 1927

Billy Haines scored twice to earn Pompey a 2-0 win away to Southampton and keep his side on track for promotion from Division Two.

SATURDAY 15TH JANUARY 1955

The First Division clash at Fratton Park between Pompey and Aston Villa was abandoned because of fog, sparking a storm of protests from the visiting team. Villa were leading 2-1 with only eleven minutes remaining when referee Mr. Pullen from Bristol had no alternative but to end the match.

SATURDAY 15TH JANUARY 2000

Wolverhampton Wanderers fought back from two goals down to win 3-2 at Fratton Park in Tony Pulis' first game as Pompey boss. The home team, without a win in thirteen matches, took the lead in the 19th minute through Sammy Igoe and Steve Claridge volleyed home minutes later. But the new manager's decision to substitute Mike Panopoulos, Pompey's most dangerous player, simply handed Wolves the initiative and they hit back with goals by Steve Sedgeley, Michael Branch and Ade Akinbiyi.

SATURDAY 16TH JANUARY 1937

Tottenham Hotspur pulled off one of the all-time shock FA Cup results by beating Pompey 5-0 at Fratton Park. Pompey were a mid-table First Division side at the time whilst Spurs were lying halfway in Division Two.

SATURDAY 16TH JANUARY 1965

Jimmy Dickinson made his 750th appearance for Pompey in a 2-2 draw with Southampton at The Dell. The Pompey captain was applauded onto the field by both teams as the band played, "For He's a Jolly Good Fellow."

SATURDAY 16TH JANUARY 1971

The fact that vouchers for the following week's FA Cup tie with Arsenal were being handed out at the turnstiles meant that the season's largest home crowd for a League game – 24,747 – was at Fratton Park to watch Pompey take on Cardiff City. The Welshmen cruised to a comfortable 3-1 victory as Pompey slipped to eighteenth place in Division Two.

MONDAY 16th JANUARY 2012

One of the Pompey supporters' most popular players of recent times, Hermann Hreidarsson, ended a four-and-a-half-year stay at Fratton Park by joining Coventry City. Hreidarsson scored eight goals in 123 appearances for the Blues and was a member of the Pompey team that won the FA Cup in 2008.

SATURDAY 17th JANUARY 1970

Pompey, with the worst goals-against total in the Second Division, clashed with Aston Villa, the side with the poorest scoring record, in a relegation battle at Villa Park. The Fratton men came out tops of an eight-goal thriller by beating the hosts 5-3 before a crowd of 21,148. It was the first time Pompey had scored five goals away from home for eight years.

TUESDAY 17th JANUARY 1989

Alan Ball was sacked as Pompey manager and replaced by John Gregory. Ball had been in charge since the summer of 1984 but Gregory's reign was to only last twelve months.

MONDAY 17th JANUARY 2005

Harry Redknapp signed Portsmouth midfielder Nigel Quashie for Southampton for a fee of £2.1m. Quashie was one of Pompey's longest-serving players, having joined the club during the summer of 2000.

THURSDAY 17th JANUARY 2008

Arsenal midfielder Lassana Diarra signed for Pompey from Arsenal for £5m. He spent a year at Fratton Park, appearing in the club's FA Cup Final win over Cardiff City and scoring Pompey's first goal in a major European competition before moving to Real Madrid for a club record £20m. On the same day Fratton favourite Matt Taylor left for Bolton Wanderers in a £3.5m deal.

SATURDAY 18th JANUARY 1908

Pompey's Southern League Division One match with Northampton Town was the first at Fratton Park to be halted by the weather. Pompey were leading 1-0 when the game was abandoned due to fog.

WEDNESDAY 18th JANUARY 1967

Pompey broke their record transfer fee by paying £25,000 for Plymouth Argyle outside-left Nick Jennings. He gave the club grand service, playing 236 games and scoring 50 goals in all competitions.

SATURDAY 18th JANUARY 1992

A last minute goal by substitute Guy Whittingham preserved Pompey's unbeaten home record. His strike against First Division leaders Blackburn Rovers earned his side a 2-2 draw.

SATURDAY 18th JANUARY 1997

It was lucky thirteen for Pompey for they beat Crystal Palace at Selhurst Park after failing in twelve attempts over a period of 31 years. They looked to be heading for another defeat when Robert Quinn put the Eagles ahead on the half-hour mark but Lee Bradbury equalised and Andy Thomson struck the winner.

SUNDAY 18th JANUARY 2009

Pompey drew 1-1 with Tottenham Hotspur at White Hart Lane as they came up against Harry Redknapp for the first time since he resigned from his second spell as manager. David Nugent scored his first Premier League goal for Pompey and former Blues' striker Jermain Defoe netted for Spurs – his first since he returned to north London.

SATURDAY 19th JANUARY 1952

A 1-1 draw away to Wolverhampton Wanderers kept Pompey top of the First Division, two points ahead of Manchester United.

SATURDAY 19th JANUARY 1957

Pompey scrambled their first league victory since 20 October with a goal by Syd McClellan four minutes from time. During the morning two Pompey players, Reg Pickett and Jackie Robertson, asked for transfers.

SATURDAY 19th JANUARY 1974

Middlesbrough fully justified their position of runaway Second Division leaders by comfortably beating Pompey 3-0 in front of 21,774 at Ayresome Park. Pompey managed to keep the scores level at half-time but Alan Foggon, Malcolm Smith and Graeme Souness all scored for Boro' after the break.

SATURDAY 19TH JANUARY 1991

Leading 2-1 away to Port Vale with five minutes to go, Pompey ended up beaten 3-2. Guy Whittingham scored twice for Pompey in the first half but after Vale equalised, Darren Beckford headed the winner.

SATURDAY 20TH JANUARY 1934

Stanley Matthews netted for Stoke City on his first appearance against Pompey which ended in a 3-1 defeat for his side. It was also the last goal he would score against Pompey in his career that was to last another 30 years.

SATURDAY 20TH JANUARY 1951

Jack Froggatt, capped twice by England at outside-left, played at centre-half for the first time in a 2-1 win at Stoke City. So successful in his new role, he remained in the centre of Pompey's half-back line for more than two years and was selected nine times for his country in the position. Froggatt eventually returned to the wing and was capped twice more.

SATURDAY 20TH JANUARY 1990

Hundreds of Pompey fans voted with their feet by boycotting the Fratton End for the home game against Bradford City which ended in a 3-0 victory. Supporters were protesting over the club's silence over the future of plans to rebuild a stand.

SATURDAY 21ST JANUARY 1928

Jack Smith scored twice on his debut to give Pompey a 2-1 win at home to West Ham United. The match came a week after the Hammers recorded a 2-0 victory at Fratton in the FA Cup third round.

SATURDAY 21ST JANUARY 1956

With a fine second-half display of attacking football, Pompey beat Arsenal 5-2 at Fratton Park. Eighteen year-old Portsmouth-born Johnny Phillips was making his home debut at right-half.

SATURDAY 21ST JANUARY 1967

Nick Jennings helped Pompey to a 3-2 win with a debut goal against Rotherham United at Fratton Park before 15,253. The £25,000 record signing converted Roy Pack's cross in the 51st minute to give Pompey a 2-1 lead. Ray Hiron was the scorer of Pompey's other two goals.

SATURDAY 21st JANUARY 1989

John Gregory's managerial reign got off to a winning start as Pompey beat Shrewsbury 2-0 at Fratton Park in front of 8,446. The goals came from Warren Aspinall (penalty) and Graeme Hogg. Making his league debut in Pompey defence was 17-year-old Kit Symons.

SATURDAY 22nd JANUARY 1927

Billy Haines scored a hat-trick as Pompey came from behind to hammer Oldham Athletic 7-2 before 15,725 at Fratton Park. The win kept Pompey second in Division Two.

SATURDAY 22nd JANUARY 1949

Pompey went three points clear at the top of Division One after Ike Clarke's strike midway through the first half secured a 1-0 victory for Pompey against Charlton Athletic at The Valley. Meanwhile at Fratton Park, Duggie Reid helped himself to five goals in Pompey Reserves' 6-0 thrashing of West Ham.

WEDNESDAY 22nd JANUARY 1969

George Smith set two records when he was transferred from Pompey to Middlesbrough in January 1969. The fee of £50,000 was the highest Boro' had paid and was also the highest Pompey had received.

SATURDAY 22nd JANUARY 2011

Pompey and Leeds United drew 2-2 at Fratton Park in a Championship encounter that was blighted by power cuts. After 52 minutes, and with the score at 1-1, some of the lighting and floodlights stopped working plunging parts of the ground into darkness while away fans chanted, "You forgot to pay the bills." It turned out to be a power cut in the city rather than anything to do with settling bills. Both sides scored again before there was more light failure and referee Anthony Taylor took the players off the field for seven minutes. The match was restarted but another power cut caused a second delay before the match reached its conclusion.

SATURDAY 23rd JANUARY 1971

Mike Trebilcock grabbed a last-minute equaliser to earn Pompey a 1-1 draw against Arsenal in the FA Cup fourth round at Fratton Park before a crowd of 39,659. Peter Storey had given the Gunners a first-half lead from the penalty spot.

SATURDAY 23rd JANUARY 1999

Leeds United took revenge for their shock FA Cup defeat by Pompey at Elland Road in 1997 by outclassing and thrashing the Blues at Fratton Park in the fourth round. Luke Nightingale gave the home side an early lead but the Premiership side ended up 5-1 winners.

SATURDAY 24th JANUARY 1925

Harry and Arthur Foxall became the first brothers to play together for Pompey in a Football League match when they both featured in the side that lost 5-0 away to Hull City. Harry, first-choice centre-half throughout his four years with the club, was joined by Arthur for just that one game.

SATURDAY 24th JANUARY 1980

Pompey let slip a two-goal lead to share a 3-3 draw at home to struggling Blackpool in Division Three. Jeff Hemmerman and Billy Rafferty had put Pompey 2-0 up by half-time, but it was up to Mick Tait to grab a late equaliser after Blackpool's revival brought them three quick goals.

SATURDAY 24th JANUARY 1987

Pompey created a club record by winning at home for the 12th successive time. An early penalty by Kevin Dillon took them a step closer to the First Division as it decided a disappointing derby match with Brighton at Fratton Park watched by 12,992. Dillon had the chance to score again from the spot but he lifted his shot over the bar.

TUESDAY 24th JANUARY 1989

The News reported that Chairman Jim Gregory was keen to build a luxurious space-age stadium on the Fratton Goods Yard. But there were many obstacles to be overcome before his dream could become reality, not least he had to acquire ownership of the 40-acre site. However, Mr Gregory hoped that the land would be bought in mid-1990 and the new stadium would be erected eighteen months later.

SATURDAY 24TH JANUARY 2009

Pompey's bid to retain the FA Cup came to an embarrassing end as they crashed out to Championship club Swansea City at Fratton Park. The Swans won 2-0, and both goals – a fine finish by loanee Nathan Dyer and a Jason Scotland penalty – came during the first half.

SATURDAY 25TH JANUARY 1958

Pompey and Wolverhampton Wanderers met in the FA Cup at Molineux for the first time since the 1939 final but there was to be no win for Pompey this time. They were 2-1 down to the First Division leaders at half-time following a first half full of thrills that included a penalty save by Norman Uprichard but totally went to pieces after the interval and were soundly beaten 5-1.

SATURDAY 25TH JANUARY 1969

Pompey met disaster, losing 4-0 to Blackburn Rovers in the FA Cup fourth round at Ewood Park. Their defensive plan fell to pieces and they were reduced to ten men when Ray Pointer was carried off on a stretcher.

SATURDAY 25TH JANUARY 1992

Darren Anderton, being watched by a large contingent of top scouts, scored two brilliant goals as Pompey defeated Orient 2-0 in the FA Cup fourth round.

SATURDAY 25TH JANUARY 1997

Pompey went through to the FA Cup fifth round after beating Reading 3-0 at Fratton Park. The introduction of substitute Mathias Svensson midway through the second-half with the score at 0-0 turned the match on its head for goals by Paul Hall, Lee Bradbury and David Hillier followed.

FRIDAY 25TH JANUARY 2011

Pompey manager Steve Cotterill announced that he would slap a £1,000 a word fine on any player leaking club information on Twitter or Facebook.

SATURDAY 26TH JANUARY 1991

Guy Whittingham blasted Harry Redknapp's Bournemouth out of the FA Cup with a sensational burst of four second-half goals in under half-an-hour in front of 15,800 at Fratton Park. Colin Clarke had given the Blues a 1-0 lead at the break.

TUESDAY 26TH JANUARY 1994

Record signing Gerry Creaney, who cost £600,000 from Celtic, made his debut in Pompey's League Cup replay with Manchester United which the visitors won 1-0.

MONDAY 26TH JANUARY 1998

Alan Ball was appointed Pompey boss for the second time. He took over a team bottom of the First Division but was able to steer them to safety.

SUNDAY 27TH JANUARY 1901

A violent storm ripped off the roof of the South Stand at Fratton Park. The cost of the damage totalled £120.

SATURDAY 27TH JANUARY 1923

Alf Strange scored five goals as Pompey thrashed Gillingham 6-1 in a Division Three (South) encounter at Fratton Park. Peter Harris (in 1958) is the only other player to hit five goals in one match for Pompey.

SUNDAY 27TH JANUARY 1974

Sunday football came to Fratton Park for the first time and a crowd of 32,838 saw Pompey and Orient draw 0-0 in the FA Cup fourth round.

TUESDAY 27TH JANUARY 1976

A crowd of 31,722 saw Pompey beaten 3-0 by Charlton Athletic at Fratton Park in an FA Cup fourth round replay. Pompey were terrible in the first half and far worse in the second during which the Londoners scored all their three goals. Manager Ian St John was at a loss to explain his team's performance. "My youth team could have beaten us," he said.

TUESDAY 27TH JANUARY 1998

Pompey's takeover negotiations were on the brink of collapse. Chairman Martin Gregory, who wanted to retain 51% share revealed that millionaire Vince Wolanin's deal to buy the club was as close as Pompey were to getting promotion. Pompey at the time were bottom of Division One.

SATURDAY 27TH JANUARY 2005

Velimir Zajec made Panathinaikos goalkeeper Konstantinos Chalkias his first signing for £100,000. The 30-year-old agreed a deal that would keep him at Fratton Park until 2008 but he agreed a pay-off that cost Pompey £300,000 in January 2007 after making just six first-team appearances.

SATURDAY 27TH JANUARY 2007

Wayne Rooney scored twice to end Pompey's brave resistance and send Manchester United in to the FA Cup fifth round at Old Trafford before 71,137. Pompey's goal in the 2-1 defeat came when Pedro Mendes' shot was deflected into the net by Kanu.

WEDNESDAY 28TH JANUARY 1931

Jimmy Allen made his debut in Pompey's 2-1 defeat by Birmingham City at St Andrews in Division One. Allen, who won two England caps, was one of the best centre-halves to represent the club but on this occasion he occupied the right-half berth in place of the injured Jimmy Nichol.

SATURDAY 28TH JANUARY 1950

Pompey eased into the FA Cup fifth round with a 5-0 home win over Second Division Grimsby Town before a crowd of 39,364. Jack Froggatt and Ike Clarke scored twice before Len Phillips grabbed the fifth.

SATURDAY 28TH JANUARY 1961

Brian Clough scored a hat-trick as Middlesbrough beat Pompey 3-0 in front of 7,272 at Fratton Park. The attendance was then the lowest for a post-war home league match.

SATURDAY 28TH JANUARY 1995

Aaron Flahavan appeared as Pompey's first substitute goalkeeper. Alan Knight was sent off for carrying the ball outside his penalty area in the FA Cup fourth round tie with Leicester City and Flahavan took to the field for his first taste of first-team action. Pompey lost the game 1-0.

TUESDAY 29TH JANUARY 1974

An argument over where the second replay of this FA Cup fourth round tie should be played lasted two hours after Pompey and Orient fought out a 1-1 draw at Brisbane Road. Orient plumped for Selhurst Park, Pompey wanted Brighton, so in the end a coin was tossed and the Os won the day. The argument should not have been necessary, for Pompey had enough chances to have won the tie. They had a dream start when Mick Mellows dived to head his first Pompey goal in the first two minutes. Orient's equaliser came from Barrie Fairbrother on 29 minutes and Pompey's Ron Davies had a goal ruled out for offside in extra time.

SATURDAY 29TH JANUARY 2000

Steve Claridge scored a hat-trick as Pompey beat high-flying Barnsley 3-0 at Fratton Park before a crowd of 12,201. In the closing stages of the game Pompey sent on Gary O'Neil who, at 16 years 256 days, became the youngest player to represent Pompey in a competitive fixture.

SATURDAY 30TH JANUARY 1954

Pompey's visit to the Old Showground for an FA Cup fourth round tie against Scunthorpe United set a ground record of 23,935. The attendance was never topped before Scunthorpe moved to Glanfield Park in 1988. The match ended in a 1-1 draw.

SATURDAY 30TH JANUARY 1960

A crowd of 7,501 saw Pompey Juniors go down 2-1 to Chelsea Juniors at Fratton Park. The Chelsea team included several future stars such as Peter Bonetti, Ron Harris, Terry Venables and Bobby Tambling.

SATURDAY 30TH JANUARY 1971

Ray Hiron earned Pompey their first win on the road for ten months when he slammed home the only goal of the Second Division clash with Hull City at Boothferry Park.

WEDNESDAY 30TH JANUARY 2008

Pompey goalkeeper David James made his 500th Premier League appearance away to Manchester United. Cristiano Ronaldo scored both goals for United in a 2-0 win that took them back to the top of the table. The Old Trafford crowd of 75,415 was the biggest to attend a league match in which Pompey were involved.

SATURDAY 31st JANUARY 1948

Two goals by Duggie Reid and another by Guy Wharton gave Pompey an emphatic 3-0 win against reigning champions Liverpool at Anfield.

SATURDAY 31st JANUARY 1970

Ray Hiron grabbed a second-half hat-trick as Pompey stormed to their biggest win of the season, 5-1 over Charlton Athletic at Fratton Park. The score was 2-1 at half-time, with Jim Storrie on target and Albert McCann netting a penalty. It was the third straight win for George Smith's side.

SATURDAY 31st JANUARY 1998

Linesman Edward Martin was knocked unconscious by a Sheffield United fan after Blades goalkeeper Simon Tracey was sent off at Fratton Park. Pompey drew the match 1-1 and stayed bottom of Division One, five points ahead of safety.

TUESDAY 31st JANUARY 2012

Pompey's fight for survival was handed a huge boost – by Prime Minister David Cameron. During Prime Minister's Question Time Portsmouth North MP Penny Mordaunt urged the PM to ask HMRC to meet club officials over its winding-up petition for unpaid tax. Mr Cameron replied that he would do all he could to keep the club in business.

PORTSMOUTH
On This Day & Miscellany

FEBRUARY

MONDAY 1st FEBRUARY 1971

Pompey produced a magnificent performance against Arsenal in the FA Cup fourth round at Highbury but were beaten 3-2. Norman Piper put Pompey ahead before Charlie George and Peter Simpson scored to give the Gunners a half-time lead. George Ley equalised for Pompey but Peter Storey settled the tie with a late penalty.

SATURDAY 1st FEBRUARY 1975

George Graham and Ken Foggo were on target as Pompey defeated Oxford United 2-1 at Fratton Park to maintain their 100% home record over the club from the Manor Ground.

WEDNESDAY 1st FEBRUARY 1995

Former Tottenham Hotspur and England defender Terry Fenwick was appointed Pompey boss just hours after Jim Smith had been sacked. Jimmy Allen, the last surviving member of Pompey's 1934 FA Cup Final team, died aged 85.

MONDAY 1st FEBRUARY 1999

After four hours of talks in London, Pompey directors and the Co-operative Bank backed a survival plan that would put Portsmouth Football Club into administration while being bankrolled by the Co-op for the rest of the season.

WEDNESDAY 1st FEBRUARY 2012

Prime Minister David Cameron backed calls for Her Majesty's Revenue and Customs to meet with Portsmouth Football Club to recoup taxes owed. Pompey had failed to pay wages to players and staff the previous month and the club had bank accounts frozen after the issuing of a winding-up petition on 3 January. Penny Mordaunt, MP for Portsmouth North, raised the issue at Prime Minister's Question Time in the House of Commons.

SATURDAY 2nd FEBRUARY 1991

Steve Wigley eased the pressure on relegation-haunted Pompey with a stunning goal that proved to be the winner against Notts County at Fratton Park. His angled shot following a run from the halfway line made the score 2-0 after Martin Kuhl had scored from the penalty spot for Pompey. Tommy Johnson later pulled a goal back for County.

SATURDAY 2ND FEBRUARY 2002

Robert Prosinecki scored a hat-trick in a 4-4 draw between Pompey and Barnsley at Fratton Park watched by 12,756. Pompey were cruising to victory when referee Philip Prosser bemused everybody in the ground by sending off Primus for a supposed elbow on Mike Sheron with seven minutes left. A penalty was awarded which Chris Lumsdon slammed into the roof of the net and Sheron headed the equaliser in injury time.

SATURDAY 2ND FEBRUARY 2008

Jermain Defoe scored on his Pompey debut to earn his new side a 1-1 draw with Chelsea at Fratton Park. This was the only point Pompey managed to take off the Londoners during their seven-year spell in the Premier League.

SATURDAY 3RD FEBRUARY 1951

Belgian outside-left Marcel Gaillard impressed as Pompey chalked up a ninth successive victory over Everton at Fratton Park before a crowd of 26,271. Pompey beat the Merseyside club in 13 consecutive home and away games between 1947 and 1956!

SUNDAY 3RD FEBRUARY 1974

Pompey's Bobby Kellard was the first player ever to be sent off on a Sunday in a professional match in England. He was ordered off during the 1-1 draw between Pompey and West Bromwich Albion at Fratton Park and Albion's David Shaw also received his marching orders later in the game.

WEDNESDAY 3RD FEBRUARY 2010

Pompey manager Avram Grant bemoaned the financial problems that had resulted in what he described as "the most tiring period of my life." He claimed that he was promised the finances to bring in new players but instead had to sell Asmir Begovic and Younes Kaboul.

SATURDAY 4TH FEBRUARY 1950

In connection with the selling of tickets for the forthcoming Manchester United v Pompey FA Cup-tie at Old Trafford, Portsmouth Police issued instructions that no queueing was to be allowed in the vicinity of Fratton Park before 8am.

SATURDAY 4TH FEBRUARY 1967

Former Burnley and England centre-forward Ray Pointer made his Pompey debut in a 1-1 draw with Millwall at The Den. Albert McCann was the Pompey goalscorer.

SATURDAY 4TH FEBRUARY 1995

Battling Pompey gave Terry Fenwick a winning start to his managerial career. Goals by Preki and Gerry Creaney set up a 2-0 victory over Stoke City at The Victoria Ground.

SATURDAY 4TH FEBRUARY 2000

Steve Claridge's 26th-minute goal gave Pompey a 1-0 win over Ipswich Town at Portman Road in Division One. The victory ended a run of three straight defeats.

SATURDAY 4TH FEBRUARY 2006

Alan Shearer broke Newcastle United's all-time goalscoring record in a Premiership fixture against Pompey at St James' Park. He scored the Magpies' second goal in the 64th minute of their 2-0 win.

THURSDAY 4TH FEBRUARY 2010

Hong Kong businessman Balram Chainrai became the new owner of Portsmouth Football Club after seizing Ali Al-Faraj's 90% stake. The deal meant Chainrai became the club's fourth owner in ten months. The 51-year-old was Al Faraj's saviour when he settled Pompey's overdue wage bill soon after he bought the club from Sulaiman Al Fahim in October.

MONDAY 5TH FEBRUARY 1962

Pompey thrashed Newport County 5-0 in a Third Division top versus bottom clash at Somerton Park. Ron Saunders (2), Tony Barton, Johnny Gordon and Dave Dodson were the Pompey goalscorers and 'keeper Dick Beattie saved a penalty from Newport's Andy Bowman.

SATURDAY 5TH FEBRUARY 1965

A crowd of 25,860 saw Pompey lose 5-2 to Southampton at Fratton Park in a Second Division encounter in which Saints' centre-forward

Norman Dean scored a hat-trick. A plank in the South Stand began to smoulder during the match but it was put out with a bucket of water before the Fire Brigade arrived.

TUESDAY 5TH FEBRUARY 1974

Chairman John Deacon stood and led the singing of the Pompey Chimes from the Selhurst Park Directors' Box as Pompey beat Orient 2-0 in the second replay of the FA Cup fourth round. They took the lead with a 20-yard shot by Bobby Kellard and Ron Davies clinched the tie four minutes from time when he beat two defenders and drove a low shot past John Jackson.

SATURDAY 6TH FEBRUARY 1971

It was a case of After the Lord Mayor's Show for after their two epic FA Cup battles with Arsenal, Pompey slumped to a disappointing 4-1 defeat against Carlisle at Fratton Park. Ray Hiron netted for the Blues to keep up his 100% home scoring record against the Cumbrians.

SATURDAY 6TH FEBRUARY 1988

Pompey recorded a 2-1 victory at home to Derby County, through goals by Vince Hilaire and Mick Quinn, as they fought to pull away from the First Division relegation zone. It was Pompey's eighth unbeaten game while it was the Rams' ninth successive defeat.

SATURDAY 6TH FEBRUARY 1993

Chris Price was sent off for a professional foul seven minutes from time on his home debut against Bristol City. The score was 2-2 at the time of his red card but Mark Gavin's shot from the free-kick brought the winning goal for the visitors.

WEDNESDAY 6TH FEBRUARY 2008

Pompey's David James was the England goalkeeper in Fabio Capello's first match in charge of the national side. England beat Switzerland 2-1 in a friendly at Wembley, the goals coming from Jermaine Jenas and Shaun Wright-Phillips.

SATURDAY 7TH FEBRUARY 1948

A rare late headed goal by Jimmy Dickinson earned Pompey victory over Second Division leaders Birmingham City in a friendly at Fratton Park before a crowd of 16,500.

SATURDAY 7TH FEBRUARY 1976

Bolton Wanderers went to the top of the Second Division and Pompey remained rooted at the bottom after Paul Went's own goal gave the visitors a narrow victory at Fratton Park watched by 8,958. The goal came after 42 minutes when John Ritson's shot appeared to be going wide of the far post until it hit Went and was deflected past Grahame Lloyd.

SATURDAY 7TH FEBRUARY 2004

A goal by Gus Poyet 78 seconds from time gave Tottenham Hotspur a 4-3 win over Pompey in a thrilling match at White Hart Lane in front of 36,107. Jermain Defoe marked his Spurs debut by netting on 13 minutes and it was a first for the club for each of Pompey's goalscorers, Eyal Berkovic, Lomana LuaLua and Ivica Mornar.

WEDNESDAY 8TH FEBRUARY 1961

Freddie Cox was sacked as Pompey manager after two and a half years in the job. The club slipped from the First Division at the end of his first season in charge and at the time of his sacking it was near certain they would be relegated to Division Three. Much criticised by Pompey supporters, Cox made three excellent signings in Ron Saunders, Harry Harris and Brian Snowdon.

SATURDAY 8TH FEBRUARY 1997

Pompey romped to their fifth consecutive victory by beating Birmingham City at St Andrews. Mathias Svensson, Lee Bradbury and Alan McLoughlin were on target for Terry Fenwick's side.

SATURDAY 8TH FEBRUARY 2003

Pompey, on their charge towards the Premiership, produced their best attacking performance for eleven years to demolish Derby County 6-2 in front of 19,503 at Fratton Park. The goalscorers were Svetoslav Todorov (2), Yakubu (2), Paul Merson and Matt Taylor.

SATURDAY 9TH FEBRUARY 1974

Malcolm Manley was carried off with a knee injury that effectively finished his career during Pompey's 4-0 defeat away to Notts County. The defender who had cost £45,000 in December, returned for one match a year later but had to admit defeat in his quest for full fitness.

THURSDAY 9TH FEBRUARY 1984

Pompey made the first concrete steps in their move to lure Kevin Keegan to Fratton Park. Chairman John Deacon posted an official request to Newcastle United asking to speak to the former England skipper who had helped the Magpies win 4-1 at Fratton Park the previous Saturday.

MONDAY 9TH FEBRUARY 2009

Tony Adams was sacked as Pompey manager. He had taken over as boss in October following the resignation of Harry Redknapp but the team had collected only ten points from the sixteen matches played under his command. Paul Hart was put in temporary charge of team affairs.

TUESDAY 9TH FEBRUARY 2010

Pompey manager Avram Grant was sent to the stand after walking onto the Fratton Park pitch at half-time to remonstrate with referee Kevin Friend. The official had awarded Sunderland a penalty which was duly converted while several penalty claims at the other end were waved aside. Darren Bent's spot kick looked to have settled the match until Aruna Dindane headed an equaliser six minutes into stoppage time.

SATURDAY 10TH FEBRUARY 1962

Two goals in four first-half minutes by Ron Saunders and Tony Barton helped Pompey to a 2-1 victory at home to Crystal Palace in Division Three. The Blues were now six points clear of second-placed Bristol City with two games in hand.

SATURDAY 10TH FEBRUARY 1973

Bobby Kellard, who had recently returned for a second spell at Fratton Park, starred in midfield as Pompey stormed to their biggest away victory for eleven years by beating Preston North End 5-0 at Deepdale. Kellard scored Pompey's second goal from 30 yards and Preston boss Alan Ball senior, who was sacked two days later, described it as, "fit to grace a World Cup Final."

SATURDAY 10TH FEBRUARY 1981

Mick Tait grabbed a hat-trick in five minutes during Pompey's 5-0 thrashing of Exeter City at Fratton Park. Frank Burrows' side led 1-0 at half-time through Steve Bryant's header and Tait's three-goal burst came around the hour. Billy Rafferty completed the scoring.

SATURDAY 10TH FEBRUARY 1996

Paul Hall kept Pompey's hopes of a First Division play-off place alive by scoring a late winner at home to Leicester City. Deon Burton equalised for the Blues after Iwan Roberts had put Leicester in front. The bad news for Pompey was that striker Paul Walsh left the field with a twisted knee – an injury which was to force his retirement.

SATURDAY 11TH FEBRUARY 1928

Pompey defeated Liverpool 1-0 on the Reds' first visit to Fratton Park. Billy Haines, who had played a massive part in helping the club climb from Division Three (South) to the First Division, was playing his last match in Pompey's colours before being transferred to Southampton.

SATURDAY 11TH FEBRUARY 1939

The Fratton Park attendance record was beaten as 47,614 watched Pompey beat West Ham 2-0 to reach the sixth round of the FA Cup. Cliff Parker and Freddie Worrall scored the goals.

SATURDAY 11TH FEBRUARY 1950

Pompey staged a dramatic recovery against Manchester United at Old Trafford, scoring two goals in the first four minutes of the second half in the FA Cup fifth round. The match ended 3-3 to set up a replay.

FRIDAY 11TH FEBRUARY 1994

Pompey slumped to a 3-1 defeat at Tranmere Rovers, stretching their dismal run to 13 matches without a win, but at least they scored. Alan McLoughlin's late consolation was the team's first in 695 minutes.

THURSDAY 11TH FEBRUARY 2010

The Pompey Supporters' Trust was given its official launch at The Rifle Club, Goldsmith Avenue. With the very existence of the Football Club hanging by a thread, two hundred diehard fans were insisting that even if the club was to go under they would be there to start it again at the bottom of the football pyramid. On the same day former manager Harry Redknapp and ex-owner Milan Mandaric both appeared in the City of Westminster Magistrates' Court as they faced charges for evasion of tax and National Insurance contributions.

SATURDAY 12TH FEBRUARY 1949

First Division leaders Pompey required extra time to see off Division Three (South) strugglers Newport County in the FA Cup fifth round at Fratton Park before a record crowd (that stood for only two weeks) of 48,581; 2-2 after 90 minutes, Jack Froggatt scored with five minutes of extra time remaining to see Pompey through to the quarter-final.

SATURDAY 12TH FEBRUARY 1955

Pompey gained a valuable and thoroughly deserved win at Sheffield Wednesday in front of 21,176. They took an early lead through Jackie Henderson and after Dennis Woodhead equalised Peter Harris restored their advantage. Gordon Dale sealed the victory with 15 minutes left.

SATURDAY 12TH FEBRUARY 1983

After leading 3-0 promotion-chasing Pompey allowed Exeter City to grab two late goals, forcing the home side to hang on desperately to claim the points in this Division Three fixture.

SATURDAY 13TH FEBRUARY 1937

Jock Anderson scored a hat-trick as depleted Pompey recorded a 4-2 victory over Stoke City at the Victoria Ground. They lost goalkeeper Jimmy Strong to an injury in the first half and his place was taken by centre-forward Johnny Weddle.

MONDAY 13TH FEBRUARY 1978

Two of England's 1966 World Cup-winning heroes, Bobby Charlton and Gordon Banks, played for Fort Lauderdale Strikers in a friendly match with Pompey at Fratton Park. The American side were managed by former Pompey winger Ron Newman. The match finished 2-2.

SATURDAY 13TH FEBRUARY 1988

Terry Connor's late goal gave Pompey a point against fellow First Division strugglers West Ham on their first league visit to Upton Park in 30 years.

SATURDAY 13TH FEBRUARY 1993

Guy Whittingham scored twice to take his tally for the season to 35 as Pompey completed a double over Birmingham City in front of a St Andrews crowd of 10,935. The other goal came from Alan McLoughlin.

MONDAY 13TH FEBRUARY 1995

Plans were revealed for a new 20,000 all-seater Fratton Park with the hope it would be in place by the summer of 1996.

SATURDAY 13TH FEBRUARY 2010

Pompey claimed their first FA Cup victory over Southampton, thrashing their south coast rivals 4-1 at St Mary's Stadium in the fifth round. The two clubs had previously met four times in the competition with Saints winning them all.

WEDNESDAY 13TH FEBRUARY 2013

Pompey set a new unwanted club record when a goalless draw at Hartlepool meant that they had gone twenty matches without sampling victory. It eclipsed the previous most wretched run during the 1975/76 season when, under Ian St John, Pompey finished bottom of Division Two.

SATURDAY 14TH FEBRUARY 1925

Billy Haines scored a hat-trick in the last six minutes of Pompey's Second Division encounter away to Wolverhampton Wanderers in the first meeting between the two clubs. His treble followed first-half goals by Dave Watson and Willie Williamson and this created the club's record away win. The five-goal margin has since been equalled several times on Pompey's travels but never bettered.

SATURDAY 14TH FEBRUARY 1931

Pompey were beaten 1-0 by Second Division West Bromwich Albion in the FA Cup fifth round at Fratton Park before a crowd of 30,891. West Brom went on to lift the trophy and become one of the few teams outside Division One to do so.

SATURDAY 14TH FEBRUARY 2009

David James celebrated his record 536th Premier League appearance by keeping a clean sheet against his former club Manchester City at Fratton Park. Goals by Glen Johnson and Hermann Hreidarsson gave Pompey a 2-0 victory in the team's first match since Tony Adams was sacked as manager.

WEDNESDAY 15TH FEBRUARY 1950

A crowd of 49,962 saw Manchester United defeat Pompey 3-1 in the FA Cup fifth round replay on a Wednesday afternoon. United led 2-0 through Charlie Mitten and Johnny Downie before Peter Harris netted for Pompey three minutes before half-time. Jimmy Delaney's strike a minute after the break ended the goalscoring.

SATURDAY 15TH FEBRUARY 1958

Derek Dougan's goal in the second minute was enough for Pompey to win a friendly match against German side The Kickers of Offenbach at Fratton Park.

SATURDAY 15TH FEBRUARY 1997

Pompey produced an FA Cup shock by beating Premiership Leeds United 3-2 at Elland Road in the fifth round. Alan McLoughlin put Pompey ahead, Lee Bowyer equalised and Matt Svensson and Lee Bradbury wrapped it up for Pompey, although Bowyer struck a second Leeds goal in the dying seconds.

THURSDAY 16TH FEBRUARY 1928

Concerned by the number of goals the Pompey team had conceded – 68 in 26 games – the club broke their transfer record by paying £5,000 for Falkirk's centre-half John McIlwaine. They let in another five goals on McIlwaine's debut but then kept seven consecutive clean sheets.

MONDAY 16TH FEBRUARY 1976

The Pompey directors urged all their supporters to buy Knorr Soup up to the following 2nd April for the club to profit by 1p from every Knorr soup, sauce or stock packet placed in collection boxes at every Portsea Island Co-op store. The club hoped to raise £10,000 from the fund-raising scheme but it brought in just £281.46. The figure would have been half that but for a decision by the company to double the amount raised.

SATURDAY 16TH FEBRUARY 1991

Paul Gascoigne scored twice in the second half for Tottenham Hotspur to earn the Londoners a 2-1 victory over Pompey in the FA Cup fifth round before a crowd of 26,049 at Fratton Park. Mark Chamberlain had put the Blues ahead just before the break.

SATURDAY 17TH FEBRUARY 1973

Ray Hiron scored his 100th league goal for Pompey in a 2-0 win at home to Nottingham Forest. His diving header just before half-time followed an earlier strike by Nick Jennings.

WEDNESDAY 17TH FEBRUARY 1988

Portsmouth FC were fighting for survival in the High Court, faced with a winding-up petition. After the 2 minutes and 27 seconds hearing, Pompey won a 14-day stay of execution and solicitor Martin Polden pronounced that chairman John Deacon would produce the money before 2nd March.

WEDNESDAY 17TH FEBRUARY 1993

Former Pompey and England star Jack Froggatt died aged 71. Froggatt, who represented both club and country at outside-left and centre-half, was due to be a guest at Fratton Park three days later for the visit of Leicester City, the club for which he left Pompey in March 1954.

TUESDAY 17TH FEBRUARY 1998

Steve Claridge's first goal for Pompey secured a win over Stockport County – the first since Boxing Day – to ease relegation worries. The second half was memorable for a wall of noise from Pompey's fans. Assistant boss Keith Waldon said, "I've never known anything like it. It was mind-blowing."

FRIDAY 17TH FEBRUARY 2012

Portsmouth Football Club entered administration for the second time in two years. Former professional footballer Trevor Birch was appointed administrator as the club was deducted ten points, leaving them above the relegation zone on goal difference.

SATURDAY 18TH FEBRUARY 1928

Jack Smith became the first Pompey player to score a hat-trick in the First Division when he scored all three of Pompey's goals in their clash with Sunderland at Fratton Park. However he was not the highest scoring player that day: David Halliday scored four for the visitors who won 5-3.

SATURDAY 18TH FEBRUARY 1967

Pompey were beaten 3-1 in the FA Cup fourth round at Tottenham Hotspur before a crowd of 57,910. Alan Gilzean (2) and Jimmy Greaves scored for eventual winners Spurs; Ron Tindall netted for the Blues.

SATURDAY 18TH FEBRUARY 1995

Stuart Doling came on as sub to rescue a draw at Roker Park before a crowd of 12,372. Ten minutes before the end, he saw a harmless looking 25-yard effort bobble past Sunderland keeper Tony Norman for a 2-2 draw.

SATURDAY 19TH FEBRUARY 1955

Bitterly cold weather and the absence of Tom Finney meant a Fratton Park crowd of only 19,830 witnessed Pompey's first win over Preston North End for six years. The result was 2-0 with Duggie Reid smashing home a free-kick and Johnny Gordon also on target.

SATURDAY 19TH FEBRUARY 1966

A first-half goal by Ray Hiron gave Pompey a 1-0 win over Bolton Wanderers at Fratton Park in front of 11,975. The match was a drab, colourless affair, but at least Pompey gained their first victory of 1966.

SATURDAY 19TH FEBRUARY 1994

Gerry Creaney scored a hat-trick in a 3-1 win over Grimsby Town at Fratton Park less than a month after signing for Pompey from Celtic for a club record £600,000. Alan Knight in the Pompey goal barely touched the ball until he had to pick it out of the net from Paul Groves' late consolation header.

THURSDAY 19TH FEBRUARY 2009

After years of announcing ambitious new stadium plans, Portsmouth Football Club outlined a scheme to redevelop Fratton Park with the intention of moving to Horsea Island put on hold. The new idea involved moving the pitch 90 degrees with the existing South Stand becoming the new "away" end.

SATURDAY 20TH FEBRUARY 1954

Reg Flewin, skipper of Pompey's double League Championship winning side of 1949 and 1950, made his final first-team appearance in an FA Cup fifth round tie against Bolton Wanderers at Burnden Park. The match ended in a goalless draw.

SATURDAY 20TH FEBRUARY 1960

Pompey dropped further into relegation trouble, losing 2-0 to Huddersfield Town at Fratton Park. The visitors' first goal was scored by Denis Law.

SATURDAY 20TH FEBRUARY 1971

Luton Town's Don Givens scored the only goal in the Second Division clash at Fratton Park between Pompey and the promotion contenders. The game was shown that evening on BBC *Match of the Day*.

FRIDAY 20TH FEBRUARY 1998

Terry Venables hit back, after accusations of leaving the club in financial ruin. He said, "They're crying like babies now it's going wrong." Chairman Martin Gregory hit back with, "In the light of his history and business failures it is hard to take anything he says on the subject seriously."

SATURDAY 21ST FEBRUARY 1948

The First Division fixture between Pompey and league leaders Arsenal at Fratton Park was postponed owing to a snow-covered pitch but along the coast at Southampton the Pompey reserve side drew 0-0 with Saints' second string.

SATURDAY 21ST FEBRUARY 1953

Peter Harris grabbed a hat-trick as Pompey hammered Sunderland in front of 29,669 at Fratton Park. Jackie Henderson and Johnny Gordon were also on target for Eddie Lever's men.

SATURDAY 21st FEBRUARY 1959

Ron Saunders scored a hat-trick as struggling Pompey shared eight goals in a thrilling match with Tottenham Hotspur at White Hart Lane. Pompey looked to have recorded their first league victory since November but Bobby Smith grabbed a last minute equaliser for Spurs. Pompey skipper Jimmy Dickinson was making his 500th league appearance for the club.

SATURDAY 22nd FEBRUARY 1947

What was expected to be a closely-fought Football Combination Cup encounter between the Pompey and Southampton reserve sides at Fratton Park turned out to be a walkover for Pompey who won 6-0.

WEDNESDAY 22nd FEBRUARY 1956

Pompey and Newcastle United made history by playing the first Football League match under floodlights at Fratton Park. The crowd of 15,800 saw the Magpies win 2-0, their goals coming from Bill Curry and Vic Keeble.

TUESDAY 22nd FEBRUARY 1972

At the Portsmouth Football Supporters' Club Annual Dinner, Pompey Chairman Dennis Collett revealed that new banking arrangements would make "not inconsiderable" money available to strengthen the playing staff in the drive to return to the First Division.

SUNDAY 22nd FEBRUARY 2004

Pompey earned their first FA Cup victory over Liverpool, winning 1-0 at Fratton Park in a fifth round replay. Richard Hughes scored the only goal and Pompey 'keeper Shaka Hislop saved a penalty from Michael Owen.

WEDNESDAY 22nd FEBRUARY 2012

Five days after entering administration Pompey revealed that they had made thirty employees redundant including Chief Executive David Lampitt and fellow board members John Redgate and Nick Byrom.

SATURDAY 23rd FEBRUARY 1929

Pompey were 3-0 down after 20 minutes of their First Division home encounter with Bolton Wanderers but they fought back to draw 4-4. The goalscorers were Dave Watson, Johnny Weddle and Freddie Cook (2).

FRIDAY 23RD FEBRUARY 2001

Graham Rix became Pompey's fourth manager in fourteen months. Chairman Milan Mandaric, who offered player-manager Steve Claridge a coaching role, promised to give his new manager millions to spend. Rix's first job was to promise that the club would not be relegated.

FRIDAY 24TH FEBRUARY 1939

Pompey signed inside-forward Bert Barlow from Wolverhampton Wanderers for £6,000. Barlow scored when Pompey beat his old club in the FA Cup Final two months later and was also a vital member of Pompey's League Championship winning side in 1948-49.

SATURDAY 24TH FEBRUARY 1996

Alan Knight saved a penalty from Sunderland's Craig Russell in a 2-2 draw at Fratton Park. Knight also saved a Sunderland spot kick when the two sides drew 0-0 at Roker Park earlier in the season.

SATURDAY 25TH FEBRUARY 1939

Bert Barlow marked his Pompey debut by scoring in a 3-3 draw with Charlton Athletic at The Valley. Pompey's other goals were scored by Freddie Worrall and Jock Anderson.

SATURDAY 25TH FEBRUARY 1950

Pompey defeated First Division bottom club Birmingham City 2-0, both goals coming from Peter Harris. The win left Pompey in fourth place only two points behind leaders Manchester United.

SATURDAY 25TH FEBRUARY 1967

Pompey were featured on BBC *Match of the Day* for the first time. Leading 2-0 at the interval thanks to goals by Cliff Portwood, they were beaten 3-2 by Division Two promotion-chasing Wolverhampton Wanderers at Fratton Park before a crowd of 23,144. Keeper John Milkins broke his arm late in the game; the injury kept him out for the rest of the season.

SATURDAY 26TH FEBRUARY 1949

A record Fratton Park crowd of 51,385, paying record receipts of £5,465 17shillings, saw Pompey beat Derby County 2-1 to reach the FA Cup semi-final. Derby had the better of the first half and Jackie

Stamps coolly nodded them in front on 41 minutes. A minute before half-time Jack Froggatt headed home Ike Clarke's corner and as the match drew to a close, Clarke thrashed home his second to book his side a semi-final place.

SATURDAY 26TH FEBRUARY 1955

Jack Hogg was selected to male his debut at outside-left, in place of the injured Gordon Dale in the First Division clash at Sheffield United, but the match was postponed because of snow and frost. Hogg returned to Fratton Park in time to play for Pompey Reserves against Arsenal Reserves in a match the Gunners' second string won 4-1. Hogg was never picked to play for Pompey again but went on to make 80 appearances for Gateshead.

SATURDAY 26TH FEBRUARY 1983

A Dean Court crowd of 13,406 saw Pompey make history by gaining their seventh successive league win as they defeated Bournemouth 2-0. The ground was a sea of blue and white and the Pompey fans were celebrating in the 21st minute when Steve Aizlewood converted a penalty. Alan Biley made the game safe with a close range header.

FRIDAY 26TH FEBRUARY 2010

Portsmouth Football Club was placed into administration by owner Balram Chainrai. This automatically incurred a nine-point penalty that came into effect three weeks later and the club was also handed a transfer embargo.

SATURDAY 27TH FEBRUARY 1954

Staging a terrific second-half recovery, Pompey came back from 2-0 down to defeat Burnley 3-2 at Fratton Park. The Pompey goalscorers were Johnny Gordon (2) and Mike Barnard.

SATURDAY 27TH FEBRUARY 1960

Pompey were still searching for their first win of the year after losing 3-2 at Fratton Park to Derby County – one of their foot-of-the-table companions. The defeat left the Blues in 20th place in Division Two.

SATURDAY 27TH FEBRUARY 1965

Ray Hiron scored twice – his first brace in league football – to earn Pompey their first away victory for twelve months. His two goals against Coventry at Highfield Road came within three minutes of Ronnie Rees putting the Sky Blues ahead midway through the first half.

SATURDAY 28TH FEBRUARY 1942

Pompey thrashed Clapton Orient 16-1 at Fratton Park in the London War League with Andy Black scoring eight of the goals.

SATURDAY 28TH FEBRUARY 1948

Without a First Division match, Pompey played a friendly against Brighton and Hove Albion at the Goldstone Ground and were held to a 1-1 draw by the Division Three (South) side. Meanwhile at Fratton Park, a crowd of 14,000 saw an FA Amateur XI beat Scottish amateur side Queens Park 4-0 in an Olympic trial match.

SATURDAY 28TH FEBRUARY 1953

Manchester City moved off the bottom of the First Division table following a 2-1 victory over Pompey at Maine Road in front of 38,537. Pompey's Peter Harris scored in the 65th minute but four minutes later City were ahead through goals by Bobby Cunliffe and Jimmy Meadows.

TUESDAY 28TH FEBRUARY 1987

Two goals by Mick Quinn and a penalty from Kevin Dillon gave Second Division leaders Pompey a comfortable 3-0 victory over Stoke City before 14,607 at Fratton Park. It was the fourteenth straight home win for Alan Ball's side.

SATURDAY 29TH FEBRUARY 1936

Jimmy Easson scored on his final appearance for Pompey in a 3-1 victory over West Bromwich Albion. It was the Scottish international's 103rd league goal for the club.

SATURDAY 29TH FEBRUARY 1992

Stunning strikes in the first eleven minutes by Chris Burns and Alan McLoughlin earned Pompey a 2-0 victory at home to Tranmere Rovers.

SUNDAY 29TH FEBRUARY 2004

Lomana LuaLua volleyed home a minute from time to earn Pompey a 1-1 draw with Newcastle United at Fratton Park. LuaLua was on loan from the Magpies and Toon boss Sir Bobby Robson was none too happy that a clause in the contract allowed the striker to play against his own club.

PORTSMOUTH
On This Day & Miscellany

MARCH

SATURDAY 1st MARCH 1952

A Fratton Park record reserve crowd of 30,289 watched Pompey Reserves thrash Charlton Athletic's second string 5-1 in a London Combination fixture. The reason for this huge attendance was that tickets for the following week's FA Cup sixth round clash at home to Newcastle United were on sale.

SATURDAY 1st MARCH 1997

After five straight wins in Division One, and seven including the FA Cup, Pompey had to settle for a 1-1 draw at home to Sheffield United. Paul Hall gave the Blues the lead but Jan Aage Fjortoft equalised for the Blades.

FRIDAY 1st MARCH 2002

Chairman Milan Mandaric refused to pay manager Graham Rix and his players because he said they weren't trying hard enough. Mandaric admitted he was playing a dangerous game but insisted he wouldn't buckle if the players threatened to go on strike.

SATURDAY 1st MARCH 2003

Pompey moved a step towards the First Division title by beating Millwall 5-0 at The New Den. Harry Redknapp's side produced an awesome performance to record their best away league victory since Preston North End were beaten by the same scoreline in February 1973.

MONDAY 2nd MARCH 1903

Fratton Park staged a Home International match between England and Wales. Pompey's Albert Houlker was making his second appearance for England who won 2-1.

MONDAY 2nd MARCH 1953

Pompey and Southampton drew 1-1 in a friendly match to launch the new Fratton Park floodlights. Harry Ferrier scored a first-half penalty to give Pompey the lead with Roy Williams netting the equaliser after the break. The historic match was watched by 22,714 and the Pompey team was: Ernie Butler, Jimmy Stephen, Harry Ferrier, Jimmy Scoular, Reg Flewin, Jimmy Dickinson, Peter Harris, Len Phillips, Jackie Henderson, Johnny Gordon, Gordon Dale.

SATURDAY 2ND MARCH 1963

Southampton defeated Pompey 4-2 at The Dell. Pompey went in front to an early Tommy Traynor own goal but Saints hit back with four goals before Ron Saunders scored a second for the Blues. Pompey were still seven points ahead of Saints in the Second Division table.

SATURDAY 2ND MARCH 1974

Millwall boss Benny Fenton was sent to the stands during a 0-0 draw against Pompey, after remonstrating with Pompey's Brian Lewis.

SATURDAY 3RD MARCH 1923

Harry Kirk scored all four goals for Exeter City in their 4-3 win over Pompey at Fratton Park in Division Three (South). John Shankly, brother of Liverpool's legendary manager Bill, netted one of Pompey's goals.

SATURDAY 3RD MARCH 1934

Pompey marched into their second FA Cup semi-final by beating Bolton Wanderers 3-0 at Burnden Park. Sep Rutherford and Johnny Weddle (2) were the goalscorers. The crowd of 52,181 paid £3,378.

SATURDAY 3RD MARCH 1962

Keith Blackburn scored the only goal as Pompey defeated Shrewsbury Town 1-0 on their first visit to Gay Meadow. The win put Pompey six points ahead of Bournemouth at the top of the Third Division table.

THURSDAY 3RD MARCH 1977

SOS Pompey closed five and a half months and £35,000 after it answered chairman John Deacon's plea for help. The appeal, initiated by *The News* when bankruptcy stalked the club, was launched to raise £25,000 by the end of October and although it narrowly missed that target, it stayed on to raise another £10,000.

SATURDAY 3RD MARCH 2007

Pompey produced their best performance for weeks but were beaten by reigning Premiership champions Chelsea before 20,219 at Fratton Park.

SATURDAY 4TH MARCH 1939

The FA Cup holders Preston were beaten by a Jock Anderson goal in the sixth round of the competition in front of 44,237. Off the field because of injury midway through the second half, Anderson returned and immediately reached a long ball before Preston goalkeeper Harry Holdcroft and planted it in the net.

SATURDAY 4TH MARCH 1961

Tony Priscott snatched a late equaliser for Pompey against promotion-chasing Liverpool at Fratton Park before 14,301. Liverpool were leading 2-1 when Priscott's shot went through a ruck of players to earn the Blues a welcome point.

SATURDAY 5TH MARCH 1932

Johnny Weddle scored all three goals as Pompey defeated West Ham United 3-0 in a First Division encounter at Fratton Park.

SATURDAY 5TH MARCH 1949

Pompey remained three points clear of Newcastle United at the top of the First Division after beating Aston Villa 3-0 at Fratton Park. Len Phillips scored twice with Jack Froggatt grabbing the third goal.

WEDNESDAY 5TH MARCH 1997

A stunning strike by Fitzroy Simpson four minutes from time earned Pompey a 1-1 draw to secure their nine-match unbeaten run against Manchester City at Maine Road before 26,051 and it also deprived his former teammates of a fifth successive win.

SATURDAY 5TH MARCH 2011

Pompey's 1-0 win at home to Sunderland equalled the club's post-war record of six consecutive clean sheets. Hermann Hreidarsson's 24th minute strike also brought the Blues their sixth straight win.

SATURDAY 6TH MARCH 1948

A crowd of 37,067 saw Pompey draw 1-1 with Blackpool at Fratton Park. Thick fog persisted throughout the game in which Stan Mortensen opened the scoring for the visitors with Duggie Reid equalising.

SUNDAY 6TH MARCH 1954

Charlton Athletic won 3-1 at the Valley, their first victory over Pompey since the war. It was their famous goalkeeper Sam Bartram's 500th league appearance. Before the home side took the lead, Bartram pulled off a superb save to deny Rodney Henwood a debut goal for Pompey.

SATURDAY 6TH MARCH 1971

Defender Colin Blant scored his only goal for Pompey and Ray Hiron also netted for the Blues as Queens Park Rangers were beaten 2-0 at Fratton Park. The victory was Pompey's first at home since December and Ron Tindall's side were still only five points off the bottom of the Second Division.

SATURDAY 6TH MARCH 2004

Pompey were ripped to shreds by Arsenal in the FA Cup sixth round at Fratton Park. Thierry Henry and Freddie Ljungberg scored twice with Kolo Toure also finding the net for the Gunners while Teddy Sheringham headed a consolation goal for Pompey in the dying seconds.

SATURDAY 6TH MARCH 2010

Two goals by Frederic Piquionne in four second-half minutes earned Pompey a 2-0 victory over Birmingham City in the FA Cup sixth round at Fratton Park.

SATURDAY 7TH MARCH 1964

Pompey's Ron Saunders scored a second-half hat-trick in a 4-3 win at home to Leyton Orient. It was the second treble the Portsmouth forward had bagged against the east London club that season, having netted three in Pompey's 6-3 win at Orient's Brisbane Road earlier in the campaign.

SATURDAY 7TH MARCH 1992

Alan McLoughlin scored in the third minute of Pompey's 1-0 FA Cup sixth round win at home to Brian Clough's Nottingham Forest. It was the first time Pompey had reached the semi-final of the competition since 1949.

SUNDAY 7TH MARCH 1999

Portsmouth United, the fans' consortium bidding to save Portsmouth Football Club, raised more than £200,000 after launching their appeal fund to the city's public. A series of presentations at the Guildhall yielded £50,000 in cash and £150,000 in pledges from fans who were desperate to see the club survive.

THURSDAY 7TH MARCH 2002

Manager Graham Rix and Director of Football Harry Redknapp agreed that Japanese goalkeeper Yoshi Kawaguchi had no future at Fratton Park. Chairman Milan Mandaric admitted the signing of Japan's captain was a gamble that backfired – and would cost him a lot of money.

SATURDAY 8TH MARCH 1952

Pompey were beaten 4-2 at home before 44,699 in the FA Cup sixth round by holders Newcastle United who went on to lift the trophy for the second successive year. Magpies legend Jackie Milburn scored a hat-trick in the match that has always been regarded as one of the finest seen at Fratton Park.

THURSDAY 8TH MARCH 1990

Pompey's youth team beat Liverpool 2-1, after extra time, to go through to the FA Youth Cup semi-final. They were watched by a crowd of 4,285 at Fratton Park.

SATURDAY 8TH MARCH 2008

A Sulley Muntari penalty was enough to secure Pompey victory over Manchester United in the FA Cup sixth round at Old Trafford in front of a crowd of 75,463. Drawn away to United in the competition for the third time in six years, Pompey claimed their first win at Old Trafford since October 1957.

TUESDAY 8TH MARCH 2011

Pompey's six-match winning run and six consecutive clean sheet sequence came to an end with a 2-1 defeat away to Bristol City. Goalkeeper Jamie Ashdown was not beaten until the 40th minute and so established a club post-war record of not conceding a goal for 636 minutes.

SATURDAY 9TH MARCH 1968

The last 40,000 plus crowd – 42,642 – to attend Fratton Park saw Pompey go down 2-1 to West Bromwich Albion in the FA Cup fifth round. Jeff Astle and Clive Clark gave the visitors a 2-0 half-time lead and Pompey pulled a goal back through Ray Hiron. West Brom went all the way to Wembley and defeated Everton 1-0 in the final.

SATURDAY 9TH MARCH 1974

Albert McCann scored his 96th and last league and cup goal for Pompey in a 2-1 win away to Swindon Town. He netted in the 18th minute of the Second Division encounter before Peter Marinello extended the lead. John McLaughlin, who would later feature in two Pompey promotion sides, grabbed a late goal for Swindon.

THURSDAY 9TH MARCH 1978

Leading scorer Dave Kemp was sold to Third Division rivals Carlisle United on transfer deadline day. The deal was worth £75,000 and it involved Carlisle's John Lathan moving to Fratton Park. Pompey also signed striker Colin Garwood from Colchester United for £25,000.

SATURDAY 10TH MARCH 1979

Pompey manager Jimmy Dickinson was angry with the supporters who hurled abuse at Derek Showers throughout the home match with Torquay United. Showers had the last laugh however for, in the dying seconds, he headed the only goal of the game.

TUESDAY 10TH MARCH 1987

Alan Ball labelled his team as "garbage" after a late Leeds goal had denied Pompey their 15th straight home league win in a match that saw nine players booked. Paul Mariner netted early for Pompey but Leeds levelled through Micky Adams.

THURSDAY 10TH MARCH 1994

Paul Walsh completed a move to Manchester City for £750,000 and the transfer sparked an angry response from Pompey supporters. Many threatened to boycott the club's next home match and a local businessman, a Pompey fan since his school days, pulled out of a £1500 sponsorship deal.

THURSDAY 11TH MARCH 1948

Pompey smashed their transfer record, paying £10,500 for Dundee centre-forward Albert Juliussen. The former Huddersfield Town player had scored 65 goals in the Scottish First Division the previous season.

SATURDAY 11TH MARCH 1950

Pompey collected two more points on their way to a second successive league championship with a 2-1 win over Burnley watched by the season's lowest crowd of 26,728. Jack Froggatt and Ike Clarke were the men on target.

MONDAY 11TH MARCH 1985

Fratton favourite Alan Biley moved to Brighton and Hove Albion for a fee of £50,000. The striker, who had helped Pompey to the Third Division title in 1983 with 23 league goals was currently Pompey's top goalscorer with 13.

SATURDAY 12TH MARCH 1938

Cliff Parker netted his only hat-trick for Pompey in a 4-1 victory at home to Brentford in Division One. Those three goals took his tally for the season to fourteen.

SATURDAY 12TH MARCH 1949

A 4-1 victory over Sunderland at Roker Park in front of 57,229 took Pompey five points clear at the top of the First Division. They had now collected 44 points from 31 matches.

SATURDAY 12TH MARCH 1960

Pompey staged a thrilling second-half recovery to secure their first win of 1960, beating Liverpool 2-1 at Fratton Park in Division Two. The visitors led at half-time through Jimmy Harrower but Pompey equalised when Alex Wilson netted his first goal in league football, then Harry Harris headed the winner.

SATURDAY 12TH MARCH 1966

Bobby Kellard was injured on his Pompey debut and replaced at half-time by Cliff Portwood. The 1-0 defeat by Birmingham City at Fratton Park pushed Pompey nearer the relegation zone.

SATURDAY 13TH MARCH 1965

Johnny Gordon was sent off late in the Second Division clash at Deepdale where Preston North End thrashed Pompey 6-1, sending George Smith's men deep into relegation trouble.

SATURDAY 13TH MARCH 1971

Pompey goalkeeper John Milkins was in outstanding form to earn his side a goalless draw with Sunderland at Roker Park.

SATURDAY 13TH MARCH 2004

Pompey were still searching for their first away victory in the Premiership after 18-year-old Wayne Rooney's first-half strike earned Everton a 1-0 victory at Goodison Park.

SATURDAY 14TH MARCH 1953

After holding Preston North End for nearly an hour, Pompey crashed to a 4-0 defeat at Deepdale, their first loss at the ground since August 1925.

FRIDAY 14TH MARCH 1958

Jackie Henderson left Pompey for Wolverhampton Wanderers. While at Fratton Park, Henderson scored 73 goals in 226 league and cup appearances and earned five Scotland caps.

THURSDAY 14TH MARCH 1974

After a week of discussions between Bobby Moore and Pompey chairman John Deacon about a possible £25,000 transfer from West Ham, England's 1966 World Cup winning captain chose not to leave London and signed for Fulham.

TUESDAY 14TH MARCH 1978

The club announced that Norman Piper was to be released. Piper, who made over 300 appearances in Pompey's colours was to re-join Fort Lauderdale Strikers, for whom he had played the previous summer.

THURSDAY 14TH MARCH 1996

Portsmouth City planners agreed to an all-seater stand being built at the Milton End. Work on the 2,450-seat structure was due to start before the end of the season.

SATURDAY 15TH MARCH 1952

A week after Newcastle United beat Pompey 4-2 in the FA Cup sixth round at Fratton Park, the two sides shared six goals in a thrilling match at St James' Park before 62,883.

SATURDAY 15TH MARCH 1958

Alex Govan scored the only goal of the First Division clash between Pompey and Aston Villa at Fratton Park. Govan signed from Birmingham City the previous evening and played at outside-left, replacing Jackie Henderson who had left for Wolves.

SATURDAY 15TH MARCH 1977

Pompey chairman John Deacon was quick to dismiss reports that the club, who owed more than £500,000, was not for sale to the Americans. An English national daily newspaper had reported that the club could go to the first American who could put up $2m.

SATURDAY 15TH MARCH 1997

Ten-man Pompey pulled off a remarkable victory at Huddersfield Town. David Hillier was sent off midway through the first half and when Marcus Stewart broke the deadlock, things looked grim for Pompey. But three goals in a four minute spell during the second half handed Pompey three points. Sammy Igoe levelled for the Blues then Paul Hall scored twice to complete an amazing comeback.

THURSDAY 16TH MARCH 1961

Caretaker-manager Bill Thompson made Johnny Gordon his second signing of the week. Portsmouth born Gordon returned to Fratton Park from Birmingham City, the club for which he left in September 1958.

FRIDAY 16TH MARCH 1962

Pompey led the Third Division by ten points after beating Reading 3-0 at Elm Park before a crowd of 22,969. Tony Barton (2) and Ron Saunders were on target

SATURDAY 16TH MARCH 1974

Peter Marinello scored twice and Ron Davies once to help Pompey to a 3-1 win at Fratton Park against Hull City in the Second Division.

SATURDAY 17TH MARCH 1900

The match between Ireland and England in Dublin included Pompey's first internationals. Danny Cunliffe turned out at inside-right for England and Matt Reilly kept goal for the hosts who won the game 2-0.

SATURDAY 17TH MARCH 1934

A hat-trick by Johnny Weddle and a goal from Sep Rutherford helped Pompey through to their second FA Cup final by beating Leicester City 4-1 at St Andrews. The crowd was 66,544 and the receipts were £5,977 and 18 shillings (90p).

SATURDAY 17TH MARCH 2007

Reading and Pompey finished goalless before a crowd of 24,087 at the Madejski Stadium in the race between two clubs chasing European football. The nearest either side came to scoring was when Pompey's Richard Hughes sent a 20-yard right foot shot crashing against the post.

SATURDAY 18TH MARCH 1961

Pompey, second from bottom in Division Two, earned their first home league victory since November, beating Leeds United 3-1 at Fratton Park. Jack Charlton put the visitors in front with a hotly disputed goal but Ron Saunders, Jimmy Campbell and Tony Priscott netted for Pompey to earn two precious points.

SATURDAY 18TH MARCH 1978

Pompey lifted their hopes of escape from relegation to Division Four with a 2-0 win over Shrewsbury at Fratton Park in front of 8,575. Colin Garwood made an impressive home debut and he grabbed the first goal on 35 minutes with a low right foot shot into the corner. Pompey's second goal was scored by Peter Denyer.

SATURDAY 18TH MARCH 2006

Pompey moved within three points of Premiership safety with a 4-2 win against West Ham at Upton Park. Lomana LuaLua, Sean Davis, Pedro Mendes and Svetoslav Todorov were on target for Pompey who were able to celebrate their first victory at Upton Park since 1929.

SATURDAY 19TH MARCH 1938

Jimmy Beattie signalled his return to the Pompey side with a hat-trick as they shared six goals with Leicester City at Filbert Street before a crowd of 16,682.

SATURDAY 19TH MARCH 1949

Pompey were still five points clear at the top of Division One after beating Derby County 1-0 at Fratton Park through a goal by Len Phillips.

SATURDAY 19TH MARCH 1960

Pompey, struggling near the foot of the Second Division table, thrashed league leaders Cardiff City 4-1 at Ninian Park. The goalscorers were Ron Newman (2), Harry Harris and Ron Saunders.

THURSDAY 19TH MARCH 1998

Jimmy Scoular, one of the heroes of Pompey's League Championship winning side of 1948-49 and 1949-50, died aged 73. Scoular scored eight times in 247 league appearances during his time at Fratton Park in an eight year spell from 1946 to 1953. He also won nine Scottish caps.

MONDAY 19TH MARCH 2007

Former Nottingham Forest manager Paul Hart was unveiled as the man charged with producing the next generation of Pompey talent. The ex-Leeds United youth supremo was named director of youth operations.

SATURDAY 20TH MARCH 1925

Harry Havelock scored four goals on his home debut for Pompey in a Second Division clash with Nottingham Forest. He had made two appearances in away games without finding the net but in his first appearance in front of the home supporters he notched a first-half hat-trick and then added another goal as Pompey ran out 5-1 winners.

SATURDAY 20TH MARCH 1948

A fortuitous strike by Jimmy Scoular – his first league goal – earned Pompey a win over Manchester City in a scrappy game watched by 29,459. The only goal of the match came six minutes from time when Scoular sent a free-kick into the goalmouth and as Frank Swift was about to collect it he was hustled by Albert Juliussen and the ball passed into the net.

SATURDAY 20TH MARCH 1971

Eoin Hand and Nick Jennings were the goalscorers as Pompey won 2-0 at Fratton Park against Second Division bottom club Charlton Athletic.

SATURDAY 20TH MARCH 1982

Trevor Senior made his league debut in Pompey's 1-1 draw at home to Fulham. Billy Rafferty put the Blues ahead just before the break but Kevin Lock equalised with a late penalty.

SATURDAY 21ST MARCH 1958

Jimmy White became the youngest player to play for Pompey when, at 16 years 291 days, he appeared at inside-right in a 1-1 draw at home to Birmingham City in a First Division match. He scored Pompey's goal and remains the club's youngest goalscorer.

WEDNESDAY 21ST MARCH 1979

Peter Mellor was attacked by a Port Vale fan during the Fourth Division encounter at Vale Park moments after the Pompey goalkeeper had enraged the home crowd with a cynical foul on Kenny Todd – a future Pompey player. The assailant was marched away by police but that wasn't the end of Mellor's problems for, as he was leaving the field at the end, he was felled by a missile thrown from the crowd and hit in the face.

SUNDAY 21ST MARCH 2004

Pompey fans invaded the pitch and hugged Yakubu after he scored the goal that secured Pompey's 1-0 win at home to Southampton. The victory, watched by 20,140, was the first over Saints at Fratton Park since 1963.

SATURDAY 22ND MARCH 1952

Charlie Dore, aged 21, made his debut in goal for Pompey, in place of Ernie Butler who was relegated to the reserves, for the home fixture against Bolton Wanderers. Pompey won 3-0 to move into third place, three points behind leaders Manchester United.

SATURDAY 22ND MARCH 1958

Everton beat Pompey 4-2 at Goodison Park. It was their first victory over the Fratton men since September 1946 and the two clubs had met on no fewer than seventeen occasions since then.

SATURDAY 23RD MARCH 1929

Jack Smith's 40th minute penalty secured a 1-0 victory over Aston Villa at Highbury in Pompey's first FA Cup semi-final. The Pompey team were lying bottom of Division One.

SATURDAY 23RD MARCH 1968

Pompey kept Second Division promotion hopes alive with a 2-0 victory at home to Middlesbrough, with George Ley and Ray Hiron on target.

TUESDAY 23RD MARCH 1993

Pompey unveiled their new away kit in a First Division promotion clash away to Tranmere Rovers. The new strip was a red and black halved shirt with baggy red shorts and the new design included the club badge, incorporating the city's coat of arms. Two goals by Guy Whittingham earned Pompey a 2-0 win and moved Jim Smith's men three points behind second-placed West Ham in the First Division table.

SATURDAY 24TH MARCH 1951

A crowd of 49,716 – the second largest league attendance in Pompey history – saw the reigning Football League Champions held to a draw by champions-elect Tottenham Hotspur at Fratton Park. Duggie Reid headed Pompey in front on seven minutes and Dennis Uphill deflected the ball past Ernie Butler on the half-hour mark for Spurs' equaliser.

SATURDAY 24TH MARCH 1962

Having beaten Third Division promotion rivals Bristol City 4-0 at Ashton Gate, Pompey went one better by winning 5-0 against City at Fratton Park. As a result Pompey's lead at the top of the table was twelve points.

TUESDAY 24TH MARCH 1976

Portsmouth Football Club president, Field Marshal the Rt Hon Viscount Montgomery of Alamein, KG, GCB, DSO, died aged 88. He had held the title of president since 1944 and was also an honorary vice-president of the Football Association.

THURSDAY 24TH MARCH 1983

Pompey made two deadline day signings. Birmingham City midfielder Kevin Dillon moved for £140,000 and £50,000 was spent on centre-forward Nicky Morgan from West Ham.

SATURDAY 24TH MARCH 1990

In a Second Division clash with Leeds United at Elland Road, Alan Knight saved a penalty from Gordon Strachan before Vinnie Jones and Lee Chapman scored to give the home side a 2-0 victory.

SATURDAY 25TH MARCH 1939

Pompey reached the FA Cup Final by beating Huddersfield Town 2-1 at Highbury in front of 60,053. Bobby Barclay gave Huddersfield a first-half lead but Bert Barlow equalised and Jock Anderson crashed home the winner with seven minutes left to set up a meeting with Wolverhampton Wanderers in the final.

SATURDAY 25TH MARCH 1950

Chasing their second successive League Championship title, Pompey turned on the style to beat Chelsea 4-0 in front of 28,574 at Fratton Park with Duggie Reid scoring a hat-trick of headers. Pompey's other goal came from Peter Harris.

FRIDAY 25TH MARCH 1966

Johnny Gordon was presented with a gold watch and cheque for £700 before Pompey's Second Division encounter with Middlesbrough at Fratton Park to mark his 400th league appearance. The team did Gordon proud, producing a memorable performance and winning 4-1.

SATURDAY 26TH MARCH 1949

One of the worst days in the club's history! Pompey – clear leaders of the First Division – were surprisingly beaten 3-1 by Second Division strugglers Leicester City in the FA Cup semi-final at Highbury. Don Revie gave Leicester a shock early lead but Peter Harris equalised. Ken Chisholm fired the Foxes back in front and it summed up Pompey's day when Harris missed an open goal from six yards. Worse was to come in the 55th minute when Revie headed in Leicester's third goal.

SATURDAY 26TH MARCH 1977

Two goals in the last five minutes earned Pompey a much-needed victory over fellow Third Division strugglers Northampton Town at Fratton Park before 9,195. In the 52nd minute the Cobblers stunned the crowd with a goal by Paul Stratford. With five minutes left, hordes of fans were streaming for the exits convinced this was another nail in Pompey's coffin when Paul Gilchrist stooped to power a header into the corner. With time running out, Dave Kemp headed a dramatic winner into the roof of the net.

SATURDAY 27TH MARCH 1948

While Pompey's first team were being defeated 2-1 by Aston Villa at Villa Park, the club was fielding two reserve teams for the first time. One team lost 2-0 to Southampton Reserves at Fratton Park while the other was beaten 3-0 by Charlton's second string at The Valley.

MONDAY 27TH MARCH 1989

Mick Quinn and Warren Aspinall gave Pompey an early 2-0 lead but John Gregory's men had to settle for a 2-2 draw at home to Watford. John Beresford, who was making his debut following a £300,000 move from Barnsley, broke an ankle in the game and didn't feature again that season.

SATURDAY 27TH MARCH 2004

Pompey pulled away from the Premiership drop zone after recording their first away victory, 2-1 against Blackburn Rovers, since achieving promotion. Teddy Sheringham and Yakubu were the Pompey goalscorers.

SATURDAY 27TH MARCH 2010

Former Pompey players Peter Crouch and Niko Kranjcar were the goalscorerers as Tottenham Hotspur beat Pompey 2-0 at White Hart Lane. There was more misery for the Blues as both Hermann Hreidarsson and Danny Webber were carried off on stretchers.

THURSDAY 27TH MARCH 2014

Manager Richie Barker parted company with the club by mutual consent. He took over a struggling side in December but, by the time of his departure, relegation was looking increasingly possible. Andy Awford immediately stepped in as caretaker-boss for the second time during the season.

WEDNESDAY 28TH MARCH 1928

Pompey won 2-0 against Arsenal on their first visit to Highbury. John Weddle and Jack Smith scored for Jack Tinn's team.

SATURDAY 28TH MARCH 1953

A Peter Harris penalty four minutes from time earned Pompey a 3-3 draw against Tottenham Hotspur at White Hart Lane. Dennis Hall was making his league debut at right-back.

SATURDAY 28TH MARCH 1987

Two goals by Vince Hilaire and another by Noel Blake restored Pompey to the top of the Second Division after beating Sunderland 3-1 in a rousing clash at Fratton Park watched by 13,371.

SATURDAY 28TH MARCH 1992

A controversial penalty, converted by John Beresford, saved Pompey from defeat against Swindon Town at Fratton Park in front of 16,007. The visitors had gone ahead four minutes into the second half through Tommy Jones.

SATURDAY 28TH MARCH 2009

The inaugural Pompey Hall of Fame ceremony was held at Fratton Park. The five former players inducted were Jimmy Dickinson, Peter Harris, Alan Knight, Guy Whittingham and Ray Hiron. Over 200 attended the ceremony which has become a highly successful annual event.

SATURDAY 29TH MARCH 1952

Duggie Reid's 74th minute header was enough to secure a home win over First Division leaders Manchester United. Pompey remained in third place but were now only a point behind Matt Busby's side.

SATURDAY 29TH MARCH 1958

A transformed Arsenal pulled back from 4-0 down to Pompey at Fratton Park only for the home side to win the match 5-4. Pompey could have added a sixth goal late on but Gunners' keeper Jack Kelsey saved a penalty from Peter Harris.

SUNDAY 29TH MARCH 1981

Pompey and Oxford United drew 1-1 in a Third Division clash at Fratton Park that was played on a Sunday as an experiment. The crowd was 12,243 which was 2,000 down on the season's average attendance so chairman John Deacon said, "From now on we will stick to Saturdays."

FRIDAY 30TH MARCH 1923

Billy Haines marked his Pompey debut with a goal as his side defeated Swindon Town 4-1 at Fratton Park. Haines became a legend at Fratton Park with his 40 goals helping the club into the First Division in 1927.

TUESDAY 30TH MARCH 1971

Ray Pointer took over in goal during the Second Division clash against Sheffield Wednesday at Hillsborough after John Milkins left the field with a groin injury with an hour gone with the score at 0-0. Wednesday ended the match 3-1 winners. Earlier in the day the general manager George Smith left Fratton Park. Appointed manager in March 1961, he moved upstairs in April 1970 when Ron Tindall was put in charge of team affairs.

FRIDAY 30TH MARCH 1979

Pompey manager Jimmy Dickinson suffered a serious heart attack in the Oakwell dressing-room following his side's Fourth Division top of the table clash with Barnsley that finished 1-1.

SATURDAY 30TH MARCH 1991

Colin Clarke scored a hat-trick as Pompey recorded their first win under caretaker-manager Tony Barton. They beat Bristol City 4-1 at Fratton Park, the other goal coming from Guy Whittingham while the Westcountrymen replied through former Pompey striker Nicky Morgan.

FRIDAY 30TH MARCH 2012

The Pompey Supporters Trust announced planes for fans to buy the club. Members of the fans' group hoped that thousands of supporters would make a minimum £1,000 commitment to give the club a fresh start – and save it from near-certain liquidation.

SATURDAY 31st MARCH 1923

A day after netting on his Pompey debut, Billy Haines scored both goals in a 2-1 victory at home to Norwich City in Division Three (South).

SATURDAY 31st MARCH 1928

Goalkeeper Dan McPhail kept a seventh consecutive clean sheet as a Johnny Weddle goal secured a 1-0 victory over Bolton Wanderers at Fratton Park.

SATURDAY 31st MARCH 1951

A Peter Harris goal was enough to secure victory over Charlton Athletic at The Valley and stretch Pompey's unbeaten run to six matches.

SATURDAY 31st MARCH 1962

Former Pompey favourite Jimmy Scoular skippered Bradford to a 2-1 victory over Pompey at Park Avenue. His old club still led the Third Division table by ten points.

PORTSMOUTH
On This Day & Miscellany

APRIL

SATURDAY 1st APRIL 1961

Pompey produced their biggest victory of the season, beating Brighton and Hove Albion 4-0 at Fratton Park in their first match after announcing that George Smith would become the new manager of the club. The goalscorers were Ron Saunders (2), Johnny Gordon and Allan Brown. Mr Smith was not in charge of the team for this game as he was not to be released from his coaching duties by Sheffield United until after the two sides met two days later.

SATURDAY 1st APRIL 1978

Millwall, banned from their own ground The Den because of crowd violence, played a home game against Bristol Rovers at Fratton Park. Rovers won the Second Division clash 3-1 before a crowd of 3,322. Meanwhile, Pompey suffered a 1-0 defeat away to Bradford City and this almost certainly consigned them to relegation from the Third Division.

SATURDAY 1st APRIL 2006

Pompey's remarkable surge towards Premiership safety continued at Craven Cottage as two goals by Gary O'Neil and another from Lomana LuaLua earned a 3-1 win over Fulham.

SATURDAY 2nd APRIL 1949

After leading 3-0 through goals by Ike Clarke, Peter Harris and Len Phillips, Pompey had to fight hard to beat Liverpool at Fratton Park before 35,013. Albert Stubbins and future Reds manager Bob Paisley pulled goals back but Pompey held on for the points.

SATURDAY 2nd APRIL 1988

Barry Horne's third goal of the season brought Pompey a valuable 1-0 victory to end their dismal run of five successive defeats as they dominated Tottenham Hotspur in a First Division clash at White Hart Lane in front of 18,616.

SATURDAY 2nd APRIL 2002

Ike Clarke, the centre-forward in Pompey's League Championship side of 1948-49 and 1949-50, died aged 87. He scored 37 goals over those two seasons including one that clinched the first title in a 2-1 win away at Bolton Wanderers.

SATURDAY 3RD APRIL 1920

Fratton Park's attendance record for a Southern League game was broken when a crowd of 24,606 witnessed a goalless draw between Pompey and Cardiff City.

SATURDAY 3RD APRIL 1965

Recovering their confidence after a run of four straight defeats, Pompey outgunned promotion-seeking Bolton Wanderers, winning 3-0. With only four matches of the season remaining Pompey were one place off the bottom of the Second Division table.

SUNDAY 3RD APRIL 2005

Pompey keeper Jamie Ashdown saved a penalty at Craven Cottage but Pompey paid for missing a host of chances, going down 3-1 to Fulham.

SATURDAY 3RD APRIL 2010

Lenny Sowah made history when he came on as a substitute for Pompey in a goalless draw against Blackburn Rovers at Fratton Park. Aged 17 years 223 days, Sowah became the first player to play in the Premier League who was born after its inception.

SATURDAY 4TH APRIL 1953

Pompey led Sheffield Wednesday 5-0 before the half-time whistle at Fratton Park, two goals each scored by Jackie Henderson and Peter Harris with Len Phillips also on target. The visitors scored twice after the interval to make the final score 5-2.

TUESDAY 4TH APRIL 1972

Seven Pompey players were put on the transfer list including centre-forward Ray Hiron. The other players up for sale were Colin Blant, Dave Munks, Tommy Youlden and Jim Storrie while Jim Standen and Mick Travers were given free transfers.

TUESDAY 4TH APRIL 1978

A crowd of only 5,825 saw a 2-0 defeat by Oxford United at Fratton Park, which consigned Pompey to relegation to Division Four.

SATURDAY 4TH APRIL 1998

Pompey met Birmingham City in Division One 100 years all but one day since the formation of the club. Many former players were invited to this vital match for Pompey were teetering on the brink of relegation to the Second Division. A defeat looked certain when Dele Adebola gave the visitors an 87th minute lead but Pompey defender Andy Thomson popped up in the last minute to stab home the equaliser.

MONDAY 5TH APRIL 1898

Portsmouth Football Club was formed. Six businessmen met at 12 High Street, Old Portsmouth, formed themselves into a syndicate and decided to buy four-and-a-half acres of agricultural land near Goldsmith Avenue for £4,950. Fratton Park would arise on this site.

SATURDAY 5TH APRIL 1952

England beat Scotland 2-1 at Hampden Park in a Home International fixture in which the entire Pompey half-back line was on duty. Jack Froggatt and Jimmy Dickinson were representing England while Jimmy Scoular lined up for Scotland.

SUNDAY 5TH APRIL 1992

Pompey could not have got closer to their first FA Cup Final since 1939 in a dramatic semi-final against Liverpool. A Highbury crowd of 41,869 saw Pompey rattle Liverpool with Bruce Grobbelaar somehow saving Alan McLoughlin's shot on 41 minutes. From that corner McLoughlin's back-heel was hacked off the line by Ray Houghton and the same Liverpool player blocked a Colin Clarke header on the line before Grobbelaar grabbed the ball. Darren Anderton put Jim Smith's side ahead in the 110th minute with a low shot. But with only three minutes left, John Barnes' free-kick struck a post and Ronnie Whelan snatched Liverpool's equaliser.

SATURDAY 5TH APRIL 2008

A second-half goal from Kanu at Wembley was enough to send Pompey through to the FA Cup final for the first time in 69 years. A crowd of 83,584 saw the striker side-foot home from close range against his old club West Bromwich Albion in the 54th minute.

WEDNESDAY 6TH APRIL 1949

First Division leaders Pompey travelled to second-placed Newcastle United and thrashed the Magpies 5-0 with the goals – all headers – shared between wingers Jack Froggatt (3) and Peter Harris (2).

SATURDAY 6TH APRIL 1963

Stanley Matthews played his last competitive match at Fratton Park – and his first since 1955 – in Second Division leaders Stoke City's 3-0 victory over Pompey.

MONDAY 7TH APRIL 1997

Former club chairman John Deacon died aged 84. Mr Deacon became a director in December 1972 and was made chairman in May 1973. He held the position for fifteen years in which Pompey sunk to Division Four, climbed up to the First Division and dropped back into Division Two.

THURSDAY 7TH APRIL 2005

Alain Perrin was appointed as the new manager of Pompey. Milan Mandaric described the Frenchman as the new Brian Clough. Meanwhile Velimir Zajec remained as the man in charge of all the club's football operations.

SATURDAY 7TH APRIL 2007

Pompey blew the Premiership title race wide open with a shock victory over leaders Manchester United at Fratton Park watched by 20,223. Matt Taylor and a Rio Ferdinand own goal were the Pompey goalscorers with John O'Shea replying for Sir Alex Ferguson's men.

SATURDAY 8TH APRIL 1950

Pompey's hopes of retaining the Football League Championship were dealt a blow when they were beaten 1-0 at home by West Bromwich Albion leaving them three points behind leaders Sunderland with five matches to play.

TUESDAY 8TH APRIL 1986

When Pompey lost 2-1 to Crystal Palace at Selhurst Park on 8 April 1986, Andy Gray scored all three goals. He headed Crystal Palace into the lead on 18 minutes then a hit-and-hope shot from the touchline gave his side a 2-0 advantage. In the second half his diving header diverted Mick Kennedy's shot past his own goalkeeper.

SATURDAY 8TH APRIL 2006

Substitute Svetoslav Todorov salvaged a priceless point for Pompey in the battle to avoid relegation and dent Blackburn's Champions League hopes. Todorov met Matt Taylor's near-post cross to make the score 2-2 after Craig Bellamy had twice put Blackburn ahead. Pompey's first goal was scored by Lomana LuaLua.

SATURDAY 9TH APRIL 1927

Pompey recorded their biggest Football League victory, beating Notts County 9-1 at Fratton Park in a Second Division clash. The goalscorers were Billy Haines (3), Jerry Mackie (2), Fred Cook (2), Reg Davies and Fred Forward. Haines' hat-trick was his second in consecutive matches.

SATURDAY 9TH APRIL 1949

Pompey's lead at the top of the First Division was cut to three points after they were beaten 1-0 by Blackpool at Bloomfield Road and second-placed Newcastle United won 4-2 away to Derby County.

SATURDAY 9TH APRIL 1960

With the half-time news that clubs below them were faring well, Pompey avoided slipping back into trouble by scoring twice in the second half to earn a 2-0 victory at Fratton Park over Rotherham United who were making their first visit to Fratton Park.

WEDNESDAY 9TH APRIL 2008

Portsmouth Football Club announced a loss of over £23m for the financial year ending 1st May 2007. The club's wage bill increased to more than £30m as the players' salaries almost doubled but it was said that financial results were in line with expectations.

SATURDAY 10TH APRIL 1954

Pompey produced a tremendous second-half display to beat Newcastle United 2-0 at Fratton Park, the goals coming from Mike Barnard and Gordon Dale. The victory eased Pompey's relegation fears.

SATURDAY 10TH APRIL 1993

Pompey stretched their unbeaten run to nine with a 2-1 win at Bristol Rovers. Benny Kristensen netted the first goal before Guy Whittingham grabbed his 43rd of the season, breaking Billy Haines' 1927 record.

SATURDAY 10TH APRIL 2004

Yakubu scored to earn Pompey a 1-1 draw against Charlton Athletic at The Valley. Shaun Bartlett had given Charlton an early lead but the introduction of Pompey substitute Eyal Berkovic changed the game and the Blues came away with a valuable point.

SATURDAY 10TH APRIL 2010

West Ham United's 1-0 win over Sunderland meant that Pompey were relegated from the Premier League with five matches of the season remaining. Pompey started the campaign by losing the first seven matches and then had nine points deducted after entering into administration.

WEDNESDAY 10TH APRIL 2014

A deal was struck between Portsmouth Football Club administrators and former owners Portpin to allow Fratton Park to be sold for £3m to the Pompey Supporters Trust. This meant that the path was clear for the Trust to buy the club out of administration.

SATURDAY 11TH APRIL 1959

Pompey were still looking for their first win at Burnley after going down 2-1 at Turf Moor. Brian Pilkington's late winner was the 100th league goal Pompey had conceded during a season which ended in relegation after 32 years in the top flight.

SATURDAY 11TH APRIL 1987

Pompey took a giant step towards the First Division as two penalties by Kevin Dillon and a goal from Mick Quinn in front of 19,708 at Fratton Park gave them a 3-0 win over Oldham Athletic and took them six points ahead of their third-placed opponents.

SATURDAY 11TH APRIL 1992

Goals by Stuart Doling and Warren Aspinall gave Pompey a 2-0 win against Grimsby Town – their first victory in five league matches – to keep their play-off dream alive at Fratton Park watched by 10,576.

SUNDAY 11TH APRIL 2010

Only 24 hours after being relegated from the Premier League, Pompey enjoyed one of the greatest days in their long history by beating Tottenham Hotspur against all odds in the FA Cup semi-final at Wembley Stadium. Managed by former Pompey boss Harry Redknapp, Spurs started with Peter Crouch and Jermain Defoe in their line-up while Niko Kranjcar later came on as a substitute. After a goalless ninety minutes Frederic Piquionne put the Blues ahead before Kevin-Prince Boateng converted a penalty to seal a famous Pompey victory.

SATURDAY 12TH APRIL 1958

Ray Crawford made a dash from his wedding at St Mary's Church, Portsea to play in a First Division game with Blackpool at Fratton Park. After the 2-1 defeat he rejoined bride Eileen and guests at the reception.

MONDAY 12TH APRIL 1982

Trevor Senior scored twice in a 3-0 win at home to Reading. Those goals were the only ones he scored for Pompey. A year later he was transferred to Reading and in two spells with the Royals hit 190 league and cup goals, becoming the Berkshire club's record goalscorer in all competitions.

MONDAY 12TH APRIL 1993

An Easter Monday crowd of 23,805 saw Pompey move within two points of First Division leaders Newcastle United by defeating Derby County 3-0 at Fratton Park. Paul Walsh scored twice after Guy Whittingham had given Jim Smith's side the lead after 85 seconds.

WEDNESDAY 12TH APRIL 2006

Lomana LuaLua's second-half header gave Pompey a valuable point in their Premiership relegation battle in front of 20,230 at Fratton Park. Thierry Henry had earlier put the Gunners in front.

WEDNESDAY 13TH APRIL 1977

Portsmouth Young Supporters' Club was launched at the Rock Gardens Pavilion, Southsea. Approximately 500 supporters and their parents crowded into the hall for the inaugural meeting of the organisation which was aimed at fans aged between eight and eighteen.

MONDAY 13TH APRIL 1992

Pompey lost their FA Cup semi-final replay with Liverpool on penalties after holding their opponents to a goalless draw after extra time. Jim Smith's side so nearly made it through to the final near the end of ninety minutes but Alan McLoughlin's shot hit the bar. Only Kit Symons found the net from the penalty spot.

WEDNESDAY 14TH APRIL 1948

Record signing Albert Juliussen scored a hat-trick in only his third Pompey outing as his new side thrashed Middlesbrough 6-1 at Fratton Park.

SATURDAY 14TH APRIL 1951

Aston Villa and Pompey played out a thrilling 3-3 draw at Villa Park. After going a goal down Pompey led 3-1 but Villa scored twice late on.

SATURDAY 14TH APRIL 1956

Peter Harris scored his 150th league goal for Pompey in the 1-1 draw with West Bromwich Albion at Fratton Park. Harris equalised after Mike Lee, playing in his only match for West Brom, netted the opening goal.

SATURDAY 14TH APRIL 1984

A second-half hat-trick by Blackburn Rovers' Simon Garner turned a sunny afternoon into an agonising tenth home league defeat for Pompey at Fratton Park before 8,915 after Bobby Campbell's team looked to have the game wrapped up at half-time. Two goals by Neil Webb had given Pompey a 2-0 half-time lead but Garner's treble and a goal by Mark Patterson completed an amazing turn-around.

SATURDAY 14TH APRIL 2007

Benjani's first goal since New Year's Day and a stunning strike from Matt Taylor earned Pompey a 2-1 victory from a game they dominated against Newcastle United at Fratton Park watched by 20,165.

SATURDAY 15TH APRIL 1950

Two goals in the last six minutes of a disappointing game against Manchester United at Old Trafford brought Pompey two valuable points in their quest for a second successive league title. Duggie Reid and Jack Froggatt were the goalscorers.

WEDNESDAY 15TH APRIL 1970

Ray Hiron scored a hat-trick as Pompey drew 3-3 with Hull City before 11,468 at Boothferry Park in their final match of the campaign. Those three goals took Hiron's tally to 18 – one better than the previous year and the most he scored in one season.

WEDNESDAY 15TH APRIL 1992

Aston Villa stadium manager Ted Small tore into Pompey fans for turning his ground into an ankle-deep waste-paper tip. He was referring to the blizzard of ticker-tape thrown during Pompey's FA Cup semi-final replay against Liverpool.

TUESDAY 15TH APRIL 2003

A goal by Svetoslav Todorov against Burnley earned Pompey the victory that clinched promotion to the Premiership at Fratton Park in front of 19,221. Paul Merson slammed a penalty against the bar in the first half but Todorov supplied the golden moment in the 72nd minute.

SATURDAY 16TH APRIL 1949

Pompey moved a step closer to winning the championship by beating FA Cup finalists Wolves 5-0 in front of 44,225 at Fratton Park.

SATURDAY 16TH APRIL 1955

A crowd of 40,230 witnessed a goalless draw between third-placed Pompey and Division One leaders Chelsea. Failure to beat the Londoners meant that any hopes of Pompey winning a third league title had realistically vanished.

FRIDAY 16TH APRIL 1982

It was announced that Pompey would be launching an ambitious scheme to bring back families to Fratton Park. A season ticket for 1982/83 a party of four – maximum two adults – for the North Stand would cost £100.

SATURDAY 17TH APRIL 1965

Pompey hung on to their hopes of avoiding the drop to the Third Division by beating Cardiff City 1-0 thanks to Cliff Portwood's 36th minute strike. They were left two points from safety but with a game in hand over 20th placed Swindon Town.

WEDNESDAY 17TH APRIL 2002

Gary O'Neil captained England under-19s in a 1-1 draw in Lithuania. He was only the second Pompey player to lead England at any level, AE Knight having skippered the national side against Wales in October 1919.

SATURDAY 17TH APRIL 2004

Steve Stone's goal just before half-time was enough to give Pompey victory over Manchester United at Fratton Park. It was a day for a lot of firsts. It was the first time Pompey had beaten the reigning league champions since 19th October 1957 when their opponents were, coincidentally, Manchester United. It was the first time the Fratton men had succeeded over a United team since that day and also the first time a team managed by Harry Redknapp defeated the Red Devils in a league match.

SATURDAY 18TH APRIL 1949

Pompey's League Championship prospects looked to have received a dent after being beaten 3-0 by Birmingham City at St Andrews, but they still led the table by four points as their closest rivals Newcastle United lost 3-2 at Middlesbrough.

SATURDAY 18TH APRIL 1959

Nat Lofthouse scored the only goal as Bolton Wanderers beat Second Division-bound Pompey in what would prove to be the last top-flight match at Fratton Park for 28 years. Pompey had only picked up one point at home since November.

WEDNESDAY 18TH APRIL 1973

Southampton and Wales centre-forward Ron Davies signed for Pompey for a fee of £38,000. He topped the goalscoring charts with 16 goals in all competitions the following season.

WEDNESDAY 19TH APRIL 1939

Reg Flewin, aged 18, was the first Portsmouth-born player to appear in Pompey's league side since the club became members of the Football League in 1920 when he played at centre-half in a 2-1 victory at home to Grimsby Town.

SATURDAY 19TH APRIL 1958

Despite losing 2-1 to Luton Town at Kenilworth Road, Pompey were made certain of First Division survival thanks to Sheffield Wednesday's 2-0 defeat by Aston Villa. Manager Eddie Lever said, "What a tremendous relief. I should have liked to have seen the lads get out of trouble in more certain fashion but one has to be thankful for small mercies."

MONDAY 19TH APRIL 1965

Jimmy Dickinson was presented with a statuette before the last home match of his career against Norwich City. The inscription on the statuette read: "Presented to Jimmy Dickinson by the players and staff on his retirement in recognition of his sterling qualities as a player for Portsmouth." After Pompey had trounced the Canaries 4-0 to give their Second Division survival hopes a tremendous boost, Dickinson was carried shoulder high on a lap of honour.

FRIDAY 19TH APRIL 2010

Pompey Supporters Trust sealed the deal to take over Portsmouth Football Club in the offices of solicitors Verisona at 1000 Lakeside, North Harbour, Portsmouth. This meant that the club was the biggest-owned community club in the country.

SATURDAY 20TH APRIL 1935

Alex Mackie made his farewell league appearance for Pompey in a 1-0 home defeat by Wolverhampton Wanderers. Mackie played in the 1929 and 1934 FA Cup finals and won two Northern Ireland caps.

SATURDAY 20TH APRIL 1963

Pompey's depressing run of nine straight defeats ended with a 3-0 victory over Leeds United at Fratton Park. Blues goalkeeper John Armstrong saved a penalty from Jack Charlton while the goalscorers were Tony Barton, Johnny Gordon and Albert McCann.

MONDAY 20TH APRIL 1987

Pompey's unbeaten home record ended with Plymouth Argyle inflicting a 1-0 defeat on Alan Ball's side. Argyle substitute Kevin Summerfield had only been on the field two minutes when he fired home the winning goal.

SATURDAY 21ST APRIL 1956

Manchester United clinched the First Division title for the fourth time by beating Pompey 1-0 at Old Trafford thanks to a goal by Dennis Viollet.

SATURDAY 21ST APRIL 1962

Oh what a let-down! This was the day Pompey should have made certain of promotion without depending on the results of others but instead crashed 3-0 at home to Peterborough United.

SATURDAY 21ST APRIL 1973

Fulham fought back with two goals by John Conway to win 2-1 in a Second Division fixture at Fratton Park to record their first-ever win over Pompey. John Cutbush had earlier put through his own goal to give Pompey the lead. Referee Ray Toseland pulled a muscle during the first half and continued the second period on the line while Ken Hunt took over the whistle.

SUNDAY 21ST APRIL 1985

Pompey manager Alan Ball completed the London Marathon in three-and-a-half hours. He said, "Whether I'll do another I don't know but I wouldn't have missed it for the world."

SUNDAY 21ST APRIL 2002

Pompey were beaten 3-1 by Manchester City on their last visit to Maine Road. There was drama in stoppage time when City's Stuart Pearce had the chance to score his 100th league goal in his last ever game but he lifted his kick over the bar.

SATURDAY 22ND APRIL 1967

Alex Wilson made his final appearance for Pompey in a goalless draw with Derby County at The Baseball Ground. Wilson, who made his debut in October 1951, was representing Pompey for the 377th time.

SUNDAY 22ND APRIL 2007

David James produced a superlative display to ensure Pompey came away from Villa Park with a point to bolster their bid for European qualification. James' display secured a new record of Premiership clean sheets – 142 – to surpass David Seaman.

SATURDAY 23RD APRIL 1949

Pompey were crowned Football League Champions following a 2-1 win away at Bolton - their first ever victory at Burnden Park. Peter Harris gave Pompey a dream start with a goal after four minutes and the outside-right then supplied the cross for Ike Clarke to double the lead with a firm header in the 25th minute. Eight minutes from time John Roberts pulled a goal back to set up a frantic finish but Pompey held on to claim the points.

SATURDAY 23RD APRIL 1955

Pompey's remaining hopes of winning the Football League Championship ended at Ninian Park when, with Chelsea beating Sheffield Wednesday 3-0 to claim their first title win, the Fratton men could only draw 1-1 with lowly Cardiff City. It meant the championship trophy going to Stamford Bridge for the first time while Pompey still had a chance of finishing runners-up.

SATURDAY 23RD APRIL 1960

A header by Harry Harris kept Pompey in Division Two. He cancelled out a goal by Hull City's Chris Morris in the penultimate match of the season at Fratton Park and the 1-1 draw also sent the Tigers down.

MONDAY 23RD APRIL 1962

A 2-1 victory over Watford at Fratton Park ensured Pompey were Third Division champions with two matches of the season remaining. Ron Saunders scored both goals to take his League tally to 26.

SATURDAY 24TH APRIL 1965

Pompey escaped relegation to Division Three when Alex Wilson equalised late in the game at Northampton Town. Jimmy Dickinson played his final match on his 40th birthday and was carried from the pitch.

SATURDAY 24TH APRIL 1971

Pompey, with five first-team regulars missing, managed to earn a 1-1 draw against Birmingham City at St Andrews. Bob Latchford gave the home side an early lead but Ray Hiron levelled in the second half.

MONDAY 24TH APRIL 1972

Second Division survival was assured when Pompey came from behind with goals by Norman Piper and Eoin Hand to win 2-1 at Blackpool.

SATURDAY 24TH APRIL 2010

Aruna Dindane scored twice to earn Pompey a 2-2 draw after being two goals down only 24 hours after his parent club Lens scrapped their £4m pay demands if the Ivory Coast international turned out for the Blues again. Dindane was desperate to play in the World Cup and, the day before his double strike, travelled to France on Eurostar to plea with Lens to allow him to appear again for Pompey.

WEDNESDAY 24TH APRIL 2013

Guy Whittingham was handed the Pompey manager's job on a permanent basis. The club's striking legend had been caretaker-boss since November when Michael Appleton left to take over at Blackpool. The team failed to make headway the following season and Whittingham was released in November.

SATURDAY 25TH APRIL 1959

Pompey completed an unbelievably poor run – no league victories since 22 November – with a 5-2 defeat by Arsenal at Highbury to bring their nightmare season to an end. Freddie Cox's men finished bottom of the First Division, eight points from safety with a record of; Played 42, Won 6, Drew 9, Lost 27, Goals Scored 64, Goals Against 112, Points 21.

SATURDAY 25TH APRIL 1998

A 3-0 home win over Huddersfield Town meant that Pompey's fate was back in their own hands. Robbie Pethick, Andy Thomson and John Durnin were on target for the Blues. A win at Bradford City on the last day would mean First Division survival.

SUNDAY 25TH APRIL 2004

Pompey stretched their unbeaten run to six and made certain of Premiership survival with a 2-1 win at Leeds United. Yakubu and Lomana LuaLua were on target before Ian Harte scored a late penalty for Leeds.

WEDNESDAY 25TH APRIL 2007

Pompey unveiled their £600m dream as they bid yet again to leave Fratton Park. A harbourside development was to see them move to The Hard with a spectacular 36,000 stadium that was set to be completed by 2011. Earlier in the day the club and its supporters were shocked to learn that former manager Alan Ball had died suddenly aged 61.

SATURDAY 26TH APRIL 1947

Manchester United earned their first ever victory at Fratton Park, beating Pompey 1-0 thanks to a goal by Jimmy Delaney.

MONDAY 26TH APRIL 1971

Pompey and Orient drew 1-1 in a Second Division encounter at Brisbane Road. Earlier in the day the club turned down a £2,000 offer from the Os for Mike Trebilcock who cost a record £40,000 in January 1968.

SATURDAY 26TH APRIL 1980

The last home match of the season ended in a 4-0 victory for Pompey over Peterborough United but promotion looked to have been lost with Frank Burrows' men in fifth place with one match remaining.

SATURDAY 27TH APRIL 1929

Pompey were beaten 2-0 in their first FA Cup Final by Bolton Wanderers at Wembley. They were forced to reshuffle their side when left-back Tommy Bell was injured close on half-time and moved to outside-left with both legs bandaged. Billy Butler scored Bolton's first goal with 12 minutes left then Harold Blackmore made certain with a terrific shot three minutes from time.

SATURDAY 27TH APRIL 1957

Although Pompey were beaten 1-0 by West Bromwich Albion at Fratton Park, Cardiff City's failure to beat Manchester United at Ninian Park made them safe from relegation.

SATURDAY 27TH APRIL 1996

Relegation to the Second Division loomed large as Pompey were beaten 1-0 at home by Ipswich Town. It meant they had to beat Huddersfield Town on the last day to have any hope of avoiding the drop. The loss sparked a noisy protest by around 500 Pompey fans who unfurled banners calling for manager Terry Fenwick to go. Several bottles were thrown with one smashing a window above the Pompey Shop.

SUNDAY 27TH APRIL 2003

A Paul Merson penalty and two goals by Svetoslav Todorov helped Pompey to a 3-2 win at Fratton Park against Rotherham United which clinched the First Division title.

SATURDAY 28TH APRIL 1934

Pompey were beaten 2-1 by Manchester City in the FA Cup Final at Wembley. Sep Rutherford gave Pompey a first-half lead but they were hit by a major blow when centre-half Jimmy Allen left the field suffering from concussion. Although he returned to action he was still concussed and City centre-forward Fred Tilson scored twice. The attendance for the game was 93,258 and the receipts were £24,950.

SATURDAY 28TH APRIL 2007

Benjani and Niko Kranjcar scored to give Pompey a 2-1 win at Fratton Park over Liverpool. The victory moved Pompey into the qualifying places for the UEFA Cup.

SATURDAY 29TH APRIL 1939

Pompey won the FA Cup, beating Wolves 4-1 at Wembley. Bert Barlow opened the scoring with a fine shot on 31 minutes and seconds before the interval Jock Anderson curled a shot just out of Bob Scott's reach. Inside a minute of the second-half, Cliff Parker added a third but Wolves hit back and after two fierce raids Dickie Dorsett reduced the deficit. Parker headed Pompey's fourth in the 72nd minute and after the match, skipper Jimmy Guthrie received the cup from King George VI.

SATURDAY 29TH APRIL 1978

Sixteen-year-old goalkeeper Alan Knight, who went on to make over 800 appearances for Pompey, made his debut as the team ended their disastrous season with a 1-0 win at Rotherham United. Already doomed to relegation it was only the seventh league win, sealed by a Peter Denyer goal.

SATURDAY 29TH APRIL 2006

Pompey completed their great escape with a 2-1 win on their first visit to the JJB Stadium which sealed their survival and sent down West Bromwich Albion and Birmingham City. Henri Camara put Wigan ahead on 34 minutes but Benjani Mwaruwari nodded home his first Pompey goal and Matt Taylor kept a cool head to slot home a winning penalty.

WEDNESDAY 30TH APRIL 1924

Pompey clinched the Third Division (South) title with an emphatic 4-1 victory over Swindon Town before 17,458 at Fratton Park. Harry Foxall (2), Dave Watson and Jimmy Martin were the goalscorers.

SATURDAY 30TH APRIL 1949

A goal in each half – from Duggie Reid and Ike Clarke – gave Pompey a 2-0 victory over Huddersfield Town at Fratton Park before 37,042. Pompey were already crowned League Champions. After the match the trophy was presented by E.J. Cearns, a member of the League Management Committee, to president Field Marshall Montgomery.

SATURDAY 30TH APRIL 1977

Pompey were left staring the Fourth Division in the face after losing 2-1 to fellow strugglers Grimsby Town in front of 10,155 at Fratton Park. After the match Pompey manager Ian St John offered his resignation.

PORTSMOUTH
On This Day & Miscellany

MAY

SATURDAY 1st MAY 1926

Freddie Cook scored on his Pompey debut two days after signing from Newport County. The outside-left, who went on to win six Welsh international caps as a Pompey player and also appear in two FA Cup Finals for the club, helped his new side to a 4-0 win at home to Chelsea in a Second Division clash on the final day of the season.

SATURDAY 1st MAY 1993

Two off and it could have been more! Guy Butters and Paul Walsh were sent off as promotion-chasing Pompey crashed 4-1 to Sunderland at Roker Park. The result meant Pompey's destiny was out of their own hands. Warren Aspinall and Benny Kristensen were lucky not to be red-carded also on what was a disastrous day for the Fratton men.

SATURDAY 1st MAY 2010

Fratton Park bade farewell to the Premier League as Pompey triumphed 3-1 over Wolverhampton Wanderers. The goalscorers were Aruna Dindane, John Utaka and Michael Brown.

THURSDAY 1st MAY 2014

Andy Awford was handed the Pompey manager's job on a permanent basis with one match of the season still to play. The team had won five and drawn one of the six matches played since the 41-year-old former Blues defender had taken over from Richie Barker.

SATURDAY 2nd MAY 1925

Pompey rounded off their first season in the Second Division with an emphatic 5-0 victory over Bradford City at Fratton Park. Jerry Mackie scored a hat-trick with the other two goals coming from Billy Haines. The win meant Pompey finished in fourth place.

SATURDAY 2nd MAY 1931

A 3-0 victory at home to Blackburn Rovers meant Pompey finished fourth in Division One. This was the highest position the club had reached and was to remain so until the Football League Championship title was attained in 1949.

SATURDAY 2ND MAY 1987

Pompey were left requiring one point to gain promotion to the First Division after beating Millwall 2-0 at Fratton Park. Paul Mariner opened the scoring on 54 minutes and Kevin O'Callaghan made certain of victory with a stunning free-kick with two minutes to go.

TUESDAY 2ND MAY 2001

Jeers echoed around Fratton Park as Pompey slumped to a 4-2 defeat at the hands of Crystal Palace. Pompey were outplayed by their fellow relegation candidates and the defeat left the Blues needing at least a draw from their final match at home to Barnsley the following Sunday to avoid the drop.

WEDNESDAY 3RD MAY 1950

Pompey went down 2-0 to Arsenal in front of 63,124 at Highbury, four days after the Gunners defeated Liverpool in the FA Cup Final at Wembley. The result still left Pompey at the top of Division One but level on points with Wolverhampton Wanderers with one match of the season remaining.

SATURDAY 3RD MAY 1980

A 2-0 victory at Northampton saw Pompey gain promotion to the Third Division after two years in soccer's basement. Backed by 8,000 supporters Pompey took the lead when Steve Davey headed them in front shortly before half-time and Ian Purdie, with his only goal for the club, made sure of victory on 73 minutes.

SUNDAY 3RD MAY 1998

Needing three points to be certain of avoiding relegation from the First Division, Alan Ball's men showed tremendous character to pull off a 3-1 victory over Bradford City before 15,890 at Valley Parade. It was the second time in three years that Pompey's fate went to the last game. John Durnin (2) and Sammy Igoe were the goalscorers with Craig Ramage netting a consolation goal for City.

SATURDAY 3RD MAY 2014

Danny Hollands scored a hat-trick as Pompey drew 3-3 at home to Plymouth Argyle on the final day of the season.

SATURDAY 4TH MAY 1968

Ipswich Town made certain of promotion to Division One with one match still to play by beating Pompey 2-1 at Fratton Park. John O'Rourke scored twice for the visitors after Albert McCann had given Pompey the lead.

FRIDAY 4TH MAY 1973

Arsenal's Peter Marinello became Pompey's first £100,000 acquisition.

TUESDAY 4TH MAY 2004

Thierry Henry pulled on a Pompey shirt to say thanks to the Fratton Park crowd that sang his name during and after Pompey's 1-1 draw with Arsenal. The Gunners striker, who was arguably the best player in the world at that time, explained, "They were singing my name asking me to sign for Portsmouth. I know I won't be coming here but I just wanted to wear the shirt for them."

FRIDAY 5TH MAY 1978

Steve Davey became Pompey's first recruit in the campaign to bounce straight out of Division Four. Signed as a striker, Davey spent most of his stint at Fratton Park in the centre of defence. The club also gave a free transfer to midfielder Mick Mellows who had spent five years as a Pompey player but had not accepted the club's new offer.

FRIDAY 5TH MAY 1982

Robbed of goalkeeper Alan Knight for the entire second half, and effectively all but the first 16 minutes, Pompey drew 3-3 against Exeter City at St James' Park. With Keith Viney acting as emergency goalkeeper, Pompey got within two minutes of their fourth away win of the season but Ray Pratt equalised for the home side.

TUESDAY 5TH MAY 1987

After a 28-year absence, Pompey were finally promoted to the First Division, less than 48 hours short of the 60th anniversary of their elevation to the top flight in 1927. However, promotion was something of an anti-climax as Pompey were not involved in a match. Oldham Athletic had a chance of sneaking into the promotion frame but their 2-0 defeat away to Shrewsbury Town meant Pompey had reached Division One with a match still to play.

WEDNESDAY 5TH MAY 1993

More than 500 angry Farlington residents packed Springfield School hall in Drayton to express their horror at the club's plans to build a £10m stadium and shopping complex with 5,000 parking spaces on 94 acres of land north of the A27.

SATURDAY 6TH MAY 1950

Pompey were crowned Football League champions for the second successive year after beating Aston Villa 5-1 before a Fratton Park crowd of 42,295. They won the title on goal average despite second-placed Wolverhampton Wanderers beating Second Division-bound Birmingham City 6-1 at Molineux. Reserve defender Bill Thompson, playing at centre-forward in place of the injured Ike Clarke, scored after only 20 seconds and he grabbed another while Duggie Reid netted his third hat-trick of the season.

SATURDAY 7TH MAY 1927

A 5-1 win over Preston North End at Fratton Park before 26,815 ensured Pompey were promoted to the First Division. Freddie Forward cancelled out Norman Robson's early strike then Billy Haines scored four to take his tally for the season to forty. Manchester City, Pompey's rivals for the runners-up spot, beat Bradford City 8-0 but Pompey pipped them by a 200th part of a goal. After the match Chairman Robert Blyth made a speech and told the jubilant fans, "I am the happiest man in England."

SATURDAY 7TH MAY 1949

The curtain came down on Pompey's first League Championship season at Maine Road where Manchester United won 3-2 in front of 39,608. Pompey had clinched the title at Bolton two weeks earlier and United's victory meant they pipped Derby County to the runners-up spot.

SATURDAY 7TH MAY 1983

With two matches of the season still to play, Pompey made certain of promotion to Division Two with a 2-0 victory over Southend United at Fratton Park watched by 17,858. Pompey were in charge for the entire 90 minutes and the first goal arrived in the 22nd minute through Kevin

Dillon. In the 69th minute Neil Webb took a corner and Alan Biley powered home a header for Pompey's second goal that sparked a mini pitch invasion. When the final whistle sounded thousands ran onto the pitch to celebrate the end of seven years in football's lower divisions.

MONDAY 8TH MAY 1939

Centre-forward Jimmy Beattie was transferred to Millwall. He had scored 28 goals in 58 league and cup matches for Pompey. A brother of Preston North End players Bob and Andy, Beattie became heavily involved in Scottish football after the war and was for a time a selector for the national team.

TUESDAY 8TH MAY 1973

Jimmy Guthrie, captain of Pompey's 1939 FA Cup-winning team, attended the ex-Portsmouth Professionals' Club Annual Dinner and got the surprise of his life. He was presented with his Cup winner's medal that he had lent to a friend more than 30 years before but had not been returned until that evening.

WEDNESDAY 9TH MAY 1945

Aston Villa defeated Pompey 4-3 at Fratton Park in a Victory Match, played to celebrate the end of World War 2. The proceeds were in aid of the Lord Mayor's Royal Navy and Merchant Navy Fund.

WEDNESDAY 9TH MAY 1973

More than 22,000 attended Albert McCann's Testimonial match at Fratton Park against West Ham that Pompey won 4-2. Pompey were parading three new big-money signings, Ron Davies, who scored a hat-trick, Phil Roberts and Peter Marinello.

TUESDAY 9TH MAY 2006

The last surviving member of Pompey's 1939 FA Cup winning team, Tommy Rowe, died in a Dorchester nursing home aged 92. He played in the final at centre-half, the position he had made his own since September 1937. He became a Royal Air Force bomber pilot during the war and in 1943 he was awarded the Distinguished Flying Cross.

THURSDAY 10TH MAY 1973

John Deacon became chairman and announced that John Mortimore would be taking control of team affairs with Ron Tindall becoming general manager. Pat Wright's main responsibility was the development of players in the midweek reserve side, chief scout Tony Barton would be given more scope with the reorganisation of the club's scouting structure whilst Alan Sefton and Ray Pointer would run the youth team.

THURSDAY 10TH MAY 1979

Frank Burrows was appointed Pompey manager immediately after the resignation of Jimmy Dickinson who relinquished his position on the advice of his doctor. Dickinson, who had suffered a serious heart attack at the end of March, was offered the role of the club's Chief Executive and he agreed to take up the appointment as soon as he felt able.

WEDNESDAY 10TH MAY 1983

A crowd of 22,244 were at Fratton Park to see Pompey beat Walsall 1-0 thanks to Steve Aizlewood's diving header. This victory meant that Pompey would be Third Division champions bar a disaster at Plymouth on the final day of the season.

SATURDAY 11TH MAY 1974

Ron Davies and Phil Roberts played for Wales in their 2-0 defeat by England at Ninian Park, Cardiff. They were the first Pompey players to appear for the Welsh national side since Freddie Cook won his last cap in November 1931.

FRIDAY 11TH MAY 1984

Bobby Campbell was sacked as Pompey manager after two years in charge. He led the club to the Third Division title in his first season but the side finished just four places above the Second Division relegation zone.

SATURDAY 11TH MAY 1985

Goals by Kevin O'Callaghan and Vince Hilaire earned Pompey a 2-0 victory away to Huddersfield Town but Manchester City's 5-1 home victory over Charlton Athletic meant they pipped Alan Ball's men to promotion to Division One on goal difference.

WEDNESDAY 11TH MAY 1988

It was announced that Jim Gregory would be buying the club from John Deacon for £2m. The deal was due to be completed on 1 June.

SUNDAY 11TH MAY 2008

Danny Murphy's 76th minute header proved enough to secure Fulham's Premier League status and consign Pompey to their fourth consecutive defeat on the last day of the season at Fratton Park.

FRIDAY 12TH MAY 1967

Pompey rounded off their season with a 1-1 draw at Fratton Park in a friendly with Scottish club Kilmarnock. Ray Pointer put the hosts in front and the equaliser came from Danish international Carl Bertelsen. Before the game manager George Smith completed the signing of West Bromwich Albion goalkeeper Ray Potter on a free transfer.

SATURDAY 12TH MAY 1984

Alan Biley scored a hat-trick as Pompey celebrated caretaker manager Alan Ball's 39th birthday by beating Swansea City 5-0 at Fratton Park in the final match of the season. Ball was subsequently handed the reins permanently. Mark Hateley and sub Nicky Morgan were also on target.

MONDAY 13TH MAY 1963

Pompey produced one of their best displays of the season to win 3-1 at Leeds Road before 12,854 to end Huddersfield Town's slender chance of promotion. Tony Barton, playing at outside-left for the first time, scored twice and Ron Saunders also netted for George Smith's side.

SATURDAY 13TH MAY 1989

It was a sweet return to Fratton Park for Chelsea manager Bobby Campbell as his runaway Second Division champions beat Pompey 3-2 before a crowd of 12,051 on the season's final day. This was Pompey's sixth consecutive defeat – a sequence not suffered since the 1975-76 campaign when they lost their Second Division status.

SATURDAY 14TH MAY 1927

John McCartney resigned as Portsmouth manager because of ill health a week after the club were promoted to the First Division. Mr McCartney was appointed manager in 1920 and led the club to the Division Three (South) title in 1924.

SATURDAY 14TH MAY 1977

Pompey celebrated Jimmy Dickinson's first home match in charge with a 3-1 victory over York City at Fratton Park to ensure Third Division survival. The goalscorers were Clive Green (2) and Dave Kemp.

SATURDAY 14TH MAY 1983

Pompey were crowned Third Division Champions as Alan Biley's 26th goal of the season was enough to secure victory over Plymouth Argyle at Home Park. They began the afternoon with the Championship trophy virtually in their hands and nothing but an absolute disaster would let it slip. Five minutes before the end the referee sent the players to their dressing rooms as hundreds of visiting fans spilled onto the field. Play later resumed but the final whistle was blown early and the Home Park pitch was soon swamped with jubilant Pompey supporters.

FRIDAY 14TH MAY 2004

The day before Pompey's final match of their first season in the Premiership, Milan Mandaric admitted he could quit. A row broke out between him and manager Harry Redknapp over the future of assistant boss Jim Smith.

SATURDAY 15TH MAY 1991

Caretaker boss Tony Barton was told by chairman Jim Gregory that he was not to be appointed manager on a permanent basis. Barton had been assured the job was his after Pompey had beaten Bristol Rovers in April to avoid relegation and that the appointment would be made official when the season ended.

SATURDAY 15TH MAY 2004

Yakubu scored four goals including a penalty in a 5-1 victory at home to Middlesbrough in the season's final game. "The Yak" had found goals difficult to come by in the first half of the campaign but eleven strikes in the last ten games took his season's tally to nineteen.

SUNDAY 15TH MAY 2005

West Bromwich Albion defeated Pompey 2-0 at The Hawthorns to retain their Premiership status. Many of the Pompey fans were celebrating with the Albion supporters afterwards because Southampton's defeat at home to Manchester United meant they dropped out of the top flight after a period of 27 years.

SATURDAY 15TH MAY 2010

Pompey were beaten 1-0 by Chelsea in the FA Cup Final at Wembley Stadium in front of 88,335. David James and Papa Bouba Diop were the only survivors from Pompey's 1-0 Wembley triumph over Cardiff City in 2008 to be in the starting line-up while Kanu, scorer of the goal against the Bluebirds, was on the bench. Chelsea hit the woodwork no less than five times in the opening 45 minutes before Kevin-Prince Boateng missed a penalty for Pompey. Didier Drogba scored the only goal with a curling 20-yard free kick and Chelsea skipper Frank Lampard placed a spot kick wide near the end. The Pompey team was: David James, Steve Finnan, Ricardo Rocha, Aaron Mokoena, Hayden Mullins (Nadir Belhadj), Michael Brown, Papa Bouba Diop (Kanu), Kevin-Prince Boateng (John Utaka), Jamie O'Hara, Frederic Piquionne, Aruna Dindane.

WEDNESDAY 16TH MAY 1923

Pompey signed left-back Joe Davison from Middlesbrough. He made 25 league appearances during the following campaign which ended with Pompey claiming the Division Three (South) title.

TUESDAY 16TH MAY 1967

Manager George Smith paid £20,000 for the Barrow midfield player of the same name. George Smith the player was at Fratton Park for one and a half seasons before joining Middlesbrough for a club record £50,000.

WEDNESDAY 16TH MAY 1984

A header by Alan Biley earned Pompey a 1-0 victory over Aston Villa in a friendly watched by 2,652 at Fratton Park.

SUNDAY 16TH MAY 1993

Pompey were beaten 1-0 by Leicester City in the first leg of the First Division play-off semi-final. Julian Joachim grabbed Leicester's goal late in the match that was played at Nottingham Forest's City Ground.

SATURDAY 17TH MAY 1941

Pompey beat Aldershot 10-5 in the Hampshire County Cup semi-final. Andy Black, Bert Barlow and Jimmy McIntosh each scored hat-tricks.

SATURDAY 17TH MAY 1947

A crowd of 37,746 saw title-chasing Manchester United beat Pompey 3-0. Old Trafford was still being rebuilt after suffering considerable war damage, so the fixture was played at Manchester City's ground.

WEDNESDAY 17TH MAY 1995

Chairman Jim Gregory's son Martin went public with the news that Portsmouth Football Club was up for sale for £7m.

SATURDAY 17TH MAY 2008

Pompey won the FA Cup by beating Cardiff City 1-0 at Wembley thanks to Kanu's first-half goal. Cardiff goalkeeper Peter Enckelman palmed a low cross by John Utaka straight to the striker who half-volleyed it into the net from three yards. The Pompey team was: David James, Glen Johnson, Sol Campbell, Sylvain Distin, Hermann Hreidarsson, John Utaka (David Nugent), Pedro Mendes (Papa Bouba Diop), Lassana Diarra, Sulley Muntari, Niko Kranjcar, Kanu (Milan Baros).

SATURDAY 18TH MAY 1963

In the final match of the season, John McClelland headed Pompey in front against Middlesbrough at Fratton Park on his club debut. Arthur Kaye equalised for Boro' and the match ended 1-1.

FRIDAY 18TH MAY 1990

Frank Burrows was appointed manager by chairman Jim Gregory. During his four months as caretaker-boss Burrows transformed a dejected relegated team into one that finished in the top half of the table.

SUNDAY 18TH MAY 2008

Up to 200,000 people lined the streets of Portsmouth to welcome home Pompey's FA Cup winning team. Fans stood six deep in places to cheer on the team that beat Cardiff City 1-0 at Wembley the previous day. The players, staff, families and the Cup travelled on three open-top buses that wended its way through the city.

WEDNESDAY 18TH MAY 2009

Pompey ended the season with an impressive 3-1 win over Sunderland at Fratton Park, the goals coming from John Utaka, a Phil Barsley own goal and Armand Traore. Asmir Begovic made a sound debut in goal while Linvoy Primus made his final club appearance as a late substitute.

WEDNESDAY 19TH MAY 1976

A Fratton Park crowd of 9,279 saw Celtic win 6-1 in a friendly arranged to raise funds for cash-stricken Pompey. The draw for a car was made at half-time by the Scottish club's legendary manager Jock Stein.

THURSDAY 19TH MAY 1988

The shock news from Fratton Park was that central defender Noel Blake was not to be offered a new contract. Manager Alan Ball said, "I know it's a drastic thing but the club is about to move in a new direction and this is the start."

WEDNESDAY 19TH MAY 1993

Pompey's hopes of Premier League football vanished at Fratton Park after a draw with Leicester City in front of 25,438 in the play-off semi-final second leg. The score was 2-2 but Leicester's first-leg victory three days earlier meant they won 3-2 on aggregate.

FRIDAY 20TH MAY 1927

Lloyd Lindbergh (Lindy) Delapenha, who appeared for Pompey during their 1948-49 League Championship campaign, was born in Kingston, Jamaica. This was also the day that Charles Lindbergh flew the Atlantic – hence Delapenha's middle name.

THURSDAY 20TH MAY 1982

Bobby Campbell finally lost his "acting manager" tag when the Pompey board confirmed the permanent appointment of the former Pompey player whose eleven-match proving period, since the departure of Frank Burrows, brought 16 points.

FRIDAY 20TH MAY 1983

Former Pompey and Scotland inside-left Jimmy Easson died aged 77. Arriving at Fratton Park in 1929, he was an automatic choice at inside-left for six seasons. He was the side's top goalscorer in 1930-31 and was in the team that lost 2-1 to Manchester City in the 1934 FA Cup Final. In December 1938 he signed for Fulham after making 293 league appearances and scoring 103 goals. He returned to the club after the war to become assistant trainer and after spells at Southampton and Aston Villa, came back to join the coaching staff at Fratton Park.

TUESDAY 20TH MAY 2008

Three days after Pompey won the FA Cup, *The News* launched a huge petition campaign – "Arise Sir Harry" – in its newspaper and on its website to ask readers to add their names to the calls for manager Harry Redknapp to be honoured with a knighthood.

THURSDAY 20TH MAY 2010

Avram Grant announced that he would be stepping down as Pompey manager. The Israeli, who led the Blues to the FA Cup Final, penned a heartfelt resignation letter explaining the decision as the toughest of his career. He was appointed boss of West Ham United the following month.

TUESDAY 21ST MAY 1963

Chelsea made certain of promotion to the First Division with an emphatic 7-0 victory over Pompey at Stamford Bridge before 54,558. Bobby Tambling scored four of the goals and Terry Venables converted a penalty.

FRIDAY 21ST MAY 1982

Bobby Doyle preserved Pompey's six month unbeaten home record by scoring two penalties against Millwall in the final match of the season as the sides played out a 2-2 draw. It stretched his run of spot kicks to a faultless dozen since arriving from Blackpool eighteen months previously. The crowd of 4,902 remains Pompey's second lowest post-war league attendance.

MONDAY 22ND MAY 1978

Jack Smith was appointed Pompey's chief scout by manager Frank Burrows. The pair were former teammates at Swindon Town.

TUESDAY 22ND MAY 1979

Pompey defenders Steve Foster and Peter Ellis both agreed terms with the club under the new freedom of contract.

SUNDAY 23RD MAY 1954

Jimmy Dickinson and Peter Harris were in the England team that was thrashed 7-1 by Hungary in Budapest. It was Dickinson's free kick that led to Ivor Broadis scoring England's goal.

WEDNESDAY 24TH MAY 1922

Pompey signed outside-right Angus Meikle from Hearts. He was ever-present in the side that won the Division Three (South) title in 1923-24.

SUNDAY 24TH MAY 1931

Jimmy Easson became the first Pompey player to score in an international match when he netted for Scotland in their 3-2 victory against Switzerland in Geneva.

SATURDAY 24TH MAY 1947

An early goal by Jimmy McAlinden gave Pompey their first victory in seven matches against Leeds United at Elland Road in front of 14,027.

SATURDAY 24TH MAY 2008

Reg Flewin, who captained Pompey to league championship triumphs in 1948-49 and 1949-50, died aged 87. He played his last match in 1954 before becoming assistant manager and left Fratton Park in 1960 to take over as boss of Stockport County and later managed Bournemouth.

TUESDAY 25TH MAY 1954

Alex Wilson made his one appearance for Scotland, playing right-back in a 2-1 defeat against Finland in Helsinki.

TUESDAY 25TH MAY 1993

It was reported that Pompey boss Jim Smith would be banned for five years from receiving FA Cup Final tickets after a top-level probe into black market dealing.

MONDAY 26TH MAY 1947

Duggie Reid scored a hat-trick of headers as Pompey defeated Chelsea at Stamford Bridge before a crowd of 26,048.

SATURDAY 26TH MAY 2001

Former Pompey player Johnny Gordon died suddenly aged 69. Gordon made his Pompey debut against Blackpool in August 1951 and made 201 league and cup appearances, scoring 74 goals before being sold to Birmingham City in September 1958. He returned to Fratton Park in March 1961 and netted a further 42 goals in 285 outings. He played his final league match in a 1-1 draw away to Huddersfield Town in May 1967. Gordon was a regular visitor to Fratton and was there to see Pompey beat Barnsley on the final day of the season and therefore avoid the drop to Division Two.

FRIDAY 26TH MAY 2006

Pompey chairman Milan Mandaric branded the £8.5m chase for Andy Johnson as crazy as Pompey pulled out of the race for the Crystal Palace striker. Mandaric said there was no way Pompey would shell out the kind of money Bolton Wanderers and Wigan Athletic had agreed to pay for the player, although he revealed they would for the right man.

TUESDAY 27TH MAY 1913

Bill Rochford, who played at left-back in Pompey's 1939 FA Cup Final triumph against Wolverhampton Wanderers, was born in Newhouse.

THURSDAY 27TH MAY 1937

Jimmy Nichol, who played in Pompey's 1929 and 1934 FA Cup Finals, returned to his former club Gillingham after ten years' service.

FRIDAY 27TH MAY 1983

Coventry City and England centre-forward Mark Hateley signed for Pompey. The fee of £190,000 was later decided at a tribunal. Hateley spent a season at Fratton Park, scoring 25 goals, before moving to AC Milan for £1m.

WEDNESDAY 27TH MAY 1987

Pompey, newly promoted to the First Division, signed midfielder Barry Horne from Wrexham for £60,000. Alan Ball's men were relegated after one season back in the top flight but Barry Horne was one of only a few bright spots during the campaign, turning in consistently good performances that won him the club's Player of the Year award.

WEDNESDAY 27TH MAY 1992

Pompey sold Darren Anderton to top-flight Tottenham Hotspur for £1.7m. He became the costliest export in Pompey's history, virtually doubling the fee that Italian giants AC Milan had paid for centre-forward Mark Hateley in 1984.

THURSDAY 27TH MAY 2004

Pompey duo Nigel Quashie and Richard Hughes made their Scotland debuts in the national side's 1-0 win away to Lithuania. It was Scotland's first away victory for two years and the Lithuania boss Arno Pjpers picked out the Pompey men as the best two players on show.

SATURDAY 28TH MAY 1927

Jack Tinn was appointed secretary-manager of Portsmouth Football Club although he was not to take up his new duties until the end of June.

WEDNESDAY 28TH MAY 2008

Three Pompey players appeared in the same England team for the first time. David James, Glen Johnson and Jermain Defoe all played in the national side's 2-0 friendly win against the USA at Wembley.

THURSDAY 28TH MAY 2009

It was announced that Arab billionaire Sulaiman Al Fahim was to take ownership of Portsmouth Football Club in a deal worth £60m.

WEDNESDAY 29TH MAY 2002

Harry Redknapp made West Ham central defender Hayden Foxe his first signing of the summer and revealed the £400,000 capture was to be the first of several signings over the next fortnight.

SATURDAY 30TH MAY 1942

Pompey lost 2-0 to Brentford in the London War Cup Final. Skipper Jimmy Guthrie scored an own goal and missed a penalty.

WEDNESDAY 30TH MAY 1962

Goalkeeper Dick Beattie was transferred to Peterborough United.

TUESDAY 30TH MAY 1989

It was announced that Havant-based electronics company Goodmans would be paying £100,000 for the privilege of having its name on Pompey's shirts for the next two years.

TUESDAY 30TH MAY 1995

Former Pompey player Bobby Stokes died suddenly aged 44. The Portsmouth-born player, most famous for his winning goal for Southampton in the 1976 FA Cup final, moved to Fratton Park in August 1977 but left towards the end of the season.

SUNDAY 30TH MAY 2004

Nigel Quashie scored Scotland's fourth goal in a 4-1 win over Trinidad and Tobago. He was the first Pompey player to find the net for the Scottish national side since Jimmy Easson in May 1931.

SATURDAY 31ST MAY 1947

Derby County fought from a goal down to beat Pompey 2-1 in front of 20,852 at Fratton Park in Jack Tinn's last match of a 20-year reign.

SATURDAY 31ST MAY 1953

Jimmy Dickinson won the 27th of his 48 England caps, representing the national side in a 2-1 defeat by Uruguay in Montevideo. Manchester United's Tommy Taylor scored for England.

WEDNESDAY 31st MAY 1989

Kenny Black became John Gregory's third £250,000 signing. The 25-year-old Heart of Midlothian midfield player, who had previously been with Rangers and Motherwell, signed a three year contract. Black made 69 league and cup appearances and scored five goals before being sold to Airdrie for £125,000 by Jim Smith in August 1991.

PORTSMOUTH
On This Day & Miscellany

JUNE

TUESDAY 1st JUNE 1988

As expected, Jim Gregory took over from John Deacon as the chairman of Portsmouth Football Club but all there was for Pompey fans for most of the day was a big silence. Mr Gregory was reported to be holidaying in the South of France with no apparent plans to return to England before the middle of the following week. The only person available for comment was manager Alan Ball who was anxiously awaiting the change in Pompey's hierarchy. He said, "I'm here at my desk every day, itching to get cracking on rebuilding the squad and can't do a thing." The deal was concluded in London with Gregory paying £2m for the club.

SUNDAY 1st JUNE 2008

Jermain Defoe became the first Pompey player to score two goals in a match for England since Jack Smith grabbed a brace in a 7-1 win against Spain at Highbury in December 1931. Defoe netted twice in a 3-0 win away to Trinidad and Tobago.

TUESDAY 1st JUNE 2010

David Lampitt was appointed the club's Chief Executive Officer. The former FA Head of Integrity made the agreeing of the Company Voluntary arrangement needed to take Pompey out of administration and the next managerial appointment his top priorities.

WEDNESDAY 1st JUNE 2011

Convers Sports Initiatives became the fifth owners of Portsmouth Football Club in two years. CSI owners Antonov, Roman Dubov and former Leeds United chief executive Chris Akers had passed the Football League's fit and proper persons' test. However CSI entered administration five months later leaving the future of the football club in very serious doubt once again.

WEDNESDAY 2nd JUNE 1982

Pompey completed the signing of former England winger Dave Thomas from Middlesbrough on a free transfer. Thomas featured in the following season's Third Division title campaign and spent two more seasons as a player at Fratton Park before becoming youth team coach.

SATURDAY 3RD JUNE 1911

Robert Brown left Sheffield Wednesday to become manager of Pompey. He led the club to the Southern League championship in 1919-20.

WEDNESDAY 3RD JUNE 1987

Kevin Dillon turned down Pompey's final take-it-or-leave-it contract offer while Mick Tait was mulling over a potential move to Brighton and Hove Albion. It seemed almost certain that the pair would be leaving Fratton but Dillon subsequently climbed down and remained with the club for two more seasons and Tait turned down the move to Brighton.

WEDNESDAY 3RD JUNE 1992

Pompey announced that fans wouldn't have to pay more for the majority of home games the next season. Games would be divided into A and B categories and a rise of £1 would occur when the bigger teams visited.

TUESDAY 3RD JUNE 2014

Portsmouth Supporters Trust was rewarded for its sterling efforts in taking over Portsmouth Football Club and its contribution to the city when members received a civic award at Portsmouth's Mayor-making ceremony. Cllr Gerald Vernon-Jackson nominated the Trust for the award and said, "Without the Trust there would be no Portsmouth Football Club. If anyone deserves this award it's the Pompey Supporters Trust."

FRIDAY 4TH JUNE 1982

Manager Bobby Campbell made Queens Park Rangers central defender Ernie Howe his second signing.

MONDAY 4TH JUNE 1984

Middlesbrough's Mick Kennedy became a Pompey player within three hours of meeting Pompey chairman John Deacon. The midfielder, who went on to win two Ireland caps while at Fratton Park, cost £100,000.

TUESDAY 5TH JUNE 1984

Alan Ball was appointed Pompey manager on a permanent basis. He had taken over as caretaker boss following the sacking of Bobby Campbell in May. It was the start of a four-and-a-half year spell which saw the former England World Cup winner lead the club to the First Division.

WEDNESDAY 6TH JUNE 1918

Fratton Park staged a game of baseball between the United States of America and Canada in aid of the Red Cross. The Americans won 4-3.

FRIDAY 6TH JUNE 2003

Liverpool's Patrik Berger became Harry Redknapp's first summer signing as Pompey prepared for their first season in the Premiership. The 29-year-old Czech midfielder signed a two-year deal.

THURSDAY 7TH JUNE 1984

Pompey won their four year battle to return to the London Combination. They originally pulled out of the competition 20 years earlier as manager George Smith began his one-team revolution to stabilise finances. When the club resumed running a reserve side in 1973 they operated in the Midweek League.

WEDNESDAY 7TH JUNE 1989

Guy Whittingham signed for Pompey. The club had been chasing Whittingham for a month and finally persuaded him to buy himself out of the army and attempt to make the grade as a professional footballer. The £450 that the club repaid Whittingham turned out to be one of the best pieces of business the club ever made for the striker went on to net over 100 goals in two spells at Fratton Park.

FRIDAY 8TH JUNE 1979

Pompey completed the signing of Doncaster Rovers midfield player Joe Laidlaw for £15,000. The former Middlesbrough and Carlisle United man was appointed team captain and he led the side to promotion from the Fourth Division in his first season.

THURSDAY 9TH JUNE 1988

Chairman Jim Gregory left for a holiday on the French Riviera but before doing so, promised that Alan Ball would continue to be Pompey's manager and that the Fratton End would be rebuilt as soon as possible.

FRIDAY 9TH JUNE 2004

One of Pompey's longest serving players, Harry Harris, died aged 69. Harris joined the club from Newport County in 1958 and when he hung up his boots in 1970 he was the last survivor of Pompey's First Division days. He took over as captain when Jimmy Dickinson retired in 1965 and led the team for two years.

FRIDAY 10TH JUNE 1988

Ron Jones, captain of the 1968 Great Britain Olympics team, was appointed Chief Executive by the club's new owner Jim Gregory.

SUNDAY 10TH JUNE 1984

Pompey striker Mark Hateley scored for England in a 2-0 victory over Brazil in a friendly in Rio before a crowd of 56,126, becoming the first Pompey player to net for England since Jack Froggatt in 1952. Terry Fenwick, who managed the club between January 1995 and 1998 and Mark Chamberlain, a Pompey player from 1988 until 1994 earned their fourth and fifth England caps respectively in the same game.

TUESDAY 10TH JUNE 1997

The News reported that fans had delivered a vote of confidence in the two Terrys – manager Terry Fenwick and chairman Terry Venables – saying, "You can lead us to the Premiership." *The News* invited supporters to have their say on Pompey in an in-depth survey and the results showed they were delighted in the club's progress over the previous twelve months. One fan reckoned the arrival of Venables was a gift from God while another forecast that El Tel would make Pompey a Premiership club.

THURSDAY 11TH JUNE 1987

Ian Baird became Pompey's record signing when he joined the club from Leeds United for £285,000. The centre-forward's stay at Fratton Park was not a success and he was sold back to Leeds at a £100,000 loss before the season was out.

WEDNESDAY 12TH JUNE 1985

Just 24 hours after a transfer request was received from Alan Knight, letters to First and Second Division clubs announcing his availability were sent.

SATURDAY 13TH JUNE 1964

It was announced that Jimmy Dickinson was to be awarded the MBE in the Queen's Birthday Honours List in recognition of his magnificent playing career – that still had one more season to run. He broke the Football League appearance record and was never in trouble with a ref.

MONDAY 13TH JUNE 2005

Pompey manager Alain Perrin made Newcastle United central defender Andy O'Brien his first signing. He made 32 appearances for the club before being transferred to Bolton Wanderers in 2007.

WEDNESDAY 14TH JUNE 1978

At the 50th annual meeting of the Pompey Supporters' Club, members received the news that they had been dreading for 12 months – a year's notice from their landlords to relinquish their clubroom at Fratton Park.

THURSDAY 15TH JUNE 1989

Pompey midfielder Kevin Dillon completed his "dream" move to Newcastle United. He returned to his native North-East on a free transfer after six years at Fratton Park.

WEDNESDAY 16TH JUNE 1971

Pompey completed the signing of Richard Reynolds from Plymouth Argyle on a free transfer. Reynolds scored 11 goals in 45 appearances in his first season at Fratton Park and won the club's Player of the Year award. He remained at Fratton Park until 1976 and scored a total of 28 goals in 160 outings.

THURSDAY 16TH JUNE 1987

Pompey striker Mick Quinn turned down a big money move to Millwall. He was offered the chance to move after the two clubs agreed a £320,000 fee but wished to play in the First Division for newly promoted Pompey rather than step down to Division Two.

FRIDAY 17TH JUNE 1954

Pompey's Jimmy Dickinson scored an own goal as England drew 4-4 with Belgium in Basle in the World Cup. Dickinson, who won 48 caps, was making his 36th international appearance.

SUNDAY 17TH JUNE 1958

Pompey goalkeeper Norman Uprichard played for Northern Ireland against Czechoslovakia in a World Cup play-off in Malmo. His side won 2-1 after extra time with Peter McParland grabbing both goals.

SUNDAY 17TH JUNE 1984

Pompey striker Mark Hateley played in England's goalless draw against Chile in Santiago. Also representing England were Mark Chamberlain, who had a six-year spell with Pompey between 1988 and 1994, and Terry Fenwick, who managed the club from January 1995 until January 1998.

TUESDAY 17TH JUNE 2003

Pompey smashed their transfer record with the signing of Dejan Stefanovic from Dutch club Vitesse Arnhem for £1.9m. The Blues beat off competition from Rangers for the central defender who had three years of his contract remaining at Vitesse.

WEDNESDAY 18TH JUNE 2008

Pompey released details and images of a new 36,000 all-seater stadium planned for Horsea Island. The club hoped that once planning permission was granted work would begin in 2010.

FRIDAY 18TH JUNE 2010

Steve Cotterill was unveiled as Pompey's new manager. The 45-year-old replaced Avram Grant who resigned in May and penned a three-year contract. His spell in charge lasted only until October 2011 when he left to take charge of Nottingham Forest.

WEDNESDAY 18TH JUNE 2011

Ipswich Town's David Norris became Steve Cotterill's first signing of the summer. The midfielder signed on a free transfer after turning down a new contract with the Tractor Boys.

MONDAY 19TH JUNE 1934

Pompey and England centre-half Jimmy Allen was transferred to Aston Villa for £10,775 – at the time, a record fee for a defender, and only £115 short of the British transfer record. The money received meant a profit of £14,961 for the year and the transfer fee went to building the North Stand, raising capacity to 58,000 with covering for 33,000.

TUESDAY 19th JUNE 1979

Pompey received their first six-figure transfer fee when centre-half Steve Foster was sold to Brighton for £150,000. Manager Frank Burrows quickly found a replacement, when he signed Swindon Town's Steve Aizlewood.

FRIDAY 20th JUNE 1930

Centre-half John McIlwaine moved from Pompey to Southampton for a fee of £2,650. He had cost Pompey a record £4,500 when he moved from Falkirk in February 1928 and made 57 league appearances as well as captaining the Pompey side against Bolton wanderers in the 1929 FA Cup Final. The £2,650 was Southampton's record transfer fee paid whilst it was the highest Pompey had received.

FRIDAY 21st JUNE 1946

Jock Anderson, one of the goalscorers when Pompey beat Wolverhampton Wanderers in the 1939 FA Cup Final, left Fratton Park for Aldershot.

WEDNESDAY 21st JUNE 1972

Pompey took their summer spending to £60,000 when manager Ron Tindall paid Peterborough United £27,600 for their Welsh under-23 international striker Peter Price.

THURSDAY 21st JUNE 2001

Harry Redknapp began a three-year contract term as Pompey's Director of Football, vowing he had no designs on becoming a manager again. Redknapp said, "I don't want the day-to-day involvement of being a manager any more and I'm more than happy to be working alongside Milan Mandaric and Graham Rix."

TUESDAY 24th JUNE 2003

Croatia and Bayer Leverkusen skipper Boris Zivkovic signed for Pompey on a four-year deal. The 27-year-old negotiated a clause in his contract relating to a fee he would receive if sold on by Pompey. Chairman Milan Mandaric said, "We're excited that we are getting a world class defender. What is good about Boris is that he can play in a variety of positions across the back and also as a defensive midfield player."

SUNDAY 24th JUNE 2007

Derek Dougan died aged 69. The former Northern Ireland international striker was most famous for his seven-year spell with Wolverhampton Wanderers but it was with Pompey, in 1957, that he began his colourful and sometimes controversial career. He also played for Blackburn Rovers, Aston Villa, Peterborough United and Leicester City.

FRIDAY 24th JUNE 2011

Jason Pearce moved from AFC Bournemouth to Fratton Park for a fee of £300,000. He returned to the club where he began as a trainee and spent ten years before his move to Dean Court in 2007.

MONDAY 25th JUNE 1979

Archie Styles, Peterborough United's former Everton and Birmingham City left-back, signed for Pompey on a free transfer. The club announced that John Lathan and Steve Davey were available for transfer.

WEDNESDAY 25th JUNE 1986

Former Chelsea, Southampton and England centre-forward Peter Osgood was appointed Pompey's youth team coach.

WEDNESDAY 26th JUNE 1991

Following Portsmouth City Council's rejection of plans for a new Milton End Stand, Southampton secretary Brian Truscott said that any idea about ground sharing with Pompey's neighbours was a non-starter.

WEDNESDAY 26th JUNE 2002

Former Pompey manager Jim Smith was confirmed as Harry Redknapp's assistant. Smith said that it only took two minutes to decide to return to Fratton Park but added, "The missus wasn't too happy."

THURSDAY 26TH JUNE 2002

Marc-Vivien Foe collapsed and died of a heart attack during Cameroon's match against Colombia in Lyon. The player was on the brink of signing for Pompey at the time of the tragedy.

TUESDAY 27TH JUNE 1951

Pompey broke their record transfer fee with the £20,000 signing of outside-left Gordon Dale from Chesterfield. On his day he was as good as any player in the country but he couldn't always produce this magical form and so spent a lot of time in the reserves. His presence would put hundreds, if not thousands, on the reserve match attendances.

MONDAY 27TH JUNE 1977

Speculation over the future of 15-year-old goalkeeper Alan Knight ended with the announcement that he would sign as an apprentice on his 16th birthday the following month. Knight had attracted the attention of a number of clubs but promised he would sign for Pompey and the club were relieved that he had kept his word. Knight went on to achieve legendary status at Fratton Park, making over 800 appearances for his only pro club.

MONDAY 28TH JUNE 1999

Torquay United postponed their 10 August League Cup first round tie with Pompey for a week because it was scheduled for the day before the Solar Eclipse and the town was expected to be inundated with visitors.

WEDNESDAY 28TH JUNE 2006

Former Arsenal and England captain Tony Adams was unveiled as manager Harry Redknapp's assistant. He was appointed Pompey boss after Redknapp left to take over Tottenham Hotspur in October 2008.

THURSDAY 29TH JUNE 1972

Mike Trebilcock, who cost Pompey a club record £40,000 from Everton in January 1968, signed for Fourth Division Torquay United on a free transfer.

MONDAY 29TH JUNE 1992

John Beresford, who had interested Liverpool since those epic semi-final clashes in April completed a move to newly-promoted Newcastle United for £700,000.

SATURDAY 30TH JUNE 1984

Exactly 48 hours after Mark Hateley left Pompey for AC Milan, the club signed Manchester United's Scott McGarvey as his replacement for a fee of £85,000.

MONDAY 30TH JUNE 1975

Ray Hiron – scorer of over 100 goals for Pompey – signed for Reading on a free transfer.

SATURDAY 30TH JUNE 1990

Harry Redknapp, then manager of AFC Bournemouth, was seriously injured in a car crash in Italy in which the Cherries' managing director Brian Tiler died.

MONDAY 30TH JUNE 2003

Former Manchester United and England striker Teddy Sheringham completed a move to Pompey from Tottenham Hotspur. He took a £1.25m-a-year drop in wages – from £40,000 a week – to join the Blues in a one year deal.

PORTSMOUTH
On This Day & Miscellany

JULY

FRIDAY 1st JULY 1966

Right-back Roy Pack signed for Pompey on a free transfer from Arsenal. The 19-year-old made 105 league and cup appearances for Pompey, his only goal coming against Hull City in an FA Cup replay during the 1966-67 campaign.

FRIDAY 1st JULY 1983

Billy Rafferty and Peter Ellis both turned down the club's offer of a year's contract. Rafferty told the PFA he was looking for a new club while Ellis still hoped to see his playing days out with the club he supported as a boy yet was holding out for an improved offer. An agreement was eventually reached and the local born defender spent one more season at Fratton Park.

WEDNESDAY 1st JULY 2009

Sean Davis moved to Bolton Wanderers on a free transfer. One of the last decisions Tony Adams made before being sacked as Pompey manager in February was to reject a £3m bid from the Trotters for the midfielder. Davis made 102 Premiership appearances while at Fratton Park.

WEDNESDAY 2nd JULY 1947

The Pompey directors provisionally appointed Bob Jackson as Pompey manager, replacing Jack Tinn who had been in charge for 20 years. Jackson was in the job for five years and led the club to two Football League titles in 1948-49 and '49-50. He left in 1952 to take charge of Hull City.

FRIDAY 2nd JULY 1982

Jeff Hemmerman moved to Cardiff City on a free transfer after four years at Pompey. The striker top scored for the Bluebirds in 1982/83, as they won promotion to Division Two, alongside Pompey.

FRIDAY 3rd JULY 1959

Pompey inside-left and Hampshire cricketer Mike Barnard moved to Chelmsford City; defender Bill Albury was transferred to Gillingham.

TUESDAY 3RD JULY 2001

Peter Crouch joined Pompey from Queens Park Rangers and signed a four year deal. The fee of £1.25m eclipsed the £1.2m the club paid Bradford City for Lee Mills the previous summer. Manager Graham Rix also signed defender Alessandro Zamperini who had been released by AS Roma.

MONDAY 3RD JULY 2006

Pompey appointed former Israel manager Avram Grant as technical director. He later managed the Club, leading them to the FA Cup Final in 2010.

FRIDAY 3RD JULY 2009

Linvoy Primus signed a one-year deal to take him into his tenth season with Portsmouth Football Club. The popular defender, who made his first appearance for two years when he came on as a late substitute during the last match of the season, was handed a far-reaching remit which encompassed playing, ambassadorial, mentoring and advisory roles.

FRIDAY 4TH JULY 1997

Builders completed the demolition of the Fratton End in order for a new 4,500-seater stand to be built.

MONDAY 4TH JULY 2005

Yakubu completed his transfer to Middlesbrough in a deal that made Pompey £4.5m richer. Boro paid around £7.5m for the 22-year-old striker leaving Pompey with £4.5m after paying Yakubu's former club Maccabi Haifa £3m – half the profit from the sale.

SATURDAY 5TH JULY 1947

The Board of Directors met in the morning and confirmed that Bob Jackson was to be the new Pompey manager. He replaced Jack Tinn who had been in charge since 1927. Tinn's official title was always that of secretary-manager but the new managerial appointment was quite separate from the secretarial post. Other appointments confirmed were: Trainer Jimmy Stewart, Assistant trainer Jimmy Easson, Reserve team manager Eddie Lever while former wing-half Dave Thackeray became a member of the groundstaff.

THURSDAY 5TH JULY 1979

Swindon Town right-back John McLaughlin completed a move to Pompey, the fee was later decided by arbitration, and winger Dave Pullar joined Exeter City for £17,000. Midfielder Steve Bryant was fined £150 by Portsmouth City Magistrates for assaulting a customer at a Southsea restaurant. He was bound over to keep the peace for 12 months.

TUESDAY 5TH JULY 1999

Pompey paid Stefani Miglioranzi's college side £150,000 to capture the 21-year-old Brazilian midfielder and they also snapped up Charlton Athletic goalkeeper Andy Petterson. Both players had impressed while on loan at Fratton Park in the latter part of the previous season.

SATURDAY 6TH JULY 1978

Billy Hunter, Pompey's assistant manager for the previous four years, left the club. A close friend of departed manager Ian St John since school days, Hunter returned to his native Scotland to become manager of First Division Queen of the South.

WEDNESDAY 7TH JULY 2004

Pompey launched a furious attack on Yakubu's agent, branding him "a waste of space." Chairman Milan Mandaric was upset at what he saw as attempts to unsettle the striker with talk of a move to Middlesbrough. Mr Mandaric also announced that the club hoped to appoint a new coach within a fortnight. He wanted to bring in extra help for Harry Redknapp but assured supporters that existing coaches Jim Smith and Kevin Bond would be staying at Fratton Park.

WEDNESDAY 7TH JULY 2010

Pompey announced that they would be scrapping their reserve side for the next season. New manager Steve Cotterill favoured sending players out on loan as he believed first-team football was more beneficial than appearing for the second string.

WEDNESDAY 8TH JULY 1987

Pompey signed Newcastle United and Northern Ireland winger Ian Stewart on a free transfer. The move turned out to be an unhappy one for the 30-year-old for his only first team appearance was as substitute on the season's opening day.

FRIDAY 8TH JULY 1988

Pompey winger Vince Hilaire moved to Leeds United. He signed from Crystal Palace for £100,000 in November 1985 and was a vital member of the Pompey side that gained promotion to the First Division in 1987.

TUESDAY 8TH JULY 2003

Paul Merson's departure from Fratton Park was nearing completion. The strain of travelling to training from his home in Birmingham was blamed for his likely exit. Blues manager Harry Redknapp said, "I would like to keep him. Everyone knows Portsmouth owes a big debt to Paul Merson. We'll never forget the job he's done for us."

WEDNESDAY 9TH JULY 2003

Harry Redknapp's Premiership plans were thrown into turmoil as the club sweated on record signing Dejan Stefanovic's work permit. The Blues appealed after the defender's work permit was turned down.

THURSDAY 9TH JULY 2009

Roberto Mancini emerged as the leading candidate for the Pompey manager's job after it was revealed that he met club representatives in Paris. Paul Hart was still caretaker boss – the role he had filled since the sacking of Tony Adams in February.

WEDNESDAY 10TH JULY 2002

A crowd of 11,553 saw Celtic win 3-2 at Fratton Park with Richard Hughes and Linvoy Primus scoring for the Blues. This is the earliest Pompey have played a pre-season friendly. As he prepared to watch his team in action, Pompey chairman Milan Mandaric admitted, "I've never been so excited about our prospects."

FRIDAY 11TH JULY 2008

Peter Crouch rejoined Pompey. The striker, who had spent most of the 2001/02 season at Fratton Park, completed his switch from Liverpool for a fee of £11m.

WEDNESDAY 12TH JULY 1989

Mick Quinn left Pompey for Newcastle United. The Magpies ended up paying £680,000 for the striker who had netted 54 league goals in 121 appearances for the Blues after the fee was later decided by tribunal.

THURSDAY 12TH JULY 2001

Milan Mandaric rushed to Fratton Park from his holiday in Greece to get to the bottom of Pompey's transfer embargo embarrassment. The multi-millionaire chairman was furious to discover that the club had been banned from buying or selling players.

THURSDAY 13TH JULY 1989

Ron Jones, Pompey's chief executive since Jim Gregory bought the club a year earlier, departed from Fratton Park. His replacement was Ray Stainton, who had recently joined as commercial manager from Waterlooville. Paul Weld, assistant secretary for 15 years, was promoted to secretary.

SUNDAY 14TH JULY 1900

Billy Haines was born in Warminster. Spotted playing for Frome Town, he signed for Pompey in 1923 and went on to score 128 goals for the club. He topped the goalscoring charts for four seasons including the 1926-27 campaign when he hit 40 goals to help Pompey into the First Division.

SATURDAY 14TH JULY 1973

Fifteen Pompey players, general manager Ron Tindall, coach Pat Wright, trainer Gordon Neave and instructors from Portsmouth Polytechnic set out for the Welsh mountains for a five-day outward bound adventure. It was Tindall's aim to breed team spirit among a vastly changed squad.

MONDAY 14TH JULY 2003

Milan Mandaric dismissed reports that he was in takeover talks with a Russian businessman. The report claimed that the Russian had made an offer for the club which the Pompey chairman was weighing up.

FRIDAY 15TH JULY 1983

England 1966 World Cup hero Alan Ball joined the Fratton Park set-up as youth team coach. "My ultimate ambition is to become a successful manager and the experience I will gain at Pompey working under Bobby Campbell will help me a great deal," said Ball.

TUESDAY 15TH JULY 1986

Chairman John Deacon spent an hour of his 74th birthday facing the players. He told them the board had instituted a new disciplinary procedure and stepped up the fines applied the previous season.

TUESDAY 15TH JULY 2008

Gosport Borough Council voted unanimously for Pompey's new state-of-the-art multi-million pound training ground complex at Lee-on-Solent. The 35-acre site in Cherque Way will house ten full-size pitches, two mini pitches and a three-quarter size pitch.

TUESDAY 16TH JULY 1996

Alan Knight was awarded an honorary Master of Science degree by the University of Portsmouth in recognition of his long service to Portsmouth Football Club and his work in the local community.

SATURDAY 16TH JULY 2005

Summer signings – Laurent Robert, Andy O'Brien and Gregory Vignal – all played some part in Pompey's comfortable win away to Yeovil Town. Ivica Mornar, Lomana LuaLua, Gary O'Neil and Svetoslav Todorov were the goalscorers.

MONDAY 17TH JULY 1978

Peter Mellor joined from Hereford United on a free transfer. Mellor, who appeared for Fulham in the 1975 FA Cup Final, spent the next three years as first-choice keeper before losing his place to Alan Knight.

THURSDAY 17TH JULY 1979

Charlton Athletic midfielder Terry Brisley completed a move to Pompey for a fee of £25,000. Brisley was a key figure in the Pompey side that won promotion to Division Three the following season, weighing in with 12 league goals from midfield.

WEDNESDAY 18TH JULY 2001

Pompey manager Graham Rix insisted he was not interested in signing Shaka Hislop from West Ham and made it clear that Aaron Flahavan was his first choice goalkeeper.

FRIDAY 18TH JULY 2003

The club announced that there would be 600 extra seats at Fratton Park ready for the start of the first season in the Premiership, taking the ground capacity to over 20,000.

WEDNESDAY 19TH JULY 2005

New signing Laurent Robert was on the mark for Pompey in their first friendly of a French tour but was unable to prevent his side slipping to defeat. The Frenchman grabbed the opening goal of the game after 18 minutes but Bordeaux came storming back to win 3-1.

THURSDAY 19TH JULY 2006

Pompey chairman Milan Mandaric sold his remaining stake in Portsmouth Football Club to joint owner Alexandre Gaydamak for a reported £32m. Mandaric, who took over in 1999, insisted that he would still be staying on at the club as non-executive chairman to offer advice and experience to the new owner. "I'm not walking away into the sunset. I'll help Alexandre any way I can. I am safe in the knowledge that I place the club in control of a person with massive ambitions," he declared. On the same day Alton Town Council honoured the memory of Jimmy Dickinson by unveiling a plaque on the wall of 13 Bow Street, the cottage where he lived as a boy. Dickinson's widow Ann attended the ceremony along with the couple's son Andrew, daughter-in-law Michelle and grandsons Edward (9) and Alexander (5) as well as representatives from Portsmouth Football Club.

FRIDAY 20TH JULY 1979

Pompey midfield player Peter Denyer was transferred to Northampton Town for £20,000.

WEDNESDAY 20TH JULY 1988

Warren Neill became Pompey's first signing of the Jim Gregory era. The Queens Park Rangers full-back signed for a fee of £100,000.

WEDNESDAY 21ST JULY 1994

A hat-trick by Gerry Creaney gave Pompey a 3-0 victory over Weymouth in their first pre-season friendly.

TUESDAY 21ST JULY 2004

Yakubu and Kevin Harper were on target as Pompey won comfortably against Wycombe Wanderers at Adams Park. After a relatively quiet summer in the transfer market by Pompey's standards, Harry Redknapp started with just two new faces, David Unsworth from Everton and Andy Griffin from Newcastle United.

TUESDAY 21ST JULY 2009

Sulaiman Al Fahim reached an agreement with Sacha Gaydamak for the sale of Pompey after being given the thumbs up by the Premier League to complete his Pompey takeover. Paul Hart, who had acted as caretaker manager since February, was handed the job on a permanent basis with a two-year contract. Chief executive Peter Storrie said, "Sulaiman is on board, the agreement is legally binding and he will lead us into a new era. It is fantastic news for everybody and we should all be excited about the future."

WEDNESDAY 22ND JULY 1931

George Clifford, ever-present at right-back during the 1926-27 Second Division promotion campaign, was transferred to Mansfield Town.

SATURDAY 22ND JULY 1944

Ray Hiron was born in Gosport. Joining Pompey from Fareham Town in 1964, he scored 110 league goals in 330 league appearances – all in the Second Division – before signing for Reading on a free transfer in May 1975.

TUESDAY 22ND JULY 1980

Pompey continued their build-up to the season with a morale-boosting 3-0 win away to the League of Ireland champions Limerick in front of 1,113. Leigh Barnard netted twice and Jeff Hemmerman also scored before Pompey 'keeper Peter Mellor made a brilliant penalty save.

FRIDAY 23RD JULY 1999

Milan Mandaric assumed full control of Portsmouth Football Club after his £5m takeover was given final clearance by the Football League. The club's new owner had been in charge for just under a month after his bid was given approval by a meeting of creditors at Fratton Park. But there were still legal requirements to complete before a deal was rubber-stamped by authorities.

FRIDAY 23RD JULY 2005

Striker Azar Karadas scored on his debut as Pompey drew with Monaco at Bayonne in the final friendly of their pre-season French tour.

TUESDAY 24TH JULY 2007

A 45th minute goal by Benjani secured a win for Pompey against Fulham in the Barclay's Asia Trophy semi-final at the Hong Kong Stadium.

TUESDAY 25TH JULY 1972

The club announced an increase in the price to watch football at Fratton Park. Following the Football League's decision to increase the minimum admission to the terraces to 40p, Pompey put up the cost for other sections of the ground with the dearest seats – in the centre of the South Stand – going up from 90p to £1.

WEDNESDAY 25TH JULY 2001

Record signing Peter Crouch scored both goals for Pompey in their 5-2 defeat to his former club Tottenham Hotspur in a pre-season friendly match at Fratton Park.

FRIDAY 25TH JULY 2008

An Airbus 319 flying Pompey players to Nigeria for a pre-season friendly trip had to abort its landing in Abuja. The pilot of the plane abandoned the descent after failing to gain clearance from the control tower. The players were instead flown around for half an hour in stormy conditions before a successful landing was made.

THURSDAY 26TH JULY 1979

Plymouth Argyle outside-left Alan Rogers signed for Pompey for a fee of £25,000 – later decided by arbitration. Rogers featured in two promotions while at Fratton Park – from Division Four in 1980 and from the Third Division in 1983 – before leaving to join Southend United in March 1984.

SATURDAY 26TH JULY 1980

Pompey's scheduled friendly away to Wimbledon – their first of the season – was called off due to a waterlogged pitch.

SATURDAY 26TH JULY 1997

A long-range strike by striker Deon Burton earned Pompey a 1-1 draw against Scottish side Dundee in an ill-tempered friendly north of the border at Dens Park.

SATURDAY 27TH JULY 1912

Portsmouth Football Company Limited was formed. At a recent shareholders meeting, Chairman George Lewin Oliver recommended that the original company, formed in 1898, should be wound up and re-constituted on more business like lines.

SATURDAY 27TH JULY 1968

Pompey's tour of Ireland got underway with a 2-1 victory over Linfield. Ray Pointer and Mike Trebilcock were the goalscorers.

FRIDAY 27TH JULY 2007

Pompey won the Barclays Asia Trophy, beating Liverpool 4-2 on penalties at the Hong Kong Stadium after the game ended 0-0 after 90 minutes.

FRIDAY 28th JULY 2001

Pompey agreed compensation of around £200,000 and a testimonial for Steve Claridge who managed the club for 22 weeks before being replaced by Graham Rix in March.

SATURDAY 28th JULY 1979

A Fratton Park crowd of 4,257 saw Pompey beat Coventry City 1-0 in their first pre-season game. New signings Archie Styles, Terry Brisley, Steve Aizlewood, John McLaughlin and Alan Rogers all played in stifling heat. The goal was scored from the penalty spot by Colin Garwood.

MONDAY 28th JULY 2008

Italian champions Inter Milan completed the signing of Pompey midfielder Sulley Muntari for a fee of £12.7m. The 23-year-old, who had spent a season at Fratton Park, signed a four-year contract.

SATURDAY 29th JULY 1972

Pompey's summer signing Peter Price scored the only goal in the team's first pre-season friendly at Griffin Park watched by 5,750.

THURSDAY 29th JULY 1982

Pompey's wrangle with Reading over the fee for Neil Webb was settled by the Football League tribunal who decided that a fee of £85,000 should be paid to the Berkshire Club.

THURSDAY 29th JULY 2010

Alex Wilson, one of Pompey's greatest-ever servants, died aged 76. The full-back made 377 appearances for his only club between 1951 and 1967 and won a Scottish cap in 1954. He scored one of the most important goals in Pompey history when he equalised against Northampton Town on the last day of the 1964/65 campaign to keep the club in Division Two.

FRIDAY 29th JULY 2011

The Pompey squad and officials were left stranded in the USA after a catering truck collided with their US Airways plane and delayed the flight home from their pre-season tour. The incident caused the postponement of the following day's planned friendly match with Real Betis at Fratton Park but, instead, the Spanish club played against Havant and Waterlooville in a hastily arranged match at West Leigh Park where they won 7-0. Pompey and Real Betis did meet a month later in Seville, the Spaniards winning 5-1.

THURSDAY 30TH JULY 1987

Record signing Ian Baird scored, and was booked, in Pompey's 3-1 win against Sandviken in the penultimate match of their Swedish tour.

WEDNESDAY 30TH JULY 1987

Chelsea beat Pompey 4-1 at Fratton Park in a pre-season friendly. The result was an exact repeat of the FA Cup sixth round tie played at Fratton in March.

THURSDAY 31ST JULY 1997

Leading goalscorer and Player of the Year Lee Bradbury was sold to Manchester City for £3m.

SUNDAY 31ST JULY 2005

Italian giants Inter Milan continued their unbeaten tour of England with a 2-0 win over Pompey at Fratton Park. Alain Perrin's side were the equals of Inter in the first half and had a headed goal by Lomana LuaLua ruled out for offside, but after the break the visitors went ahead through a David Pizarro penalty before Dejan Stankovic slotted home the second goal.

SATURDAY 31ST JULY 2010

Fratton Park held a testimonial match between Pompey and Fulham for long-serving defender Linvoy Primus. Blues' Marc Wilson headed the only goal in the first half of the game that saw Primus take part for twelve minutes. The fans' favourite undertook a lap of honour after Chief Executive David Lampitt announced that the Milton End would be renamed the Linvoy Primus Community Stand.

PORTSMOUTH
On This Day & Miscellany

AUGUST

SATURDAY 1st AUGUST 1970

Pompey were beaten 2-0 by West Ham in their opening pre-season friendly at Fratton Park. Harry Redknapp came on as substitute for the Hammers, replacing Trevor Brooking. The club's present goalkeeper David James was also born on this day.

TUESDAY 1st AUGUST 1989

Kenny Black marked his Pompey debut with a goal to earn Pompey's first team a win against Bognor in a pre-season friendly at Nyewood Lane. Steve Wicks resigned as Pompey's assistant manager to take up a post with First Artists Management handling players' affairs.

THURSDAY 1st AUGUST 1991

Neither chairman Jim Gregory nor his son Martin attended the club's Annual General Meeting because of business commitments. The meeting, which lasted only fifteen minutes, was chaired by director David Deacon who told shareholders that the club was making a fresh attempt to build an all-seater stand at the Milton End.

SATURDAY 2nd AUGUST 1997

Pompey were sent to defeat by a controversial goal by Steve Thompson in a pre-season friendly against Woking at Kingfield Stadium.

SATURDAY 2nd AUGUST 2003

Pompey's Scottish tour came to a disappointing end as an early second-half goal by Dunfermline's Barry Nicholson condemned them to a 1-0 defeat at East End Park.

SATURDAY 3rd AUGUST 2002

Pompey's first £1m signing, striker Rory Allen, scored for the first time in more than two years in a 1-1 draw with Spanish side Alaves. Allen's performance was the highlight of a low-key game.

SATURDAY 4th AUGUST 2001

A late goal by Rowan Vine earned Pompey a 2-1 victory against Premiership Leicester City at Fratton Park in a friendly watched by 6,804. The young striker had only been on the pitch for two minutes when he coolly slotted the ball home from an acute angle.

MONDAY 4TH AUGUST 2014

On the centenary of the beginning of World War I Portsmouth Football Club unveiled its new strip, honouring every member of the Pompey Pals who fell during the four years of hostilities by including their name on the shirts. The Pompey Pals, the 14th and 15th battalions of the Hampshire Regiment, recruited heavily from Fratton Park. They went on to suffer heavy losses at the Great War with more than 1,400 making the ultimate sacrifice.

MONDAY 5TH AUGUST 1974

Former Pompey defender Tommy Youlden scored the only goal to sink his old club in a friendly at Elm Park watched by 2,746. Youlden was fouled by Alan Stephenson 20 yards from goal in the 73rd minute and his free-kick struck Pompey's defensive wall and spun wide of David Best.

SATURDAY 5TH AUGUST 1995

Pompey ended their tour of Scotland with the best of their performances north of the border with a victory against Falkirk at Brockville. Defender Guy Butters headed his second goal of the tour with Pompey's other goals coming from Deon Burton and Lee Bradbury.

SUNDAY 5TH AUGUST 2001

Pompey's 25-year-old goalkeeper Aaron Flahavan was killed in a car accident during the early hours of the morning. Flahavan had been handed the Number One squad shirt and was expected to be in goal for the opening match of the season at Wolverhampton the following Saturday.

THURSDAY 5TH AUGUST 2010

Portsmouth Football Club won its battle against the taxman at the High Court. Judge Justice Mann read a summary of his 49-page ruling and said that he could not back the taxman on any of the five points over which it had gone to court. The decision meant that the club could move out of administration, paving the way for a new buyer to take over.

SATURDAY 6TH AUGUST 1977

A crowd of 3,424 saw Pompey and Millwall draw 1-1 in an entertaining friendly at Fratton Park. Ian Pearson put the Lions ahead and Pompey's equaliser came from a header by Paul Gilchrist.

TUESDAY 6TH AUGUST 1985

Pompey midfielder Mick Tait was sent off and Bournemouth's Robbie Savage suffered a broken leg following a 27th minute incident in the Hampshire Professional Cup Final at Dean Court. Pompey were already a goal up through Vince Hilaire's header when the two players clashed.

SATURDAY 6TH AUGUST 1994

Ludek Miklosko prevented Pompey from beating West Ham comfortably in a friendly at Fratton Park before a crowd of 4,622. The goalkeeper produced a string of brilliant saves before he was beaten by Creaney who cancelled out a 25th minute lob by Steve Jones.

TUESDAY 6TH AUGUST 2002

Paul Merson completed his free transfer move from Aston Villa to Pompey on a two year deal worth around £10,000 a week in wages.

SATURDAY 6TH AUGUST 2011

Luke Varney marked his Pompey League debut by grabbing a last minute equaliser to secure a 2-2 draw against Middlesbrough at the Riverside Stadium. Pompey's first goal was scored by David Norris who was also playing his first match in Pompey's colours.

WEDNESDAY 7TH AUGUST 1985

Neil Webb returned to Fratton Park to score for Nottingham Forest in his side's 3-1 victory in a friendly two months after leaving the club.

FRIDAY 7TH AUGUST 1987

Mick Kennedy became the most heavily fined player in the history of British football when he was ordered to pay £5,000 by the FA following two articles which appeared in *The Sun* at the end of 1986.

THURSDAY 7TH AUGUST 1997

Deon Burton was reunited with his former Pompey boss Jim Smith when he signed for Derby County for £1m.

SATURDAY 7TH AUGUST 1999

The Milan Mandaric era got underway with a 2-0 home win over Sheffield United. Scorers were Stefani Miglioranzi and Guy Whittingham.

SATURDAY 7TH AUGUST 2010

Pompey's first League match outside the top flight for seven years ended in a 2-0 defeat away to Coventry City. This was also manager Steve Cotterill's first game in charge.

SATURDAY 8TH AUGUST 1970

Colin Sullivan and Steve Davey, both of whom would later move to Fratton Park, were in the Plymouth Argyle side that beat Pompey 4-3 in a friendly at Home Park.

SUNDAY 8TH AUGUST 1982

A 15,355 crowd saw Ian Rush score twice and Phil Neal score a penalty, as champions Liverpool beat Pompey 3-0 at Fratton Park in a friendly.

TUESDAY 8TH AUGUST 1989

Rio de Janiero state champions Botafogo beat Pompey 2-0 at Fratton Park in the first pre-season friendly of the Brazilian club's tour of England.

SATURDAY 8TH AUGUST 1998

The new season began with Watford defeating Pompey 2-1 at Fratton Park. Pompey's goal was scored by John Aloisi.

TUESDAY 8TH AUGUST 2006

Arsenal and England central-defender Sol Campbell joined Pompey from Arsenal on a free transfer. Within two years he was collecting the FA Cup trophy on Pompey's behalf at Wembley.

SATURDAY 9TH AUGUST 1969

Albert McCann missed a penalty as Pompey were defeated 2-1 by Blackpool at Bloomfield Road on the first day of the season.

SATURDAY 9TH AUGUST 1980

A goal by Joe Laidlaw gave Pompey victory over Plymouth Argyle in the League Cup first round first leg before a crowd of 7,036 at Home Park.

SATURDAY 9TH AUGUST 1997

Paul Hall grabbed a late equaliser to earn Pompey a 2-2 draw against Manchester City at Maine Road in the season's opener in front of 30,474. John Aloisi marked his debut with a goal in the first five minutes.

TUESDAY 9TH AUGUST 2011

Pompey crashed out of the Carling Cup, going down 1-0 to League Two side Barnet on the north London club's first visit to Fratton Park. This was the first time that Pompey had gone out of the competition in the first round for ten years. Better news for supporters was that new owners Convers Sports Initiatives agreed to spend £100,000 on ground improvements.

MONDAY 10TH AUGUST 1959

Pompey signed goalkeeper Dick Beattie from Celtic making him the club's first choice 'keeper over the next three years. He made 132 appearances before being transferred to Peterborough United.

FRIDAY 10TH AUGUST 1973

Bob Ingram, a local 21-year-old supporter, was named winner of the "Design a new strip for Pompey" competition. The club decided to go for his idea of white shirts with two vertical blue stripes, blue shorts and white socks with red and blue tops. Mr Ingram received two free season tickets as his prize.

SATURDAY 10TH AUGUST 1996

Former England and Spurs manager Terry Venables agreed to become Pompey's director of football.

SATURDAY 10TH AUGUST 2002

What turned out to be Pompey's First Division championship-winning season got underway with a 2-0 win over Nottingham Forest at Fratton Park. The Pompey goalscorers were Deon Burton and Vincent Pericard. Shaka Hislop, Hayden Foxe, Arjan De Zeeuw, Carl Robinson, Paul Merson and Pericard were all making their debuts for the club while Burton was playing his first match since re-joining the club on loan from Derby County.

SUNDAY 10th AUGUST 2008

Pompey were beaten 3-1 on penalties by Manchester United in the Community Shield at Wembley Stadium after the match had ended goalless.

TUESDAY 11th AUGUST 1970

Pompey played their fourth and last pre-season friendly at Fratton Park before a crowd of 5,382 and Fulham inflicted the fourth defeat on Ron Tindall's men, winning 3-1. One bright spot for Pompey was the display of Norman Piper who was playing his first match since his £40,000 move from Plymouth Argyle.

SATURDAY 11th AUGUST 1979

Alan Rogers scored on his debut in a 1-1 draw with Swindon Town at Fratton Park in the League Cup first round first leg, watched by 9,978.

SATURDAY 11th AUGUST 2001

Pompey produced a battling display at Molineux in front of 23,012 to draw 2-2 with Wolverhampton Wanderers at the end of one of the worst weeks in the club's history. The Blues dedicated their performance to goalkeeper Aaron Flahavan who was killed in a car accident six days earlier. Record signing Peter Crouch marked his debut by scoring with a glancing header after only eight minutes.

FRIDAY 11th AUGUST 2006

Manchester City goalkeeper David James became Pompey's fourth signing of the summer. Manager Harry Redknapp described James as "one of the best around."

SATURDAY 12th AUGUST 1950

A week before the opening game of the season, a crowd of 9,094 saw Pompey's League Championship winning side beat the reserves 2-1 in the annual public practice match at Fratton Park. Goalkeeper Ernie Butler damaged a hand during the game resulting in him missing the opening seven league matches.

SATURDAY 12th AUGUST 1972

Norman Piper missed a 40th minute penalty in a goalless draw at Nottingham Forest on the season's opening day.

SATURDAY 12TH AUGUST 2000

Lee Mills, Pompey's recent £1.2m record signing, made his debut in a 2-0 defeat by Sheffield United at Bramall Lane.

SATURDAY 12TH AUGUST 2006

David James joined Pompey from Manchester City for a fee of £1.2m. During his four years at Fratton Park the goalkeeper appeared in two FA Cup finals for the club, won 19 caps for England and broke two Premier League records.

TUESDAY 13TH AUGUST 1968

Three days after opening the season with a 0-0 draw at Huddersfield, Pompey claimed another away point at Brunton Park where their meeting with Carlisle United also ended goalless.

WEDNESDAY 13TH AUGUST 1969

A 20-yard drive by Alex Dawson sent Pompey out of the League Cup at the first hurdle at the Goldstone Ground in front of 19,787. Pompey were outfought by their Third Division opponents and Brighton goalkeeper Geoff Sidebottom was only really tested by a couple of long range efforts.

SATURDAY 13TH AUGUST 1994

Kit Symons gave Pompey a flying start to the new season with a winning diving header in added time against Notts County before 10,487 at Fratton Park. Darryl Powell gave Pompey an early lead when he powered past Dean Yates to smash a low shot into the bottom corner before Paul Sherlock brought County level on 70 minutes with a controversial penalty.

SATURDAY 13TH AUGUST 2011

Benjani Mwaruwari returned to Fratton Park, penning a one-year deal after turning down a contract at Blackburn Rovers. The surprise re-appearance of the popular striker diverted attention from a painful defeat by Brighton & Hove Albion at Fratton Park. Craig Mackail-Smith scored the only goal on the stroke of half-time with Liam Lawrence missing a penalty for the Blues five minutes into stoppage time.

SATURDAY 14TH AUGUST 1971

An 89th minute goal by Albert McCann earned Pompey a 2-1 win at home to Middlesbrough at Fratton Park on the opening day of the season. Jim Storrie had put the Blues ahead before Johnny Vincent equalised for Boro.

SATURDAY 14TH AUGUST 1993

Chris Allen put Oxford ahead after 19 minutes in the season's opening fixture but Lee Chapman, on his Pompey debut, calmly lifted the ball over goalkeeper Paul Kee for the equaliser five minutes later. Allen grabbed his second goal with a curling shot only for Chapman to level the scores once again before half-time. Pompey were looking good for at least a point until Oxford were awarded a disputed penalty on 62 minutes which Jim Magilton drove past Alan Knight to settle the match.

SATURDAY 14TH AUGUST 2004

A David Unsworth penalty earned Pompey a 1-1 draw against Birmingham City at Fratton Park on the opening day of the Premiership season.

TUESDAY 14TH AUGUST 2012

Pompey fielded their youngest-ever side for a competitive fixture against Plymouth Argyle in the League Cup first round at Home Park watched by 5,318. Only two of the starting line-up, Adam Webster and Ashley Harris, had made a competitive appearance for the Club and only goalkeeper Simon Eastwood at 23 and 35-year-old first team coach Ashley Westwood who had come out of retirement were aged over 18. Woeful finishing by Argyle allowed Pompey's youngsters to settle and they held out until Johnny Gorman scored with a left-foot shot on the stroke of half- time. Argyle scored twice during the second half to record a 3-0 win. The Pompey team was: Simon Eastwood, Adam Webster, Alex Grant, Ashley Westwood (Jack Maloney), Dan Butler, Jed Wallace, Sam Magri, George Colson, Andy Higgins (Bradley Tarbuck), Ashley Harris, Dan Thompson.

SATURDAY 15TH AUGUST 1970

Ron Tindall's first match in charge ended in a 1-1 draw away to Norwich City. Norman Piper marked his debut with an equaliser four minutes from time.

SATURDAY 15TH AUGUST 1987

Pompey were beaten 4-2 by Oxford United at The Manor Ground on their first match in Division One for 28 years. Paul Mariner had the distinction of scoring the club's first goal back in the top flight.

SATURDAY 15TH AUGUST 1992

Guy Whittingham scored a hat-trick as Pompey drew 3-3 with Bristol City at Ashton Gate on the opening day.

WEDNESDAY 15TH AUGUST 2007

A header from Benjani denied Manchester United their first win of the league campaign before 20,510 at Fratton Park as both sides ended the match with ten men. Paul Scholes scored for United before Benjani equalised with a superb header. Pompey midfielder Sulley Muntari picked up a second yellow card while Cristiano Ronaldo was also sent off.

FRIDAY 15TH AUGUST 2008

Pedro Mendes joined Scottish giants Rangers for a fee of £3m, manager Harry Redknapp admitting the sale was purely to balance the Pompey books. On the same day Jerome Thomas arrived from Charlton Athletic on a one-year loan. The loan actually lasted for six days because Pompey then paid the London club £500,000 to make it a permanent deal.

SATURDAY 16TH AUGUST 1969

A Fratton Park crowd of 19,107 saw Pompey outfought and outclassed by Sheffield United who inflicted the heaviest home defeat – 5-1 – on their hosts since September 1958. This was the first home game of the season and the embarrassing defeat followed losses in the opening league fixture and a League Cup tie.

SATURDAY 16TH AUGUST 1997

Swedish striker Mathias Svensson scored twice and John Aloisi was also on target as Pompey beat Port Vale 3-1 before 10,605 at Fratton Park.

SATURDAY 16TH AUGUST 2003

Pompey won their first Premiership fixture 2-1 at home to Aston Villa with Teddy Sheringham giving Pompey the lead three minutes before half-time and Patrik Berger adding a second on 63 minutes. Gareth

Barry pulled a goal back with a disputed penalty six minutes from time but Pompey held out for a deserved win.

MONDAY 17TH AUGUST 1981

Not one, but two full Pompey teams were beaten by an Isle of Wight Select XI at Ryde in what assistant manager Stan Harland admitted, "was a very disappointing display." Pompey played 22 players, changing their side completely at half-time against an Island team that made only one substitution.

WEDNESDAY 17TH AUGUST 1988

Warren Aspinall became Pompey's costliest player when he moved from Aston Villa for £315,000 – £30,000 more than was paid to Leeds United for Ian Baird a year previously.

SATURDAY 17TH AUGUST 1996

Andy Awford and Aaron Flahavan were both sent off in a 3-1 defeat away to Bradford City on the opening day.

SATURDAY 17TH AUGUST 2002

The introduction of sub Jason Crowe inspired one of Pompey's greatest comebacks. Losing 2-0 at Crystal Palace, shortly after Crowe entered the action, Hayden Foxe headed a goal. Within 60 seconds Crowe equalised, and three minutes later scored the winner.

SATURDAY 18TH AUGUST 1951

Keeper Ernie Butler was the hero as Pompey started the season with a hard-fought 2-0 victory over Liverpool watched by 42,250 at Anfield. Butler saved well from Kevin Baron and Billy Liddell early on and Pompey went on to score twice through Albert Mundy and Len Phillips.

SATURDAY 18TH AUGUST 1962

Dave Dodson scored a hat-trick as Pompey celebrated their return to the Second Division by beating Walsall 4-1 in the opening game of the season. The outside-left was the first of only two players – Guy Whittingham being the other – to notch three goals on the opening day of a season.

TUESDAY 18TH AUGUST 1987

Years of longing and dreaming finally ended when Fratton Park staged a First Division fixture for the first time since 1959. Chelsea were the visitors and defeated Pompey 3-0.

SATURDAY 19TH AUGUST 1950

A sun-baked crowd of 44,070 saw Football League champions Pompey kick off the new season with a 1-1 draw against Middlesbrough in a superb match at Fratton Park. The match remained goalless until Duggie Reid thundered in a tremendous shot ten minutes from time and in the 87th minute a quick break by the visitors led to Wilf Mannion flicking the ball over Ron Humpston for the equaliser.

SATURDAY 19TH AUGUST 1967

Pompey kicked off with a 1-1 draw at home to newly-promoted Queens Park Rangers. Instead of facing the usual heatwave start to the new season, the Fratton Park staff had to use brushes and mops to clear the flooded passageway under the south stand as the drains were unable to cope with a pre-match downpour. The match finished 1-1 with Roger Morgan giving QPR the lead and Ray Pointer equalising for the Pompey.

FRIDAY 19TH AUGUST 1988

The pub on the doorstep of Fratton Park – The Pompey – closed its doors for the last time. The favourite watering hole for many of the club's fans was transformed into the new Pompey Shop.

SATURDAY 19TH AUGUST 2006

Blackburn Rovers keeper Brad Friedel denied Kanu a debut hat-trick with a last-minute penalty save. Kanu had stepped off the bench and scored two headers, to add to Svetoslav Todorov's first-half strike, and would have been the first Pompey debutant to score three in his first game.

SATURDAY 20TH AUGUST 1949

Pompey opened their season as reigning League Champions with a well-deserved 3-1 victory over Newcastle United at St James' Park before 54,258. Len Phillips, Ike Clarke and Peter Harris scored for Pompey before George Robledo pulled a goal back for the Magpies. It was Pompey's last win at St James' Park until November 2007.

SATURDAY 20TH AUGUST 1955

Pat Neil became the youngest player to play for Pompey when, aged 17 years 300 days he played at outside-right in the opening match of the season that ended in a 1-0 defeat by Huddersfield Town at Leeds Road.

SATURDAY 21ST AUGUST 1948

Pompey's first league championship-winning season and Golden Jubilee year began with a 2-2 draw away to Preston North End. The home side led 2-0 but goals by Duggie Reid and Bert Barlow secured a point.

SATURDAY 21ST AUGUST 1954

Pompey overcame appalling conditions to beat Manchester United 3-1 in the opening game of the 1954-55 campaign, watched by 38,203 at Old Trafford. The goalscorers were Gordon Dale, Jackie Henderson and an Allenby Chilton own goal.

SATURDAY 21ST AUGUST 1965

Pompey made a fine start to the season by beating Plymouth Argyle 4-1 at Fratton Park in a one-sided "battle of the ports." This was the first day that substitutes were allowed in the Football League and Plymouth, because of injury and sickness, were without one.

MONDAY 21ST AUGUST 1989

Pompey's Annual Meeting began at 6.30pm – and by 6.37pm it was all over. Eleven minutes later the extraordinary general meeting to approve a rights issue of 850,000 shares had also been whistled through.

TUESDAY 21ST AUGUST 2012

Jordan Obita scored with his first touch for Pompey seconds after coming off the bench to replace Jack Compton in a 2-2 draw away to Colchester United. The player signed on the morning of the match and only met his new team-mates on the coach travelling to the game. Obita became the third player to score with his first touch for Pompey – Dave Dodson and Kanu being the others.

SATURDAY 22ND AUGUST 1964

Pompey's new plan, with the accent on tight defence, was ripped apart at Brisbane Road by Leyton Orient who won the opening game of the season 5-2. All their goals came from headers.

SATURDAY 22ND AUGUST 1970

Albert McCann scored after only 24 seconds against Bolton Wanderers in the first home league match of the season. Pompey went on to win 4-0 with two goals by Ray Hiron and another from Nick Jennings.

SATURDAY 22ND AUGUST 1987

Pompey collected their first point in Division One for 28 years by drawing 2-2 with Southampton at Fratton Park in what was the first top flight meeting between the two sides. Vince Hilaire opened the scoring for Pompey, Colin Clarke netted twice for Saints before Clive Whitehead grabbed the equaliser. The match was watched by 20,161.

SATURDAY 22ND AUGUST 2007

Goalkeeper David James became the first Pompey player to play for England since Mark Hateley in 1984. He played the whole of the second half, as substitute for Paul Robinson, in a 2-1 defeat by Germany at Wembley Stadium.

SATURDAY 23RD AUGUST 1952

Johnny Gordon made his league debut at inside-right in Pompey's 2-0 defeat at home to Blackpool in front of 43,072. Pompey had only beaten the Seasiders once in thirteen meetings since the war.

SATURDAY 23RD AUGUST 1958

West Ham celebrated their return to the First Division after an absence of 26 years by beating Pompey 2-1 at Fratton Park.

MONDAY 23RD AUGUST 1982

The European Cup was paraded round Fratton Park in August 1982 when holders Aston Villa played Pompey in a testimonial match for Alex Cropley, a former player for both clubs.

SATURDAY 23RD AUGUST 2003

Pompey were the visitors when Manchester City played their first league fixture at the City of Manchester Stadium. Playing their first away fixture in the Premiership, Pompey went ahead through Yakubu on 24 minutes and looked to have wrecked the party. But with only five seconds of normal time remaining, David Sommeil headed an equaliser for City.

SATURDAY 24TH AUGUST 1963

Pompey started the 1963-64 campaign with a 2-0 win over newly-relegated Manchester City in front of 21,822 fans at Maine Road. Pompey went ahead after three minutes through an own goal by Alf Wood and then Ron Saunders scored with a brilliant header.

SATURDAY 24TH AUGUST 1968

Birmingham City overwhelmed Pompey at St Andrews, winning 5-2. The hosts, who had lost their first three matches, took the lead after only thirteen seconds through Fred Pickering.

SATURDAY 24TH AUGUST 1974

A policeman was taken to hospital after fighting broke out on the Fratton Park terraces during a Second Division clash between Pompey and Nottingham Forest. Pompey won 2-0 with Mick Mellows and Richard Reynolds the goalscorers.

SATURDAY 25TH AUGUST 1928

The Fratton Park ground record was broken when a crowd of 33,475 attended Pompey's opening match of the 1928-29 season against Huddersfield Town. Johnny Weddle scored the only goal of the match in which Dave Thackeray, who was to captain Pompey in the 1934 FA Cup, made his debut for the club.

SATURDAY 25TH AUGUST 1956

Pompey recorded their first win of the season by beating Sheffield Wednesday in front of 23,730 at Fratton Park. Before the start of the game, Sir Leslie Bowker, vice-chairman of the Football Association, officially opened the new West Stand. Pompey won 3-1 with goals from Johnny Gordon (2) and Jackie Henderson.

SATURDAY 26TH AUGUST 1972

A crowd of 12,421 saw Pompey end Millwall's run of 29 home matches without defeat at The Den thanks to two goals by Brian Lewis.

MONDAY 26TH AUGUST 1996

TV pundit Mark Lawrenson warned Pompey that the arrival of Terry Venables alone would not rescue the club's fortunes. The former Liverpool defender said, "Money talks in the modern game and however much the arrival of Terry Venables will lift the players and supporters initially, in the long term, Pompey will only improve if they can bring in new faces."

MONDAY 26TH AUGUST 2002

Pompey went top of the First Division after a goal by Mark Burchill gave them a 1-0 win away to Grimsby Town.

TUESDAY 26TH AUGUST 2003

Teddy Sheringham scored a hat-trick as Pompey went top of the Premiership for the first time with a splendid second-half display to beat Bolton Wanderers, before a Fratton Park crowd of 20,113. Goalless at half-time, Steve Stone opened the scoring before Sheringham's header rounded off a fine move. With two minutes to go Sheringham scored again. Suddenly Pompey were in touching distance of the top for the first time since January 1952. In the last minute, Vincent Pericard was brought down in the box; Sheringham completed his hat-trick from the spot.

SATURDAY 27TH AUGUST 1927

Sunderland hit back from three goals down in front of 35,106 at Roker Park to deny Pompey a victory in their first match in Division One. Freddie Cook gave Pompey a dream start, flashing a shot high into the net on four minutes and Jerry Mackie pounced to double the advantage. Billy Haines shot through a crowd of players on 24 minutes but Bobby Marshall pulled a goal back for the home side before half-time. After the break Dave Halliday scored with a cross-shot and with Sunderland going all out for the equaliser, Billy Moffat planted the ball into his own net when attempting to clear. The Pompey team was: Dan McPhail, George Clifford, Jock McColgan, Reg Davies, Harry Foxall, Billy Moffat, Fred Forward, Jerry Mackie, Billy Haines, Dave Watson, Freddie Cook.

SATURDAY 27th AUGUST 1949

A late goal by Stan Mortensen – his second of the match – earned a 3-2 win for Blackpool, making the Seasiders the first team to beat Pompey at Fratton Park since Boxing Day 1947. The attendance was 47,260.

SATURDAY 27th AUGUST 1988

Substitute Mark Kelly scored the winner against Shrewsbury Town at Gay Meadow to give Pompey victory in their first match of the season. Terry Connor had nodded Pompey in front from a Warren Neill corner before Bernard McNally drew the Shrews level from the penalty spot. The home side were the more dangerous after the break but Kelly's strike meant that Jim Gregory's chairmanship began with a win.

SATURDAY 28th AUGUST 1920

Pompey won their first Football League match, triumphing 3-0 over Swansea Town. Billy James had the distinction of scoring the club's first Football League goal when he netted after 22 minutes.

SATURDAY 28th AUGUST 1926

A then-record crowd of 27,896 saw Pompey's Second Division promotion-winning season begin with a 3-1 home win over Southampton.

TUESDAY 28th AUGUST 1973

Ron Davies scored his first competitive goal for Pompey in a 2-1 victory over Southend United at Fratton Park in the League Cup first round.

SATURDAY 29th AUGUST 1925

The new season opened with a visit to Fratton Park by Middlesbrough and the new South Stand was opened at 3pm by Football League President Mr. John McKenna. The match, won by the visitors 5-1, kicked off at 3.15pm.

SATURDAY 29th AUGUST 1953

Pompey extended their disastrous start to the season, losing their fourth consecutive match, this time 5-1 away to Huddersfield Town. Not surprisingly they were bottom of Division One.

SATURDAY 29TH AUGUST 1964

Ron Saunders played his last match for Pompey, in which he scored two goals in a 3-2 defeat at home to Charlton Athletic. Those two strikes took his Pompey goal tally to 158.

SATURDAY 29TH AUGUST 1981

This was the first game which could potentially provide three points, under the new points system, but it took a late goal by Billy Rafferty to earn Pompey just one, with a 1-1 draw at home to Lincoln City.

SATURDAY 29TH AUGUST 1987

Pompey were hammered by Arsenal in front of 30,865 at Highbury. The Gunners thrashed Alan Ball's men 6-0; Alan Smith scored a hat-trick.

TUESDAY 29TH AUGUST 1989

Seven and a half years after being fired as Pompey manager, Frank Burrows returned to Fratton Park to become assistant to John Gregory.

SATURDAY 29TH AUGUST 1998

Alan McLoughlin scored a last minute penalty to earn Pompey a draw away to Huddersfield Town, seconds after Wayne Allison had given the home side a 3-2 lead.

SATURDAY 30TH AUGUST 1924

Goals by Jerry Mackie and Harry Foxall earned Pompey victory away to South Shields in the club's first match in Division Two.

THURSDAY 30TH AUGUST 1962

Coventry City inside-forward Albert McCann signed for Pompey for a fee of £3,000. He spent the next 12 years at Fratton Park, scoring 96 goals in 377 league and cup appearances.

SATURDAY 30TH AUGUST 1969

Bill Atkins scored his first goal for Pompey and his 100th in league football when he netted for the Blues in a 2-0 home victory over Blackburn Rovers in Division Two.

WEDNESDAY 30TH AUGUST 1972

Huddersfield Town wrecked Pompey's chances of going top of Division Two by winning 2-1 at Fratton Park, both their goals coming from former Manchester United player Alan Gowling. The Pompey goalscorer was Richie Reynolds.

TUESDAY 30TH AUGUST 1977

Pompey of the Third Division beat First Division Leicester City 2-0 at Fratton Park in a League Cup second round tie.

MONDAY 30TH AUGUST 2004

Pompey held on for victory despite a spirited Fulham comeback to win 4-3 in a thrilling match at Fratton Park attended by 19,728. Eyal Berkovic's volley gave them the lead before Yakubu grabbed a hat-trick.

WEDNESDAY 31ST AUGUST 1927

Pompey celebrated their first home match in the First Division by beating Aston Villa 3-1 and Freddie Cook had the distinction of being the first player to net for the Blues at Fratton Park in the top flight. The attendance of 32,050 set a new ground record.

SATURDAY 31ST AUGUST 1929

Reigning Football League champions Sheffield Wednesday thrashed Pompey 4-0 at Fratton Park on the opening day of the season. Jack Tinn's side never looked like salvaging anything from the game once Ellis Rimmer had put Wednesday ahead after only three minutes, as they made a miserable start to the new season.

SATURDAY 31ST AUGUST 1946

Duggie Reid scored twice as Pompey defeated Blackburn Rovers at Fratton Park in their first league match of the post-war era. Two Pompey greats, Jimmy Dickinson and Peter Harris, were making their Football League debuts in the game that was watched by a crowd of 30,962.

MONDAY 31ST AUGUST 1964

Ron Saunders was transferred to Watford. He had been the team's leading goalscorer for the past six seasons.

FRIDAY 31st AUGUST 1974

Bobby Fisher's first-half own goal was enough to gift Pompey their first league win of the season against Orient at Brisbane Road.

MONDAY 31st AUGUST 1987

Two goals by Kevin Dillon – the second a penalty – against West Ham United at Fratton Park, earned Pompey a 2-1 victory. It was their first win since returning to the First Division.

MONDAY 31st AUGUST 1998

Pompey claimed their first three points of the season by defeating Queens Park Rangers 3-0 at Fratton Park. John Aloisi gave them a first-half lead with his seventh goal of the season and Martin Phillips stepped off the substitute's bench to set up a goal for Alan McLoughlin before scoring himself in the last minute.

SATURDAY 31st AUGUST 2002

Three former Pompey men, Andy Petterson, Robbie Pethick and Guy Butters, were in the Brighton and Hove Albion team that were beaten 4-2 by Pompey in front of 19,031. Matt Taylor put away his first goal for the Blues in the third minute and the win kept his side top of Division One.

THURSDAY 31st AUGUST 2006

It was a busy transfer deadline day for Pompey with four players on the move. Pompey signed striker Andy Cole on a two-year deal, Croatia's Niko Kranjcar from Hajduk Split and they also signed winger Roudolphe Douala from Sporting Lisbon on a season-long loan. Going in the other direction was Svetoslav Todorov who joined Wigan Athletic on loan.

TUESDAY 31st AUGUST 2010

On a frantic transfer deadline day at Fratton Park, Dave Kitson and Liam Lawrence arrived from Stoke City who also paid £1.5m for Blues skipper Marc Wilson. Two other players to leave Fratton were Tommy Smith who joined Queens Park Rangers for £1.5m and youngster Marlon Pack who joined Cheltenham on loan.

PORTSMOUTH
On This Day & Miscellany

SEPTEMBER

WEDNESDAY 1st SEPTEMBER 1928

A Dixie Dean hat-trick helped reigning League Champions Everton to a 4-1 victory over Pompey at Goodison Park.

WEDNESDAY 1st SEPTEMBER 1948

A week after beating Everton 4-0 at Fratton Park, Pompey went one better against the Toffees at Goodison. Jack Froggatt scored twice with the other goals coming from Peter Harris, Duggie Reid and Bert Barlow.

SATURDAY 1st SEPTEMBER 1973

Billy Wilson was sent off after receiving two bookings during a 1-1 draw away to Cardiff City in Pompey's second league match of the campaign.

SATURDAY 1st SEPTEMBER 1979

Pompey came from behind to make it four wins in a row against Wigan Athletic at Springfield Park in front of 8,198. They went a goal down after ten minutes but hit back through Terry Brisley and Colin Garwood.

TUESDAY 1st SEPTEMBER 2009

Pompey signed defender Mike Williamson from Watford for a fee of £2m rising to £3m after he had played a certain number of matches. Due to Pompey's financial problems Williamson made no appearances and was sold to Newcastle in January. The fee was undisclosed.

SATURDAY 2nd SEPTEMBER 1899

Fifteen months after the formation of Portsmouth Football Club, the team played their first league match at Chatham in the Southern League. They wore salmon pink shirts with maroon collars and cuffs and were dubbed "The Shrimps." They won 1-0 with Harold "Nobby" Clarke being credited with the goal, although the ball entered the net off a Chatham defender.

SATURDAY 2nd SEPTEMBER 1931

Fred Worrall, who was to win the FA Cup with Pompey in 1939 as well as represent the club in the 1934 final, made his debut at outside-right in a 3-0 home defeat by Everton. Tommy White, deputising at centre-forward for the Toffees in place of the injured Dixie Dean, scored all three goals.

SATURDAY 2ND SEPTEMBER 1950

Newcastle United gained their first point at Fratton Park by holding Pompey to a goalless draw in an intense battle watched by 43,244.

WEDNESDAY 2ND SEPTEMBER 1970

Ray Hiron equalised five minutes from time to earn Pompey a 1-1 draw with Orient at Fratton Park.

SATURDAY 3RD SEPTEMBER 1949

A hat-trick by Peter Harris in the last fifteen minutes helped Pompey to a 5-1 victory over Middlesbrough at Ayresome Park.

SATURDAY 3RD SEPTEMBER 1955

Pompey produced one of their greatest performances of all time to defeat League Champions Chelsea 5-1 at Stamford Bridge before a crowd of 48,273. Peter Harris and Derek Rees both scored twice and Jackie Henderson also netted for Eddie Lever's side.

WEDNESDAY 3RD SEPTEMBER 1958

Peter Harris scored all five goals as Pompey beat Aston Villa 5-2 before a crowd of 24,200 at Fratton Park. The home team produced some of their best football for several years and yet it was Villa who took the lead through Gerry Hitchens after only two minutes. Harris equalised with a twice-taken penalty and the former England outside-right went on to score four more goals before Leslie Smith pulled a goal back for Villa.

SATURDAY 3RD SEPTEMBER 1988

Pompey won 4-0 at Fratton Park in a Second Division clash against Leeds United who included three former Blues – Noel Blake, Vince Hilaire and Ian Baird, the latter receiving his marching orders late on.

SATURDAY 4TH SEPTEMBER 1937

Johnny Weddle played his last match for Pompey in a 2-2 draw away to Birmingham City. He had represented the club on 396 occasions in league and cup and scored 181 goals – both club records until Jimmy Dickinson overtook his number of appearances in November 1955 and Peter Harris notched his 182nd goal.

SATURDAY 4th SEPTEMBER 1948

Pompey went top of Division One for the first time since the war, beating Stoke City 1-0 through a 37th minute goal by Peter Harris. Regular skipper Reg Flewin was injured so the team was led by Phil Rookes.

SATURDAY 4th SEPTEMBER 1993

John Durnin scored in the third minute of his full debut in a home fixture against Stoke City that ended 3-3.

SATURDAY 5th SEPTEMBER 1903

The *Sports Mail*, which has been an institution in the Portsmouth area for over one hundred years, was first produced. Cricket, darts, snooker and bowls are just some of the sports that take their place in the paper but chiefly the publication covers football and Pompey in particular. The first edition, then known as the *Football Mail*, reported on Pompey's 2-1 Southern League defeat away to Reading.

SATURDAY 5th SEPTEMBER 1925

Pompey secured their first Football League victory over Southampton, winning 3-1 in a Second Division clash at The Dell. The goalscorers were Jerry Mackie, Alex Merrie and Willie Beedie.

SATURDAY 5th SEPTEMBER 1970

Pompey took their unbeaten start to five matches with a 2-0 win at home to Sheffield Wednesday thanks to Ray Hiron and Nick Jennings goals.

WEDNESDAY 6th SEPTEMBER 1899

Fratton Park staged its first football match – a friendly between Portsmouth and Southampton. Pompey won 2-0.

SATURDAY 6th SEPTEMBER 1924

Pompey and Derby County drew 1-1 in the first Second Division match to be played at Fratton Park.

SATURDAY 6th SEPTEMBER 1952

Johnny Gordon scored the first of his 118 Pompey goals in the 2-0 victory at home to reigning League Champions Manchester United.

WEDNESDAY 6TH SEPTEMBER 1972

"There are no words to describe how I feel right now," said Pompey manager Ron Tindall after seeing his side plumb the depths in slumping to their third home defeat in eight days, this time 1-0 to Third Division Chesterfield in the second round of the League Cup.

SATURDAY 6TH SEPTEMBER 1975

Seventeen-year-old Chris Kamara made his league debut in Pompey's midfield in a 2-0 defeat by Luton Town.

FRIDAY 6TH SEPTEMBER 1963

The Portsmouth Ex-Championship XI was registered with the Hampshire Football Association. The team consisted of Pompey's championship-winning veterans and, as time moved on, other former players of the club. A sum of around £100,000 was raised for numerous charities over a period of 30 years.

WEDNESDAY 7TH SEPTEMBER 1932

Freddie Cook played his last match for Pompey. The Welsh international outside-left collapsed with a knee injury after taking a corner kick during the 4-4 draw with Chelsea at Stamford Bridge.

SATURDAY 7TH SEPTEMBER 1935

John McKenna, President of the Football League, officially opened the new North Stand at Fratton Park before Pompey's First Division clash with Aston Villa which was won 3-0 by the home side. It was fitting that Villa should have been the opposition for it was the money received from the Midlands club for captain Jimmy Allen in June 1934 that enabled Pompey to build the stand.

SATURDAY 7TH SEPTEMBER 1974

Sir Alf Ramsey received a personal call from chairman John Deacon – but declined his invitation – to become Pompey manager. Deacon was prepared to pay him £20,000 a year – roughly three times the amount he earned as England boss – to replace the departed John Mortimore. On the pitch that afternoon Pompey were beaten 3-1 at home by West Bromwich Albion.

SATURDAY 7TH SEPTEMBER 2002

Pompey made it six wins out of seven against Gillingham at the Priestfield Stadium. Paul Merson, Mark Burchill and Gary O'Neil scored in the 3-1 victory.

SUNDAY 8TH SEPTEMBER 1946

Returning home by coach from the previous day's 1-0 defeat at Bolton Wanderers, the Pompey party were involved in an accident at Wickham at 3.30am when the driver was unable to avoid the obstruction of an American service vehicle. Manager Jack Tinn and trainer Jimmy Stewart who occupied the front seats were badly bruised but fortunately none of the players were injured.

SATURDAY 8TH SEPTEMBER 1956

Pompey were beaten 3-2 by Arsenal at Fratton Park, the Gunners' winner coming two minutes from time. Pompey had come back to level after being 2-0 down after only four minutes.

SATURDAY 9TH SEPTEMBER 1950

Reigning champions Pompey suffered their heaviest defeat in 11 years, going down 5-0 to West Bromwich Albion in a First Division encounter before a crowd of 34,460 at The Hawthorns.

SATURDAY 9TH SEPTEMBER 1961

Portsmouth celebrated Jimmy Dickinson's 600th league appearance for the club by beating Barnsley 3-2 at Fratton Park in Division Two before 16,014. Reg Cutler scored from a penalty and Pompey's other goalscorers were Harry Middleton and Ron Saunders.

SATURDAY 9TH SEPTEMBER 1978

First-half goals by Steve Davey and John Lathan earned Pompey their first away success in Division Four – a 2-0 victory over Rochdale. The crowd of 1,479 was then the smallest to watch Pompey in a league match.

SATURDAY 9TH SEPTEMBER 1989

Guy Whittingham came on as sub to score his first goal for Pompey since buying himself out of the army. He opened the scoring in a 2-2 draw with Hull City at Fratton Park before a crowd of 6,469.

WEDNESDAY 9TH SEPTEMBER 1992

Centre-forward Colin Clarke broke the Northern Ireland goalscoring record when he netted in his country's 3-0 win over Albania in a World Cup qualifying match. The goal took his tally to 13.

SATURDAY 10TH SEPTEMBER 1949

Pompey claimed their biggest league victory for 22 years by beating Everton 7-0 before a crowd of 36,012 at Fratton Park. Their five forwards, Peter Harris, Duggie Reid, Ike Clarke, Len Phillips and Jack Froggatt all found the net. The result remains the club's biggest win in the top flight and this was the last time Pompey scored seven goals until Reading were beaten 7-4 at Fratton Park in September 2007.

SATURDAY 10TH SEPTEMBER 1960

Two goals by Ron Saunders gave Pompey a 2-1 victory at home to Sunderland. Pompey were to be relegated from the Second Division at the end of the season but this victory moved them into fourth spot.

SATURDAY 11TH SEPTEMBER 1937

Jimmy Guthrie, who skippered Pompey to victory in the 1939 FA Cup final, made his debut in the 2-0 defeat at home to Middlesbrough.

SATURDAY 11TH SEPTEMBER 1948

Duggie Reid scored all three goals in a 3-1 victory over Charlton Athletic at Fratton Park watched by 39,459 putting Pompey three points clear at the top of the First Division.

SATURDAY 11TH SEPTEMBER 1971

Goals by Mike Trebilcock, Eoin Hand and Ray Hiron earned Pompey a 3-2 win at home to Orient.

SATURDAY 11TH SEPTEMBER 1976

Former Pompey player Ray Hiron, so desperate to turn out for Reading against his former club at Fratton Park despite suffering from a leg injury, started the match but clearly was not fit. He limped off after just three minutes of the game. The visitors won the Third Division fixture 2-0.

SATURDAY 11TH SEPTEMBER 2004

Pompey's 3-1 victory before 20,019 at Fratton Park kept Crystal Palace bottom of the Premiership. Ricardo Fuller struck his only Pompey goal after three minutes, Patrik Berger scored from 25 yards and Tony Popovic put Steve Stone's cross into his own net.

SATURDAY 12TH SEPTEMBER 1970

Pompey's unbeaten start to the season came to an end at the County Ground where Swindon Town overcame Ron Tindall's side 2-1.

TUESDAY 12TH SEPTEMBER 1989

The Pompey players trailed down the tunnel to chants of "what a load of rubbish" after losing 3-0 at home to Plymouth Argyle.

SATURDAY 12TH SEPTEMBER 1998

Two goals apiece for striker John Aloisi and midfielder Sammy Igoe, with another from Steve Claridge helped Pompey to a 5-2 victory at home to Swindon Town.

SATURDAY 13TH SEPTEMBER 1947

A goal by Duggie Reid four minutes from time earned Pompey a 1-0 victory over the reigning League Champions Liverpool at Fratton Park.

FRIDAY 13TH SEPTEMBER 1974

Former Liverpool and Scotland centre-forward Ian St John agreed to become Pompey manager even though he had not even seen Fratton Park. Chairman John Deacon commented, "I can't wait for him to get started. I'm absolutely convinced this is the start of a great new era for Pompey."

MONDAY 13TH SEPTEMBER 1976

An appeal fund to save Portsmouth Football Club – S.O.S. Pompey – was launched by the Portsmouth local newspaper *The News*. Club chairman John Deacon said, "I commend the efforts of *The News* and hope people will support it." The campaign aimed to raise £25,000 as quickly as possible to meet the club's most pressing debts.

SATURDAY 13TH SEPTEMBER 2003

A disputed penalty denied Pompey a first victory over Arsenal at Highbury since 1955. Replays showed there was no contact from Dejan Stefanovic as Robert Pires went to ground in the 40th minute, but ref Alan Wiley awarded a penalty (he later admitted he was the wrong) and Thierry Henry scored with a re-taken kick. Pompey had gone ahead on 26 minutes when Teddy Sheringham powered home Steve Stone's cross from the right. Unfortunately, although Stefanovic's yellow card was later rescinded, the result of the match stood, depriving Pompey of a long awaited victory.

SATURDAY 13TH SEPTEMBER 2010

Jermain Defoe capped a stunning second-half performance as Pompey picked up their first win at Fratton Park for six months. The striker scored twice to give Pompey a 2-1 victory over Middlesbrough.

MONDAY 14TH SEPTEMBER 1964

Boss George Smith signed Ron Tindall from Reading on a free transfer. The former Chelsea and West Ham man gave the club great service over the next ten years, becoming captain, player-manager and manager.

SATURDAY 14TH SEPTEMBER 2002

Svetoslav Todorov's goal earned a 1-0 home win over Millwall and gave Pompey their best start to a season. Seven wins and a draw from eight eclipsed the starts of 1922/23 and 1948/49. The win over the Lions was followed by a 4-1 victory at home to Wimbledon but the team suffered a first defeat of the campaign the next week, losing 1-0 at Norwich City.

SATURDAY 15TH SEPTEMBER 1951

Pompey were beaten 3-2 at home in a highly entertaining match with Wolverhampton Wanderers watched by 30,759. All the goals came in the second half.

SATURDAY 15TH SEPTEMBER 1973

Goalkeeper Ron Tilsed played the last 20 minutes of Pompey's 3-3 draw away to Luton Town in September 1973 with a broken arm. Centre-forward Ron Davies, back helping out the defence, struck the goalkeeper's arm while attempting to clear the ball but Tilsed, obviously in severe pain, defiantly refused to leave the field and helped Pompey to a point.

SATURDAY 15TH SEPTEMBER 2001

Pompey moved into second place in Division One after beating Crystal Palace at Fratton Park. The goals were scored by Alessandro Zamperini, Robert Prosinecki, Mark Burchill and Peter Crouch.

SATURDAY 16TH SEPTEMBER 1950

A second-half Duggie Reid hat-trick helped Pompey beat Stoke City 5-1 in front of a Fratton Park crowd of 33,973. Pompey's other goals came from Ike Clarke and a Harry Ferrier penalty.

SATURDAY 16TH SEPTEMBER 1967

Nicky Jennings grabbed a hat-trick – the only one of his career – as Pompey maintained their unbeaten start with a 3-1 victory over Norwich City in front of 11,802 at Carrow Road.

SATURDAY 16TH SEPTEMBER 1995

Alan McLoughlin's stoppage-time header earned Pompey a 2-2 draw against Jim Smith's Derby County at Fratton Park. The crowd of 14,434 was 6,000 up on the previous home game, mainly due to the fact that Paul Walsh was making his first appearance since returning to the club.

SATURDAY 16TH SEPTEMBER 2006

Lomana LuaLua came off the bench to score the only goal against Charlton Athletic at The Valley. Pompey's defence remained intact for the fifth successive game and the victory put them at the top of the Premiership table.

WEDNESDAY 17TH SEPTEMBER 1930

Johnny Weddle netted his second hat-trick to help Pompey beat Blackpool 4-3 in a First Division fixture at Fratton Park.

WEDNESDAY 17TH SEPTEMBER 1947

Jack Froggatt scored a second-half hat-trick for Pompey in a 6-0 win at home to Sheffield United. The other goals came from Duggie Reid, Peter Harris and a Dick Young own goal.

SATURDAY 17TH SEPTEMBER 1955

Pompey came from a goal down to beat Arsenal in front of 48,816 at Highbury. Doug Lishman put the Gunners in the lead but Pompey hit back with two goals by Peter Harris and another by Derek Rees. This was the last time that Pompey won at Arsenal.

WEDNESDAY 17TH SEPTEMBER 1975

Jon Sammels' goal two minutes before the end of added time gave Leicester City victory over Pompey in a League Cup second round replay.

SATURDAY 18TH SEPTEMBER 1948

Pompey stretched their unbeaten start to the season to nine matches and remained top of the First Division by drawing 1-1 with Manchester City. They fell behind in the first minute through an Eddie McMorran header but Pompey's perseverance was rewarded in the 65th minute when Duggie Reid levelled from close range.

SATURDAY 18TH SEPTEMBER 1971

Pompey moved up to sixth in the Second Division table after claiming their first away victory of the season – 3-1 against Hull City. Goals by Norman Piper, Eoin Hand and Albert McCann came in a five minute burst midway through the second half before Stuart Pearson netted a consolation for the Tigers.

TUESDAY 18TH SEPTEMBER 1979

Two goals each from Terry Brisley and Jeff Hemmerman gave Pompey an easy home win over Bournemouth who were reduced to ten men after 43 minutes when Ian Cunningham was sent off for kicking out at Alan Rogers. The win took Frank Burrows' side to the top of Division Four.

THURSDAY 18TH SEPTEMBER 2008

Pompey marked their debut in the UEFA Cup competition with a 2-0 victory over Portuguese club Vitoria Guimaraes at Fratton Park before a crowd of 19,612. Lassana Diarra played a one-two with Jermain Defoe and scored with a left-foot volley on 39 minutes to break the deadlock. Three minutes later Guimaraes' Jose Paulo Fajardo blazed a penalty over the bar. After the break Defoe also missed a penalty but made amends on the hour mark by sealing victory with a superb volley. The

Pompey team that evening was: David James, Glen Johnson, Sylvain Distin, Nadir Belhadj, Sol Campbell, Lassana Diarra, Sean Davis, John Utaka (Papa Boupa Diop), Armand Traore (Hermann Hreidarsson), Peter Crouch (Kanu), Jermain Defoe.

SATURDAY 19TH SEPTEMBER 1936

Pompey went top of the First Division following a 2-1 win at home to Manchester City thanks to goals by Johnny Weddle and Cliff Parker. They held the position for two months.

SATURDAY 19TH SEPTEMBER 1964

After failing to score in their previous three matches, Pompey trounced Swindon Town 5-0 with all the goals coming in the first half. John McClelland and Cliff Portwood each scored twice with the other goal coming from Albert McCann.

TUESDAY 19TH SEPTEMBER 2006

Premiership leaders Pompey held out against a spirited second-half display from League Two Mansfield Town to win 2-1 before 6,646 at Field Mill and book their place in the League Cup third round. Manuel Fernandes marked his Pompey debut by scoring the first goal. Stags substitute Danny Reet became the first player to score against Pompey since May.

SATURDAY 20TH SEPTEMBER 1952

Pompey recorded their first away win of the season, 5-0 at Bolton Wanderers. The scorers were Peter Harris (2), Duggie Reid, Johnny Gordon and Len Phillips. It was also Bolton's first home defeat.

SATURDAY 20TH SEPTEMBER 1958

Ron Saunders scored twice in the second half as Pompey came from behind to defeat Blackburn Rovers 2-1 at Fratton Park.

FRIDAY 20TH SEPTEMBER 1974

Chairman John Deacon believed a "new Fratton Park" could be in existence at the former City Airport within five years. He said, "The project is at the stage where drawings are being made for a multi-purpose sports centre based on a new Fratton Park." However, a corporation spokesman said, "I know nothing of our being within five years of the project."

TUESDAY 20TH SEPTEMBER 2005

Pompey fans turned on manager Alain Perrin after Pompey were beaten 3-2 by Gillingham in the League Cup second round after extra time at The Priestfield Stadium.

SATURDAY 21ST SEPTEMBER 1946

After four consecutive defeats and without scoring a goal, Pompey got back to winning ways by beating Huddersfield Town 3-1 at Fratton Park. The goals came from Cliff Parker (2) and Jack Froggatt.

SATURDAY 21ST SEPTEMBER 1957

Jimmy Stewart, the club's chief scout, retired. He joined the club as trainer in 1935, the position he held throughout the double League Championship years of 1949 and 1950, and had been chief scout for the two years before his retirement. On the same day, Pompey were beaten 4-1 at home by Nottingham Forest.

SATURDAY 21ST SEPTEMBER 1974

Ian St John's first match as Pompey manager ended in a 2-2 draw with Cardiff City at Fratton Park. They pulled back from a 2-0 half-time deficit thanks to goals from Mick Mellows and Norman Piper.

SUNDAY 21ST SEPTEMBER 2008

Pompey suffered their heaviest defeat during their seven-year Premiership existence, losing 6-0 to Manchester City at Eastlands.

SATURDAY 22ND SEPTEMBER 1956

A 2-2 draw at home to Preston North End left Pompey at the bottom of the First Division with only four points from nine matches. Pompey were awarded a penalty after only fifteen seconds which Peter Harris, playing his 400th league and cup match, converted. Jackie Henderson made it 2-0 three minutes later but Preston scored twice in the second half to deny the Blues their second win of the season.

SATURDAY 22ND SEPTEMBER 1973

John Milkins saved three penalties from three different players in a 2-1 home defeat by Notts County. First, Kevin Randall's spot kick was saved by Milkins but the referee decided that the goalkeeper had moved. Up stepped Don Masson and Milkins deflected his shot against the crossbar. The referee again decided Milkins had moved and this time Brian Stubbs took the kick which the Pompey 'keeper turned over the bar.

SATURDAY 22ND SEPTEMBER 1999

Alan Knight appeared as a late substitute for Andy Petterson in a 3-1 defeat away to Blackburn Rovers in the League Cup second round second leg to chalk up his 800th Pompey appearance.

SATURDAY 23RD SEPTEMBER 1967

Pompey hung on to their unbeaten record by scraping a 1-1 draw at Fratton Park with lowly Rotherham United in Division Two. The below-par Blues took the lead courtesy of an Albert McCann penalty but Laurie Sheffield provided the equaliser for the visitors. The result kept Pompey in seventh place with eleven points from seven games.

SATURDAY 23RD SEPTEMBER 1978

Aldershot's unbeaten home run stretching back to April 1977 was ended as Jeff Hemmerman and John Lathan netted for Pompey in a 2-0 win at the Recreation Ground.

WEDNESDAY 23RD SEPTEMBER 1981

Pompey collected three points for the first time. Three points for a win instead of two had been introduced at the start of the 1981-82 season to encourage more attacking football and Pompey had to wait until their sixth league match to win their first three points when they defeated Oxford United 2-0 at the Manor Ground in a Division Three fixture.

SATURDAY 23RD SEPTEMBER 1989

The pressure on manager John Gregory eased a little as Pompey won their first league game of the season, beating Middlesbrough 3-1 at Fratton Park. It had been the worst start by a Pompey side since 1973.

SATURDAY 24TH SEPTEMBER 1949

A crowd of 35,765 saw Pompey and Bolton Wanderers draw 1-1 at Fratton Park. Ike Clarke put Pompey ahead before Nat Lofthouse levelled.

SATURDAY 24TH SEPTEMBER 1955

Seventeen-year-old Pat Neil scored the only goal in Pompey's First Division home clash with Everton.

SATURDAY 24TH SEPTEMBER 1960

Pompey kept up a 100% home record, beating Norwich City 3-0 at Fratton Park before 17,946. Tony Priscott, Reg Cutler (penalty) and Ron Saunders were the men on target. At half-time a testimonial cheque was presented to ex-Pompey winger Peter Harris who had recently been forced to retire through ill health.

FRIDAY 24TH SEPTEMBER 2010

After collecting only two points from their first seven matches of the season Pompey thrashed Leicester City 6-1 at Fratton Park to move off the bottom of the Championship table. Liam Lawrence netted twice including a penalty, Dave Kitson also grabbed a brace and the other goals were scored by David Nugent and Michael Brown.

SATURDAY 25TH SEPTEMBER 1926

Billy Haines scored a hat-trick and had a hand in two more goals as Pompey beat Blackpool 5-0 in the Second Division at Fratton Park.

SATURDAY 25TH SEPTEMBER 1948

Pompey remained at the top of the First Division table following a 3-0 victory at home to Sheffield United. Although not at their best they were in command from the moment Len Phillips scored his first goal of the season after nine minutes. Peter Harris added a couple of goals and Phillips hit a post late on.

SATURDAY 25TH SEPTEMBER 1965

Pompey maintained their unbeaten home record when they ploughed their way through the havy rain to beat lowly Leyton Orient 4-1 at Fratton Park. Ray Hiron and Dennis Edwards scored two apiece.

TUESDAY 25TH SEPTEMBER 1984

Pompey won their League Cup second round second leg meeting with Brian Clough's Nottingham Forest at Fratton Park thanks to a second-half header by Alan Biley.

SATURDAY 26TH SEPTEMBER 1959

Ipswich Town, with the former Pompey players Ray Crawford and Reg Pickett in their line-up, recorded a 2-0 victory on their first visit to Fratton Park. It was Pompey's seventh successive league defeat.

SATURDAY 26TH SEPTEMBER 1970

Pompey were defeated 2-0 by Leicester City at Filbert Street but were denied a legitimate goal that would have given them the lead. Jim Storrie's header entered the net but bounced back into play and the referee, thinking the ball had hit the crossbar, allowed the game to continue.

TUESDAY 26TH SEPTEMBER 2000

The 1-1 draw with Blackburn Rovers at Fratton Park in the League Cup second round second leg was watched by only 2,731 – Pompey's lowest home attendance for a competitive fixture. Supporters could have been excused for their lack of interest as Blackburn had gone into the match with a healthy lead having won 4-0 at Ewood Park in the first leg.

SATURDAY 26TH SEPTEMBER 2009

Pompey were left still without a point after Louis Saha's first-half strike was enough to secure Everton victory over the Blues at Goodison Park. It was Pompey's seventh straight defeat – the worst start by a top-flight club since Manchester United lost their first twelve matches of the 1931/32 campaign.

SATURDAY 27TH SEPTEMBER 1924

The first meeting in Division Two between Pompey and Southampton ended goalless at The Dell.

TUESDAY 27TH SEPTEMBER 1978

A late goal by Steve Davey was enough for Pompey to beat Wigan Athletic in a Fourth Division clash before a crowd of 13,902 at Fratton Park in the first meeting between the two sides.

TUESDAY 27TH SEPTEMBER 2004

Tim Cahill's late header gave Everton a 1-0 victory at Fratton Park in front of 20,125.

SATURDAY 28TH SEPTEMBER 1929

Dixie Dean scored his third hat-trick against Pompey, helping the Toffees to a 4-1 victory at Fratton Park.

SATURDAY 28TH SEPTEMBER 1963

Pompey gained their first home victory of the season by beating Southampton 2-0 in front of 29,459 at Fratton Park. Ron Saunders headed Pompey in front after only 20 seconds and Brian Lewis netted a second goal on eleven minutes. Saints suffered another blow four minutes later when they lost goalkeeper Ron Reynolds with a shoulder injury and Cliff Huxford took over between the sticks.

SATURDAY 28TH SEPTEMBER 1968

A crowd of 18,998 was treated to a thrilling match at Fratton Park in which Pompey and Crystal Palace shared six goals. Pompey led twice but it took a 35-yard shot by Harry Harris to save a point for the Blues.

FRIDAY 28TH SEPTEMBER 1990

Ten days after being dropped from the Pompey team for the first time in a decade, Alan Knight handed in a written transfer request.

WEDNESDAY 28TH SEPTEMBER 1994

Pompey's fine 2-0 win away to West Bromwich Albion saw them shoot ten places up the First Division table but the evening was marred when Andy Awford broke his leg and Tony Dobson was sent off.

SATURDAY 29TH SEPTEMBER 1962

Bobby Tambling scored both goals as Chelsea won 2-0 at Fratton Park in what was Jimmy Dickinson's 650th league appearance for Pompey.

SATURDAY 29TH SEPTEMBER 1973

Pompey had collected only five points from eight matches after being beaten 2-1 by Preston North End at Deepdale but manager John Mortimore said, "I have not seen a better side than us all season."

SATURDAY 29TH SEPTEMBER 1990

Colin Clarke scored twice and Martin Kuhl was also on target as Pompey gained a 3-1 victory over Plymouth Argyle in front of 8,636 at Fratton Park. England under-21 central defender Guy Butters was making his debut after a £325,000 move from Tottenham Hotspur.

SATURDAY 29TH SEPTEMBER 2007

Benjani Mwaruwari scored a hat-trick as Pompey beat Reading 7-4 in a Premier League meeting at Fratton Park. It was the first time eleven goals had been scored in a Premier League match and was also the most goals scored in a first class match at Fratton Park. However, there could have been more goals for Pompey had one disallowed and goalkeeper David James saved a penalty. It was the first time Pompey had hit seven since September 1949 and, curiously, Pompey failed to find the net at home until January when another Benjani treble earned a 3-1 win against Derby County.

SATURDAY 30TH SEPTEMBER 1961

Johnny Gordon scored four minutes from time to secure a 1-1 draw for Pompey against Bournemouth in a Third Division clash at Fratton Park before a crowd of 25,672.

SATURDAY 30TH SEPTEMBER 1967

A goal by George Smith yielded Pompey a 1-0 victory over Derby County at the Baseball Ground to move them up to fourth place in the Second Division. The attendance was 27,043.

WEDNESDAY 30TH SEPTEMBER 1970

Pompey crashed to a 5-1 home defeat by Sheffield United. It was the second time in thirteen months that the Blades had triumphed at Fratton Park by that scoreline.

SATURDAY 30TH SEPTEMBER 1972

Goals by Richard Reynolds and Norman Piper secured a 2-0 win for Pompey at home to Brighton and Hove Albion in the first league meeting between the two clubs since 1961.

TUESDAY 30TH SEPTEMBER 1980

Goals by Dave Gregory and Steve Perrin in a 2-0 win over Bristol Rovers in the League Cup set up a fourth round tie at Liverpool.

PORTSMOUTH
On This Day & Miscellany

OCTOBER

SATURDAY 1st OCTOBER 1927

Pompey were thrashed 8-2 by Liverpool on their first visit to Anfield. Pompey goalkeeper John Jarvie, making his first appearance in a year, was beaten six times by the interval. Jerry Mackie pulled a goal back after the break and Freddie Cook, the one Pompey player to show anything like his true form, snatched a second, but Liverpool restored their six-goal advantage.

SATURDAY 1st OCTOBER 1949

The biggest crowd to attend Fratton Park for a league match – 50,248 – saw reigning champions Pompey and FA Cup holders Wolverhampton Wanderers fight out a 1-1 draw. Playing sparkling football in the first half, Pompey thoroughly deserved their lead that came after half an hour through a Duggie Reid penalty. Wolves fought back strongly after the break and Jesse Pye crashed home the equaliser.

TUESDAY 1st OCTOBER 1991

Kit Symons became the youngest Pompey captain. The central-defender was 20 when he led the side against Plymouth Argyle at Home Park in the first round of the Zenith Data Systems Cup. Argyle won the match 1-0.

SATURDAY 2nd OCTOBER 1948

Len Phillips scored the only goal as Pompey defeated Newcastle United before a crowd of 45,827 at Fratton Park. This was the Magpies' first visit to Fratton Park in fifteen years and the victory kept Pompey at the top of the First Division.

TUESDAY 2nd OCTOBER 1973

Two goals by Eoin Hand in a 2-1 win over Carlisle United gave Pompey their first home win of the season. The new Fratton Park floodlights, which produced four times the power of the old system, were officially opened by Supporters' Club Chairman Bill Davis before the game.

THURSDAY 2nd OCTOBER 1997

Terry Venables, Pompey chairman and manager of the Australian national side, was told by an anonymous caller that he would be murdered if he played Mark Viduka in Australia's friendly in Tunisia. Viduka did play – and scored – but Venables was shaken by the call and informed the police.

THURSDAY 2ND OCTOBER 2008

Two extra-time goals by Peter Crouch ensured Pompey won their first UEFA Cup tie. Portuguese club Vitoria Guimaraes, beaten 2-0 in the first leg at Fratton Park, led by the same score after ninety minutes but Crouch's brace saw Pompey to victory.

SATURDAY 3RD OCTOBER 1959

Pompey took a 3-0 lead against Huddersfield Town after only thirteen minutes of their Second Division encounter at Leeds Road but ended up losing the match 6-3.

SATURDAY 3RD OCTOBER 1970

A real game of two halves as Mike Trebilcock, playing in his first match for six months, celebrated his return by firing a second-half hat-trick to help Pompey hammer Watford 5-0 at Fratton Park. The other goalscorers were Nick Jennings and Norman Piper; their strikes also came after the break, as all five goals came in the second half of the game.

SATURDAY 3RD OCTOBER 1987

Liverpool steamrollered their way to another victory, beating Pompey 4-0 in front of 44,366 at Anfield in the first league meeting between the two clubs since 1961.

SATURDAY 3RD OCTOBER 1992

Guy Whittingham's second hat-trick of the season helped Pompey to an impressive 4-1 win away to Luton Town. It was Portsmouth's first victory at Kenilworth Road since 1921. Northern Ireland international Colin Clarke added Pompey's other goal.

SATURDAY 3RD OCTOBER 2009

Pompey collected their first points of the season by winning 1-0 away to Wolverhampton Wanderers, ending a run of seven straight defeats. The goal was scored by French Algerian Hassan Yebda who was on loan from Benfica.

SATURDAY 4TH OCTOBER 1952

Playing without skipper Reg Flewin for an hour, Pompey held Sunderland to a draw at Roker Park in front of 45,145. Flewin was taken to hospital with concussion following a collision with Trevor Ford but was able to return home with the Pompey party.

SATURDAY 4TH OCTOBER 1958

Pompey created enough chances to have beaten Tottenham Hotspur at Fratton Park before 26,402 but had to be content with a 1-1 draw.

TUESDAY 4TH OCTOBER 1983

Aston Villa of the First Division scored twice in the last five minutes to draw 2-2 with Second Division Pompey in the League Cup second round first leg at Fratton Park in front of 18,484.

SATURDAY 5TH OCTOBER 1968

Mike Trebilcock became the first Pompey substitute to score two goals in a match when he helped his side to a 3-0 win at home to Oxford United in the first Football League meeting between the two clubs. Ray Pointer added Pompey's other goal. Former manager, 90-year-old Jack Tinn, was Guest of Honour.

SATURDAY 5TH OCTOBER 1991

Pompey defeated Newcastle United 3-1 at Fratton Park. Jim Smith's men had not conceded a goal at Fratton Park all season and former Blues striker Mick Quinn promised to be the first player to put the ball past Alan Knight. Quinn kept his promise but with unfortunate repercussions. Colliding with a post as he forced the ball over the line he sustained an injury that would keep him out of action for five months.

SATURDAY 6TH OCTOBER 1928

Dave Watson scored all three goals in Pompey's 3-2 victory at home to Sheffield Wednesday.

SATURDAY 6TH OCTOBER 1979

Phil Ashworth, a free transfer signing from Rochdale, scored twice on his debut in a 4-3 victory over Darlington at Fratton Park. The Fourth Division clash was watched by 16,692.

TUESDAY 6TH OCTOBER 1981

Pompey's first experience of playing on an artificial pitch was not a happy one. Queens Park Rangers thrashed them 5-0 in the League Cup second round first leg at Loftus Road.

SATURDAY 6TH OCTOBER 1984

"We were pathetic," claimed manager Alan Ball, despite his side beating Cardiff City 2-1 at Ninian Park and going joint top of Division Two.

SATURDAY 7TH OCTOBER 1922

Bert Batten was the first player of the season to score past Pompey goalkeeper Tommy Newton when he netted for Plymouth Argyle in his side's 2-1 victory at Fratton Park. Newton had kept clean sheets in all Pompey's first eight matches of the campaign – still a club record.

SATURDAY 7TH OCTOBER 1961

Pompey lost their unbeaten record, going down 2-1 to Notts County at Meadow Lane in Division Three before 9,889. Peter Bircumshaw scored both goals for County while Johnny Gordon netted for Pompey.

SATURDAY 7TH OCTOBER 1967

John McClelland and Ray Hiron were on target after Bobby Kellard had missed a penalty as Pompey beat Carlisle United 2-1 at Fratton Park in a Second Division encounter in front of 21,864. Hugh McIlmoyle replied for Carlisle.

WEDNESDAY 7TH OCTOBER 1970

Bobby Charlton scored from long range to give Manchester United a 1-0 victory in the League Cup third round at Old Trafford. Charlton was the only player on the field to have featured in Pompey's previous visit to United's home in March 1959 when they were thrashed 6-1 by Matt Busby's team.

SATURDAY 7TH OCTOBER 2007

Hermann Hreidarsson scored his first goal for Pompey in a 2-0 victory over Fulham at Craven Cottage. Benjani netted the other goal.

WEDNESDAY 7th OCTOBER 2009

Avram Grant was installed Pompey's Director of Football. The former Chelsea manager had spent the 2006/07 season at Fratton Park as Technical Director. Grant was to replace Paul Hart as Pompey manager two months later.

SATURDAY 8th OCTOBER 1927

The first meeting between Pompey and Arsenal ended in a 3-2 victory at Fratton Park for the Gunners.

SATURDAY 8th OCTOBER 1949

Pompey claimed their first win over Birmingham City at St Andrews at the 16th attempt. Two goals by Ike Clarke and one from Duggie Reid helped them to a 3-0 victory and moved them to sixth in Division One.

SUNDAY 8th OCTOBER 2000

Pompey conceded an 88th minute equalising goal for the third successive match against Stockport at Edgeley Park in front of 6,212. Lee Mills netted in the 15th minute but barely ten minutes later the goalscorer was stretchered off with knee ligament damage. With two minutes to go Kevin Cooper fired past Russell Hoult to deny Pompey victory and at the same time bring an end to Tony Pulis' reign as manager at Fratton Park.

SATURDAY 9th OCTOBER 1954

Peter Harris became the first Pompey player to score four goals in a match after the war as his side thrashed Sheffield United 6-2 at Fratton Park. Pompey's other goals were both scored by Johnny Gordon.

SATURDAY 9th OCTOBER 1971

John Milkins saved a twice-taken penalty from Preston North End's Hugh McIlmoyle during a 1-1 draw at Fratton Park. The Preston striker equalised after Mike Trebilcock had put the Blues ahead with a brilliant shot.

SATURDAY 9th OCTOBER 1976

A late penalty by Norman Piper, in Pompey's Third Division home fixture with Walsall, sparked off remarkable scenes with jubilant fans swarming onto the pitch to celebrate the escape of a fourth successive defeat. Alan Buckley had given the Saddlers a first-half lead.

SATURDAY 9TH OCTOBER 1982

Pompey goalkeeper Alan Knight had hundreds of pounds' worth of gloves stolen from his goal net during the 1-1 draw at Huddersfield Town.

WEDNESDAY 10TH OCTOBER 1984

After entering the match with a 1-0 lead from the first leg, Pompey went down 3-1 on aggregate to Nottingham Forest in the League Cup second round second leg after extra time. Forest's second goal was scored by future Pompey winger Steve Wigley.

SATURDAY 11TH OCTOBER 1952

Arthur (AE) Knight captained the England team that lost 2-1 to Wales at Cardiff in one of four Victory international matches.

SATURDAY 11TH OCTOBER 1952

Peter Harris scored both goals as Pompey beat Manchester City 2-1 at Fratton Park.

WEDNESDAY 11TH OCTOBER 2000

Tony Pulis was sacked as Pompey boss after just nine months in charge. Two wins from eleven games was deemed unacceptable by chairman Milan Mandaric who gave Steve Claridge the job of player-manager.

SATURDAY 12TH OCTOBER 1946

One of the great players of Pompey's post-war period, Jimmy Scoular, made his league debut in a 1-1 draw away to Aston Villa.

SATURDAY 12TH OCTOBER 1963

Ron Saunders scored a hat-trick in Pompey's 5-2 victory over Newcastle United at Fratton Park.

SATURDAY 12TH OCTOBER 1988

Pompey were beaten – or rather humiliated – 3-1 by Scarborough in the League Cup second round second leg. The Yorkshire club went through to the third round 5-3 on aggregate. After the match Pompey boss Alan Ball said to waiting reporters, "I've nowt to say except that I'm responsible for that shambles."

SATURDAY 13TH OCTOBER 1951

Peter Harris scored seven minutes from time to earn Pompey a 5-4 win over Middlesbrough at Fratton Park watched by 33,631. Len Phillips (2), Jackie Henderson and Duggie Reid were the other scorers.

SATURDAY 13TH OCTOBER 1962

Two finely taken goals capped a dour struggle between Pompey and their south coast neighbours at Fratton Park in front of 32,407. Tony Barton rocketed a first-time shot into the roof of the net to give Pompey the lead and the Saints equaliser came when George O'Brien rose spectacularly to head Terry Paine's corner past John Milkins.

SATURDAY 13TH OCTOBER 1979

"So set 'em up Joe" was the *Sports Mail* headline after Joe Laidlaw starred in Pompey's Fourth Division clash with fellow promotion-chasers Huddersfield Town at Leeds Road. The Pompey skipper scored twice in his side's 3-1 victory which moved them to the top of the table.

SATURDAY 14TH OCTOBER 1967

A 20-yard drive by George Ley a minute from time earned Pompey a 2-2 draw against Birmingham City at St Andrews in a Second Division clash. Nick Jennings scored Pompey's first goal while Fred Pickering and Geoff Vowden were on target for Birmingham.

SATURDAY 14TH OCTOBER 1972

Stuart Pearson was the last player to score four against Pompey in a match when he helped Hull City to a 5-1 win at Boothferry Park. Phil Holme had opened the scoring for the Tigers while Peter Price grabbed Pompey's consolation goal.

SATURDAY 14TH OCTOBER 1995

Steve Claridge netted the only goal of the game for Birmingham City in his side's victory over Pompey at Fratton Park.

SATURDAY 14TH OCTOBER 2000

Portsmouth celebrated Steve Claridge's first match as player-manager by beating Sheffield Wednesday 2-1 at Fratton Park in front of 13,376.

Claridge scored Pompey's second goal after Thomas Thogersen had given them the lead. Clinton Morrison pulled a goal back for Palace.

SATURDAY 14th OCTOBER 2006

Pompey bounced back from two straight defeats to beat West Ham in an ill-tempered game at Fratton Park watched by 20,142. Kanu headed his sixth goal of the season in the 24th minute and Andy Cole fired home his first Pompey goal late on.

FRIDAY 14th OCTOBER 2011

Steve Cotterill left Fratton Park after Pompey agreed a compensation package with Nottingham Forest for their manager. Cotterill had been in charge since June 2010. First team coaches Guy Whittingham and Stuart Gray were immediately put in charge of team affairs.

SATURDAY 15th OCTOBER 1921

Percy Cherrett became the first player to score a Football League hat-trick for Pompey when he bagged three goals in a 4-1 victory at home to Gillingham in Division Three (South).

SATURDAY 15th OCTOBER 1966

Bobby Kellard scored twice against his old club Ipswich Town as Pompey won 4-2 at Fratton Park. Ipswich have since visited Fratton to play eleven competitive matches as well as three friendlies but have yet to be on the losing side.

TUESDAY 15th OCTOBER 1974

A crowd of 25,608 saw Pompey and Manchester United battle out a goalless draw in the first Football League meeting between the two sides at Fratton Park since March 1959 and the first in Division Two since November 1924.

WEDNESDAY 16th OCTOBER 1946

Fratton Park staged a friendly between Pompey and Clyde that the home side won 3-1. The match was originally arranged in 1939 but when war broke out the two clubs agreed to play the match as soon as was possible. During the morning of the game the Clyde party were received by the Lord Mayor of Portsmouth and given a tour of HMS Victory.

SATURDAY 16TH OCTOBER 1948

Pompey cruised to a 3-0 win over Sunderland at Fratton Park to remain two points clear at the top of the table with Jack Froggatt, Peter Harris and Duggie Reid on target. Froggatt was later forced to limp off but even with ten men Pompey were fully in command and were unfortunate not to double their tally.

SATURDAY 16TH OCTOBER 1954

England international Peter Harris scored the decisive goal as Pompey defeated Arsenal 1-0 in front of 44,866 at Highbury.

SATURDAY 16TH OCTOBER 1993

Pompey came from behind to beat Derby County 3-2 at Fratton Park and stretch their unbeaten run to 12 matches – thanks largely to Alan Knight. The Pompey goalkeeper, who received a silver salver and medallion before the match to mark his 500th league appearance, produced several fine saves to deny the Rams.

SATURDAY 17TH OCTOBER 1936

Scot Symon scored twice as Pompey defeated Manchester United 2-1 at Fratton Park to remain top of the First Division.

SATURDAY 17TH OCTOBER 1970

Pompey turned in a disappointing display at Fratton Park and were deservedly beaten 2-0 by Norwich City.

TUESDAY 17TH OCTOBER 1989

Guy Whittingham fashioned an astonishing escape from defeat for Pompey before 10,269 disbelieving spectators. With 89 minutes gone Pompey were trailing 3-1 at home to Leeds United but Whittingham struck twice to earn his side a 3-3 draw.

SATURDAY 17TH OCTOBER 2009

Former Pompey striker Jermain Defoe was sent off as Tottenham Hotspur defeated Pompey 2-1 on Harry Redknapp's first visit to Fratton Park since leaving to take over at White Hart Lane. Defoe scored Spurs' second goal after Ledley King put the visitors ahead and former Tottenham man Kevin-Prince Boateng pulled a goal back for Pompey.

SATURDAY 18TH OCTOBER 1997

Despite a tremendous fightback, Pompey slipped to a 3-2 defeat – their sixth loss in succession – against West Bromwich Albion in front of 9,158 home supporters.

SATURDAY 18TH OCTOBER 2003

A Fratton Park crowd of 20,123 saw former Liverpool midfielder Patrik Berger score 190 seconds into the game to earn Pompey their first victory over the Reds since 1960. Pompey were desperate for a second goal to kill the game off and it nearly came near the end when Yakubu's shot crashed down off the underside of the bar. The final whistle heralded scenes of joy at a memorable win.

SATURDAY 19TH OCTOBER 1935

Jimmy Easson became the third player to score 100 Football League goals for Pompey when he netted the winner in a 2-1 win at home to Arsenal.

WEDNESDAY 19TH OCTOBER 1949

Pompey and Wolverhampton Wanderers drew 1-1 at Highbury in the Charity Shield before a crowd of 35,140. Duggie Reid gave Pompey the lead but Wolves equalised through a Johnny Hancocks penalty.

SATURDAY 19TH OCTOBER 1957

Derek Dougan made his league debut as Pompey beat reigning champions Manchester United 3-0 in front of an Old Trafford crowd of 39,423. Jackie Henderson, Ron Newman and Peter Harris scored the goals that all came in the first half.

SATURDAY 19TH OCTOBER 1963

Ron Saunders grabbed a hat-trick in a 5-2 victory over Newcastle United in a Second Division fixture watched by 14,998 at Fratton Park. Albert McCann and John McClelland were also on target in a fine win for Pompey.

TUESDAY 19TH OCTOBER 1982

Alan Biley's second-half strike gave Pompey a win over Wigan Athletic at Springfield Park before 4,504. Pompey looked in a different class to a Latics side beaten at home only once in the previous 12 months.

SATURDAY 20TH OCTOBER 1928

Pompey suffered their biggest-ever Football League defeat, going down 10-0 to Leicester City at Filbert Street. Centre-forward Arthur Chandler scored six of the Foxes' goals.

SATURDAY 20TH OCTOBER 1979

Phil Ashworth, a free transfer signing from Rochdale, took his goal tally to four in two games as Pompey defeated Bradford City 4-1 at Fratton Park in a Fourth Division top of the table clash in front of 23,871. Alan Rogers and Colin Garwood also netted for Frank Burrows' side.

SATURDAY 20TH OCTOBER 1984

Pompey, the only unbeaten team in the Football League, lost 3-2 to Wimbledon at Plough Lane but they had nobody to blame but themselves. As well as Kevin Dillon missing a penalty, they scored the most bizarre own goal imaginable. After going 1-0 down they worked the ball back to Noel Blake from the kick-off and from 30 yards the centre-half played it back to goalkeeper Alan Knight. But Knight was rubbing his injured knee and, to the disbelieving delight of the home fans, the ball trickled past him and into the net.

WEDNESDAY 21ST OCTOBER 1937

Pompey were knocked off the top of Division One following a 4-0 defeat by Everton at Goodison Park. They had topped the table for two months.

SATURDAY 21ST OCTOBER 1950

Manchester United and Pompey fought out a goalless draw at Old Trafford before a crowd of 41,842.

TUESDAY 21ST OCTOBER 1986

Mick Quinn grabbed a second-half hat-trick to earn Pompey a 3-1 win at home to Derby County. The victory took them to the top of the Second Division table. The Rams led at the break courtesy of John Gregory who would manage Pompey for twelve months from January 1989.

SATURDAY 21st OCTOBER 1989

Guy Whittingham netted the only goal as Pompey beat Bournemouth at Dean Court in Division Two.

SATURDAY 22nd OCTOBER 1955

Pompey were crushed 6-1 at The Valley in front of 15,859 but had the excuse that they played without goalkeeper Norman Uprichard for all but ten minutes of the game. Uprichard was replaced between the sticks by Reg Pickett after being injured in a vain bid to stop Jimmy Gauld putting the home side in front.

FRIDAY 22nd OCTOBER 1999

Chairman Milan Mandaric unveiled plans to build a 35,000 all-seater stadium at a cost of £25,000,000. The new stadium was to be built in Fratton Goods Yard and partially overlap the existing Fratton Park. It was hoped to have it ready for the start of the 2002-03 season.

SUNDAY 23rd OCTOBER 1955

The day before his 18th birthday, Pompey's amateur international schoolboy Pat Neil played for Great Britain in a 1956 Olympic qualifying fixture against Bulgaria in Sofia.

SATURDAY 23rd OCTOBER 1965

Pompey hit three goals in seventeen second-half minutes to record a 4-1 win over Carlisle United at Fratton Park in the first meeting between the two clubs. They led through a Dennis Edwards second-minute tap-in but their play had been lacklustre before Johnny Gordon's move upfield midway through the second half changed everything. The switch brought goals from Brian Lewis, Ray Hiron and Albert McCann.

FRIDAY 23rd OCTOBER 1981

Chris Kamara was controversially allowed to join Brentford in a straight swap deal that saw winger David Crown move to Fratton Park. Kamara had only returned to the club that gave him his league debut a little more than two months earlier.

SATURDAY 23RD OCTOBER 1982

Billy Rafferty scored a hat-trick in a 3-1 win over Preston North End at Fratton Park in a match that was transformed after Alan Rogers switched from the right of midfield to outside-left. At the time of his positional change Pompey had looked anything but promotion contenders but they ended the match in full control.

THURSDAY 23RD OCTOBER 2008

Pompey suffered their first UEFA Cup defeat as they were beaten by Portuguese club Braga before 12,000 at the Axa in the first fixture of the group phase.

SATURDAY 24TH OCTOBER 1925

Pompey suffered their heaviest Football League defeat up to that time, going down 7-1 at Darlington in a Division Two clash.

SATURDAY 24TH OCTOBER 1934

Preston North End were beaten 4-0 in a First Division game at Fratton Park thanks to a Johnny Weddle hat-trick and a goal from Fred Worrall.

SATURDAY 24TH OCTOBER 1953

After being twice two goals in arrears, Pompey fought back to draw 4-4 with Sheffield Wednesday at Hillsborough with Johnny Gordon claiming the only hat-trick of his career.

SATURDAY 24TH OCTOBER 2004

Diomansy Kamara scored his first league goal for Pompey but their wait for a first away win continued after Middlesbrough broke their resistance to earn a 1-1 draw at the Riverside Stadium in front of 30,964.

SATURDAY 25TH OCTOBER 1952

Pompey crashed to a 5-2 defeat by Preston North End at Fratton Park watched by 31,865. Two of the Preston goals were scored by their greatest-ever player Tom Finney.

SATURDAY 25TH OCTOBER 1986

Two second-half goals by Vince Hilaire earned Pompey a 2-1 victory over West Bromwich Albion at Fratton Park. Mick Quinn and Paul Wood were cautioned by police after the game for swearing at a linesman.

THURSDAY 25TH OCTOBER 1990

Chairman Jim Gregory unveiled plans for a £1.6m stand at the Fratton End. The stand was to accommodate 6,000 seats and incorporate hospitality boxes. Mr Gregory hoped it would be open for the start of the 1991-92 season.

SUNDAY 25TH OCTOBER 1992

Zillwood (Zach) March, who played three league matches for Pompey in the early 1920s, celebrated his 100th birthday with a party at the Bognor Regis nursing home where he lived.

SATURDAY 25TH OCTOBER 2008

Pompey manager Harry Redknapp ended his second spell as Pompey manager, walking out on the club to take over at Tottenham Hotspur following the sacking of Juande Ramos and his backroom staff. Redknapp claimed he would not be taking assistants Tony Adams and Joe Jordan. Adams was unveiled as Pompey's new boss within little more than 48 hours while Jordan later rejoined his former boss at White Hart Lane.

MONDAY 25TH OCTOBER 2010

Portsmouth Football Club exited administration after a period of almost eight months during which the club had been relegated from the Premiership and had also reached the FA Cup Final.

SATURDAY 26TH OCTOBER 1963

Ron Saunders scored his second hat-trick in consecutive games as Pompey produced the most amazing comeback by winning 6-3, despite being 3-0 down to Leyton Orient at Brisbane Road. Pompey's first five goals were recorded between the 43rd and 55th minutes.

SATURDAY 26TH OCTOBER 1985

Pompey made it five wins in a row by winning 4-0 against Millwall at The Den. The win put Pompey eight points clear at the top of Division Two. The first goal was scored by Kevin O'Callaghan and that earned Pompey £750 from Canon, the Football League sponsors, for being the first team to score 25 league goals.

TUESDAY 26TH OCTOBER 2004

Diomansy Kamara claimed his third goal in four to help Pompey beat Leeds United and put them into the fourth round of the League Cup.

FRIDAY 26TH OCTOBER 2007

Pompey unveiled plans for a new stadium at Horsea Island. Plans included setting aside 15 acres for a £75m state of the art ground with the remainder of the land being allocated for 1,500-2,000 homes. It was hoped that the Club would be in its new home ready for the 2011/12 season.

SUNDAY 26TH OCTOBER 2008

Less than 24 hours after Harry Redknapp had been announced as manager of Tottenham Hotspur, Pompey drew 1-1 with Fulham at Fratton Park. Peter Crouch gave the Blues the lead but Clint Dempsey struck a late equaliser for the Cottagers.

SATURDAY 27TH OCTOBER 1928

After being trounced 10-0 by Leicester City in their previous game, Pompey recorded a 4-1 win over Bury at Fratton Park. Alex Mackie, who was to earn two Northern Ireland caps as a Pompey player and appear in both the 1929 and 1934 FA Cup finals, was making his club debut at right-back.

SATURDAY 27TH OCTOBER 1951

Two goals by Duggie Reid – the first being his 100th for the club – and another from Len Phillips, gave Pompey a 3-1 victory at home to Newcastle United. Phil Gunter made his league debut at right-back in the match that was the very first to be broadcast on Hospital Radio. The service went on to broadcast every successive Saturday home match, and some away matches, and continues to do so.

SATURDAY 27TH OCTOBER 1962

Pompey took a two-goal lead after only four minutes of their Second Division home clash with Bury – the quickest they have ever done so. Tony Barton shot them ahead in the second minute and this was followed by a goal by David Dodson two minutes later. That was the end of Pompey's goalscoring for the day as they won the match 2-1.

SATURDAY 28TH OCTOBER 1961

A Fratton Park crowd of 18,811 saw Pompey defeat Reading in a hard-fought encounter – the first competitive match between the clubs since 1924. Johnny Gordon gave Pompey the perfect start and Ron Saunders stabbed home Pompey's second goal in the 75th minute.

TUESDAY 28TH OCTOBER 1980

Around 12,000 Pompey fans travelled to Anfield to watch their team take on reigning League Champions Liverpool in the fourth round of the Football League Cup. They out-sang the famous Liverpool Kop choir as Pompey, then a Third Division side, produced a gallant performance. Kenny Dalglish gave Liverpool the lead on 22 minutes but Alan Kennedy then put through his own goal 14 minutes later. David Johnson gave Liverpool a 2-1 half-time lead and Pompey spent the entire second half battling for another equaliser until Johnson scored Liverpool's third with ten minutes left. Graeme Souness volleyed the fourth in the last minute.

SATURDAY 28TH OCTOBER 1989

The Pompey and Ipswich Town players left the field because of a severe hailstorm midway through the second half of a Second Division fixture at Fratton Park. The 7,914 crowd saw Ipswich eventually win 3-2, their goals coming from Simon Milton (2) and Jason Dozzell. The Pompey men on target were Warren Neill, his first for the club, and Martin Kuhl.

TUESDAY 28TH OCTOBER 2008

Harry Redknapp was made a Freeman of the City of Portsmouth. The club's FA Cup-winning boss, who had left Fratton Park at the weekend to take charge of Tottenham Hotspur, returned to the city to receive his award at the Guildhall. On the same day Tony Adams made the step up from assistant manager to take over following Redknapp's shock departure. The former Arsenal and England skipper lasted less than four months in the job, being sacked after the team won only twice in sixteen matches.

SATURDAY 29TH OCTOBER 1927

Dixie Dean scored a hat-trick as Everton beat Pompey 3-1 in Division One, on the Toffees' first visit to Fratton Park. Harry Foxall headed Pompey in front but there was no stopping the England centre-forward.

SATURDAY 29TH OCTOBER 1966

Bursting into life in the second half with two goals in three minutes, Pompey gained five points out of six when they beat Carlisle 2-1 at Fratton Park before 11,674 in a match that was seldom lacking incident.

TUESDAY 29TH OCTOBER 2002

Pompey took another step towards the Premiership by beating Preston 3-2 at Fratton Park in front of 18,637. Steve Stone netted on his debut, Paul Merson scored a penalty and Matt Taylor was also on target.

WEDNESDAY 29TH OCTOBER 2008

Tony Adams' term as Pompey manager got off to a losing start as his side were beaten by Liverpool at Anfield. The only goal of the game was a Steven Gerrard penalty after 75 minutes.

FRIDAY 29TH OCTOBER 2010

It was announced that Balram Chainrai, Deepak Cainrai and Levi Kushnir were officially the new owners of Portsmouth Football Club after the Football League rubber-stamped the purchase.

WEDNESDAY 30TH OCTOBER 1991

Six thousand Pompey fans travelled to Old Trafford to watch their team go down 3-1 to Manchester United in the third round of the League Cup. Minutes after Mark Robins had given United a flattering lead John Beresford drifted a glorious 25-yard shot over the stranded Peter Schmeichel. United regained their lead through Bryan Robson and Mark Robins grabbed their third goal in the dying seconds.

SATURDAY 30TH OCTOBER 1993

Pompey's charge up the First Division table gathered momentum as they stretched their unbeaten run to fifteen matches following a 2-0 home win over Tranmere. Tony Dobson put Pompey in front with a glancing header before Paul Walsh put away his fifth goal in six matches.

SATURDAY 30TH OCTOBER 2004

Pompey claimed their second home victory over Manchester United in just over six months by winning 2-0 in front of 20,190. United laid seige on the Pompey goal in the early stages but the defence held firm and the home side grew stronger as the game went on. David Unsworth thumped home a penalty early in the second half and Yakubu sealed the win on 72 minutes.

TUESDAY 30TH OCTOBER 2007

Pompey manager Harry Redknapp was handed a £700,000 a year pay rise and a three and a half year contract to establish the club as a European force. The deal was agreed between Redknapp, club owner Sacha Gaydamak and chief executive Peter Storrie over a cup of coffee in a Wigan restaurant prior to Pompey's 2-0 victory over the Latics three days earlier.

SATURDAY 31ST OCTOBER 1970

Mike Trebilcock scored three goals – his second hat-trick of the month – as Pompey overcame Blackburn Rovers 4-1 in a Second Division clash at Fratton Park. Ray Pointer grabbed Pompey's fourth goal while Blackburn replied through Ken Knighton.

FRIDAY 31ST OCTOBER 1997

The new 4,500–seat Fratton End stand, built at a cost of £2.5m, was opened before the home clash with Swindon Town – a game that ended in a 1-0 defeat for Pompey.

SATURDAY 31ST OCTOBER 2009

Aruna Dindane scored a hat-trick in Pompey's 4-0 home victory over Wigan Athletic in the Championship. The other goal was scored by Frederic Piquionne. Only four days earlier Pompey beat Stoke City in the Carling Cup at Fratton Park by the same scoreline.

PORTSMOUTH
On This Day & Miscellany

NOVEMBER

WEDNESDAY 1st NOVEMBER 1961

Harry Middleton scored all four goals in a 4-2 win away to Derby County in a second round League Cup tie.

SATURDAY 1st NOVEMBER 1969

Pompey reserve goalkeeper Ray Potter, playing only his second game in two years, broke two fingers in a 3-3 draw away to Carlisle United and the injury forced his retirement from the game.

TUESDAY 1st NOVEMBER 1983

Mark Hateley scored the first of two consecutive hat-tricks in Pompey's 5-0 home win over Cambridge United.

SATURDAY 1st NOVEMBER 2003

A crowd of 67,639 – a Premiership record at the time – saw Manchester United defeat Pompey 3-0 at Old Trafford.

SATURDAY 2nd NOVEMBER 1946

Peter Harris scored his first Football League goal in a 4-1 win at home to Leeds United. Harris holds Pompey's all-time goalscoring record with 205 in league and cup.

WEDNESDAY 2nd NOVEMBER 1960

Pompey's first match in the Football League Cup ended in a 2-0 victory over Coventry City at Fratton Park. Tony Priscott became Pompey's first goalscorer in the new competition and the Blues' second strike came from Ron Saunders.

SATURDAY 2nd NOVEMBER 1976

Pompey's young side defeated Chester City 2-1 at Fratton Park to claim their first two points since August. Chris Kamara and Norman Piper were the goalscorers.

SATURDAY 2nd NOVEMBER 2002

First Division leaders Pompey were beaten 2-0 by second-placed Leicester City at Fratton Park. What should have been the match of the season turned out to be a farce as incessant rain turned the pitch into something resembling a swimming pool.

SATURDAY 3RD NOVEMBER 1934

Johnny Weddle scored a hat-trick – his second in consecutive home games – as Pompey thrashed Huddersfield Town 5-0.

SATURDAY 3RD NOVEMBER 1992

Three goals up with fifteen minutes left against Oxford United at The Manor Ground and still two goals up with a minute left but Pompey managed to drop two points. The final score was 5-5 – the only occasion on which Pompey have finished a Football League match with that scoreline.

SATURDAY 3RD NOVEMBER 2001

Keeper Yoshikatsu Kawaguchi had a bad start to his Pompey career, conceding after 26 seconds in a First Division clash away to Sheffield Wednesday. He finished on the winning side as Pompey won 3-2.

SATURDAY 3RD NOVEMBER 2007

Pompey defeated Newcastle United 4-1 at St James' Park – their first win at the Magpies' home since August 1949. How Pompey made up for the 58-year wait! Noe Pamarot opened the scoring after eight minutes, Benjani netted a minute later and with only eleven minutes gone John Utaka had given Harry Redknapp's side a 3-0 lead. Sol Campbell put through his own goal but Niko Kranjcar scored in the second half to seal Pompey's fifth consecutive away victory.

SATURDAY 4TH NOVEMBER 1967

Pompey went top of Division Two for the first time since being relegated from the First Division in 1959 following a 3-0 victory over Hull City at Fratton Park. Nick Jennings gave the Blues a 1-0 half-time lead and Albert McCann struck twice after the break.

TUESDAY 4TH NOVEMBER 1986

Kevin Dillon scored a hat-trick of penalties in Pompey's 3-2 win at home to Millwall in the Full Members' Cup second round tie. The score was 1-1 after ninety minutes so two of Dillon's spot kicks came in extra time.

TUESDAY 4TH NOVEMBER 2003

The Blue of Pompey was seen at neighbours Southampton's St Mary's Stadium for the first time. A youthful Pompey reserve side managed to earn a 1-1 draw with Saints' second string in front of a crowd of 3,201.

SATURDAY 5TH NOVEMBER 1932

Sep Rutherford grabbed all three goals as Pompey defeated West Bromwich Albion 3-0 at Fratton Park in a First Division clash.

SATURDAY 5TH NOVEMBER 1955

Jackie Henderson received a telegram calling him up for Scotland prior to kick off against Sheffield United at Bramall Lane in front of 23,834 and Pompey celebrated by winning 3-1. Pompey have visited Bramall Lane on 24 occasions since then but have yet to come away with another victory.

SATURDAY 5TH NOVEMBER 1977

Pompey nosedived from the luxury of a 2-0 lead over Tranmere Rovers at Fratton Park to the devastation of a 5-2 defeat to plummet to the bottom of the Third Division.

SATURDAY 5TH NOVEMBER 1983

Mark Hateley's second hat-trick in five days helped Pompey to a 4-0 victory over Grimsby Town in Division Two.

SATURDAY 5TH NOVEMBER 1991

Guy Whittingham scored his first goal of the season after only five minutes to give Pompey a 1-0 victory at home to Leicester City.

SATURDAY 5TH NOVEMBER 2011

Nottingham Forest manager Steve Cotterill suffered a nightmare return to Fratton Park as his side were thumped 3-0 by Pompey. Cotterill, who had left the Blues to take over at the City Ground three weeks earlier saw his side dominate the first 45 minutes but end up well beaten.

SATURDAY 5TH NOVEMBER 2012

Former Pompey and Scotland full-back Jimmy Stephen died aged 90. Stephen was the oldest surviving Pompey player and was one of the few remaining players to have played pre-war League football although his three appearances for Bradford Park Avenue at the start of the 1939/40 season were expunged from League records owing to the outbreak of war causing the suspension of the League competition. He cost Pompey £15,000 from Bradford – a then record for a full-back – and made 103 appearances for the club.

SATURDAY 7TH NOVEMBER 1964

Ipswich Town recorded their biggest league victory by beating Pompey 7-0. The record still stands although the Tractor Boys have since defeated Southampton and West Bromwich Albion by the same scoreline.

SATURDAY 7TH NOVEMBER 1970

Charlton Athletic substitute Mike Kenning equalised in the dying seconds to deny Pompey victory after they were leading 2-1 at The Valley through goals by Brian Bromley and Nick Jennings.

SATURDAY 7TH NOVEMBER 1998

More than 3,000 Pompey fans travelled to Selhurst Park hoping to see their team put one over the two Terrys, Venables and Fenwick, who were in charge of Crystal Palace, but came away disappointed as the home side won 4-1. Former Pompey man Craig Foster scored Palace's first goal.

WEDNESDAY 7TH NOVEMBER 2012

Pompey manager Michael Appleton left the club to take over at Blackpool, three days short of a year after replacing Steve Cotterill in the Fratton hot seat. Appleton experienced perils and pitfalls no other Pompey boss had ever endured, as for all but nineteen days of his tenure the club was in administration. Guy Whittingham was placed in temporary charge of team affairs.

SATURDAY 8TH NOVEMBER 1947

Ike Clarke scored within six minutes of his Pompey debut at home to Aston Villa. Harry Ferrier scored Pompey's second goal with a free-kick from near the halfway flag – a distance of approximately 70 yards. That goal gave Pompey a 2-0 lead but they lost the match 4-2.

SATURDAY 8TH NOVEMBER 1952

Northern Ireland international goalkeeper Norman Uprichard made his Pompey debut against Tottenham Hotspur at Fratton Park watched by 40,867. He was unfortunate to score an own goal in his first match but goals by Peter Harris and Duggie Reid secured a 2-1 win.

MONDAY 8TH NOVEMBER 1982

Former player and manager Jimmy Dickinson died suddenly at his home in Alton, Hampshire, aged 57. He made a record 822 league and cup appearances for Portsmouth and was capped 48 times for England.

SATURDAY 8TH NOVEMBER 2003

Pompey thrashed Leeds United 6-1 in the Premiership at Fratton Park, inflicting the heaviest defeat on the Yorkshire club since 1959. There was a strong fear the game might not go ahead after an electrical failure at Fratton Park. The match had already been put back ten minutes following traffic congestion when the floodlights failed. Eventually power was restored at 3.20pm and the game kicked off half an hour late.

SATURDAY 9TH NOVEMBER 1957

Derek Dougan scored the first goal of his career when he netted for Pompey in a 1-1 draw with Wolverhampton Wanderers at Fratton Park.

SATURDAY 9TH NOVEMBER 1974

Former Pompey goalkeeper John Milkins was between the sticks for Oxford United at the Manor Ground in their 1-0 victory over his old club. It was the sixth match in which Pompey failed to hit the target.

SATURDAY 9TH NOVEMBER 1996

David Hillier was sent off on his debut at Oldham Athletic, a week after his £250,000 transfer from Arsenal. He saw red in the 64th minute of a goalless draw after he stamped on Oldham's Nick Henry.

SATURDAY 10TH NOVEMBER 1962

A last minute goal by Ron Saunders earned Pompey a 3-3 draw with Charlton Athletic after they fought back from two goals down at Fratton Park before a crowd of 15,026.

SATURDAY 10TH NOVEMBER 1984

Scott McGarvey went a long way towards winning over his critics by scoring twice in Pompey's 3-1 win at home to Notts County. The striker had found life difficult after moving to Fratton Park to fill the boots left by Mark Hateley.

MONDAY 10TH NOVEMBER 2011

Michael Appleton was appointed manager of Pompey. The 35-year-old, who had been assistant to Roy Hodgson at West Bromwich Albion, penned a three-and-a-half year deal.

SATURDAY 11TH NOVEMBER 1950

Pompey were held to a 3-3 draw at home by Charlton Athletic after leading 3-1 at half-time in front of 32,755. Jimmy Scoular, Jimmy Dickinson and Duggie Reid scored for Pompey with John Evans grabbing a hat-trick for the visitors.

SATURDAY 11TH NOVEMBER 1961

The only Football League match to be played at Fratton Park between Pompey and Bradford Park Avenue – watched by 11,546 – finished 4-2 to the home side. The Pompey goals came from Ron Saunders (2), Johnny Gordon and Harry Harris while Norman Bleanch scored both goals for Bradford. The visitors were captained by Pompey's former Scottish international wing-half Jimmy Scoular who was at that time the Bradford player-manager.

SATURDAY 11TH NOVEMBER 1972

A crowd of 7,571 saw Luton Town fight back with an own goal by Alan Stephenson and a strike by Rodney Fern to earn a 2-2 draw at Fratton Park after Norman Piper and Nick Jennings had given Pompey a 2-0 lead after 12 minutes.

SATURDAY 11TH NOVEMBER 2006

Andy Cole scrambled the ball home in the 74th minute against his former club opponents Fulham to grab a draw for Pompey in a match that the hosts should have won comfortably. Antti Niemi produced a brilliant save from a Lomana LuaLua free-kick, Sean Davis saw a header hit the post and Kanu scuffed an easy chance as Pompey dominated the first half.

SATURDAY 12TH NOVEMBER 1955

A goal by Tom Finney after 15 minutes and a masterly display that followed from the England winger, saw Pompey sink to a 2-0 defeat against Preston at Fratton Park.

MONDAY 12TH NOVEMBER 1962

The Football League Management Committee fined Pompey £50 for fielding a weakened team in a League Cup tie away to Brighton and Hove Albion on 25 September. Weakened or not, Pompey won 5-1.

SATURDAY 12TH NOVEMBER 1967

Pompey came from behind with goals by Ray Hiron and Albert McCann to beat Bolton Wanderers 2-1 at Fratton Park.

TUESDAY 12TH NOVEMBER 2002

Pompey's first £1m player, Rory Allen, sensationally quit football – to watch cricket. Allen flew to Australia to watch England in the Ashes series after offering his resignation in a letter saying that he no longer wanted to play football. The Blues' striker retired at the age of 25 after battling against injury for four years during which he had undergone eight operations.

SATURDAY 12TH NOVEMBER 2011

Michael Appleton's managerial reign got off to a bad start as Pompey were beaten 2-0 by Watford at Vicarage Road.

SATURDAY 13TH NOVEMBER 1948

Jamaican Lindy Delapenha made his debut in the Pompey side that drew 1-1 at home to Blackpool before a crowd of 44,869. Stan Mortensen put the Seasiders ahead from the penalty spot but Peter Harris found the net late on to preserve Pompey's unbeaten home record.

TUESDAY 13TH NOVEMBER 1973

Fratton Park was the venue for England under-23s 100th match that ended 1-1 with Denmark. The Danes took the lead through Jan Pettersson and England – whose side included three future Pompey players in Colin Sullivan, Gerry Francis and Dave Thomas – equalised eight minutes from time with a goal by Bob Latchford.

SATURDAY 13TH NOVEMBER 1982

Pompey crashed to their heaviest defeat of the season – 5-1 away to Bristol Rovers, and had it not been for Alan Knight's heroics between the posts the home side could have reached double figures.

SATURDAY 14TH NOVEMBER 1970

Pompey hit back from a goal down with strikes by Mike Trebilcock and Ray Hiron to defeat Sunderland 2-1 at Fratton Park.

SATURDAY 14TH NOVEMBER 1987

Nottingham Forest thrashed Pompey 5-0 at the City Ground with old boy Neil Webb one of the Forest goalscorers.

SATURDAY 15TH NOVEMBER 1952

Pompey came out the better in a seven goal thriller to win 4-3 against Sheffield Wednesday in front of 44,187 at Hillsborough.

SATURDAY 15TH NOVEMBER 1975

Pompey dropped to the bottom of the Sercond Division after Ken Beamish's late strike gave Blackburn Rovers victory at Fratton Park before a crowd of 7,323. Pompey dominated the match but things came to nothing in front of goal.

SATURDAY 16TH NOVEMBER 1985

Pompey celebrated Jimmy Dickinson's 700th league appearance for the club in style by beating Charlton Athletic 4-1 at Fratton Park. Before the game Dickinson opened telegrams of congratulations including one from the Pompey League Championship side in which Dickinson was a member. In the boardroom there were two giant 700th anniversary cakes in the shape of football pitches – one from each club.

SATURDAY 16TH NOVEMBER 1985

Former England striker Mick Channon made his 700th league appearance in Pompey's Second Division fixture against Grimsby Town at Blundell Park – but his big day was spoiled by the hosts. The Mariners won 1-0 through a second-half Phil Bonnyman penalty.

TUESDAY 16th NOVEMBER 2004

Velimir Zajec was appointed as Pompey's new director of football. Manager Harry Redknapp agreed to stay on as the club's boss after initially saying he couldn't see himself working alongside the former Yugoslavia international.

SATURDAY 17th NOVEMBER 1951

Pompey moved to the top of the First Division after beating Manchester United 3-1 at Old Trafford before a crowd of 35,914 thanks to goals by Jackie Henderson, Marcel Gaillard and an own goal by Henry Cockburn.

TUESDAY 17th NOVEMBER 1987

"If I go the club goes," was chairman John Deacon's message to the fans who had called for his resignation three days earlier at the City Ground where Nottingham Forest trounced Pompey 5-0. Chants of "Deacon out" could be heard above the public address system after the match.

TUESDAY 17th NOVEMBER 1992

After a week of speculation Pompey chairman Jim Gregory announced that he would not be selling the club and his ambition was to see a new 20,000-plus all-seater stadium as soon as possible with him in charge.

WEDNESDAY 17th NOVEMBER 1993

Alan McLoughlin scored the goal that put the Republic of Ireland into the 1994 World Cup Finals. Six minutes after coming on as substitute against Northern Ireland at Windsor Park with the Republic 1-0 down, the Pompey midfielder sent a curling shot into the net to send his national side to the USA.

SATURDAY 18th NOVEMBER 1967

A 3-0 victory over Bolton Wanderers at Fratton Park, watched by a crowd of 21,437, kept Pompey in second place in Division Two. The goalscorers were Mick Travers, Harry Harris and Albert McCann.

SATURDAY 18TH NOVEMBER 1972

Pompey drew 0-0 against Fulham at Craven Cottage in a Second Division fixture. Fulham went very close to recording their first Football League win over Pompey when their striker John Mitchell hit the post in the dying seconds.

SATURDAY 18TH NOVEMBER 1978

A Colin Garwood penalty and further goals by Steve Foster and John Lathan earned a 3-0 win at home to Hartlepool United which kept Pompey in fourth place in Division Four.

SATURDAY 19TH NOVEMBER 1949

Bert Barlow scored on his last appearance for Pompey in a 2-1 defeat at Burnley. Barlow, who had been at Fratton Park for over ten years, was the only player to win both an FA Cup winners' medal and League Championship medal with the Club.

SATURDAY 19TH NOVEMBER 1966

Pompey stretched their unbeaten run to six, beating Charlton Athletic 2-0 at the Valley. John McClelland and Ray Hiron scored against a side who until then had only conceded two home goals all season.

SATURDAY 19TH NOVEMBER 1988

A 3-0 win at home to Barnsley put Pompey alphabetically on top of Division Two. Both they and Watford shared 30 points and both had identical goal differences. Barry Horne (2) and Mick Quinn were the goalscorers while Alan Knight saved a penalty from David Currie.

TUESDAY 19TH NOVEMBER 1996

Terry Venables announced he was the new Pompey chairman. He had previously been described as the club's director of football.

SATURDAY 20TH NOVEMBER 1937

Pompey at last won a match. Their 16th match of the season brought their first victory, 4-0 at home to Derby County.

SATURDAY 20TH NOVEMBER 1971

The floodlights went out at Fratton Park while Pompey and Oxford United were playing out a boring match that had failed to produce any hint of a goal. The duty electrician had set the lights to go out at 4.10pm – an hour earlier than intended. He broke the seal, reset the mechanism and light was restored. The game then exploded into positive action and Pompey went on to win 2-0 through goals by Nick Jennings and Mike Trebilcock.

SATURDAY 20TH NOVEMBER 2004

Shaun Wright-Phillips was Manchester City's inspiration as they inflicted a third successive Premiership defeat on Pompey at Fratton Park before 20,101. The England winger set up two of City's goals in their 3-0 victory in the last match of Harry Redknapp's first stint as Pompey manager.

TUESDAY 21ST NOVEMBER 1967

Pompey beat Arsenal 2-0 at Fratton Park in a joint testimonial match for long serving players Johnny Gordon and Alex Wilson who had both been released at the end of the previous season.

SATURDAY 21ST NOVEMBER 1970

Manager Ron Tindall described Pompey's defending as comical after watching his side go down 2-1 to Luton Town at Kenilworth Road. The Pompey goal was scored by Albert McCann.

WEDNESDAY 21ST NOVEMBER 2007

Pompey's Niko Kranjcar scored for Croatia from 30 yards in the eighth minute of a European Qualifying tie against England at Wembley. Pompey's Sol Campbell was in the England line-up while David James was on the bench. Croatia won the match 3-2, meaning that England failed to qualify for the competition for the first time in 24 years and manager Steve Mclaren was sacked the following day.

SATURDAY 22ND NOVEMBER 1958

Pompey let a two-goal lead slip but recovered to beat Burnley 4-2 at Fratton Park in front of 17,320. This was the last time Pompey won a league match all season – in fact they only collected four points from the remaining 24 matches.

SATURDAY 22ND NOVEMBER 1986

Paul Mariner's first competitive Pompey goal and a header from Noel Blake helped Pompey to beat Grimsby Town 2-1 at Fratton Park.

SATURDAY 23RD NOVEMBER 1946

Pompey staged a thrilling second-half recovery to share six goals with Middlesbrough watched by 31,824 fans at Ayresome Park. Wilf Mannion's hat-trick gave Boro' a 3-0 lead but Pompey replied with two goals by Duggie Reid and another from Bert Barlow. Reid rounded off a smart left-wing move by scoring a delightful goal. A minute later, Bert Barlow and Reid combined to set up Jack Froggatt to score Pompey's second, and as Boro' lost their grip on the game, Reid volleyed home Barlow's centre for a stunning equaliser.

SATURDAY 23RD NOVEMBER 2002

Pompey took another step towards the Premiership by beating Sheffield Wednesday 3-1 to claim their seventh away victory of the season.

FRIDAY 23RD NOVEMBER 2007

Following the sacking of England manager Steve McClaren, Pompey chief executive Peter Storrie said that any approach from the FA for Harry Redknapp to replace him wouldn't be welcome.

SATURDAY 24TH NOVEMBER 1962

Pompey scored three goals after the interval and beat Sunderland 3-1 in front of 15,000 at Fratton Park.

WEDNESDAY 24TH NOVEMBER 2004

Harry Redknapp resigned as Pompey manager saying he wanted a break from the game and not because of Velimir Zajec's arrival at Fratton Park. Assistant boss Jim Smith also walked out on the club.

THURSDAY 24TH NOVEMBER 2005

Alain Perrin was sacked as Pompey boss after less than eight months in charge. He managed just four wins in his time as manager and the current season's return was ten points from thirteen games. Perrin was the club's seventh manager in six and a half years.

TUESDAY 24TH NOVEMBER 2009

Paul Hart was sacked as Pompey manager after failing to lift the club out of the relegation zone. Hart became caretaker manager following the dismissal of Tony Adams in February and was handed the job on a permanent basis in July. He was offered the chance to work with the club's 18- to 21-year-olds but rejected the invitation.

SATURDAY 25TH NOVEMBER 1950

Terry Ryder rescued a point for Pompey with a late goal against Aston Villa before 30,399 at Fratton Park. Ryder scored his first league goal before Duggie Reid doubled the score. Villa hit back to go 3-2 ahead but with five minutes remaining Ryder hit the equaliser.

SATURDAY 25TH NOVEMBER 1967

A 2-2 draw against Blackburn Rovers at Ewood Park watched by 13,081 put Pompey top of the Second Division. The Pompey goalscorers were Keith Newton (own goal) and George Ley.

SATURDAY 25TH NOVEMBER 1978

Two second-half goals by Jeff Hemmerman gave Pompey a 2-0 win at home to Northampton Town in the FA Cup first round.

SATURDAY 25TH NOVEMBER 1995

A 25-yard free-kick by Neil Thompson in injury time gave Ipswich Town a 3-2 victory over Pompey at Portman Road in Division One. Paul Walsh and Martin Allen scored for Pompey.

SATURDAY 25TH NOVEMBER 2000

A mistake by Pompey goalkeeper Russell Hoult allowed Barnsley's Bruce Dyer to score the only goal of a First Division clash at Oakwell.

MONDAY 25TH NOVEMBER 2013

Guy Whittingham was sacked as Pompey manager. He had been in charge for a year, the first five months as caretaker-boss. The team was struggling in League Two and had lost the last three matches.

SATURDAY 26TH NOVEMBER 1927

Jimmy Nichol, the first major acquisition of Jack Tinn's 20-year managerial reign, made his debut in a 2-2 draw at home to Birmingham City. Nichol, who signed from Gillingham, appeared in two FA Cup Finals during his ten years as a Pompey player and clocked up 383 league and cup appearances before rejoining the Kent club.

MONDAY 26TH NOVEMBER 1934

Johnny Weddle's two goals against Aston Villa at Villa Park took his tally to eleven in the last six matches but his brace failed to help Pompey to a win for they were beaten 5-4.

SATURDAY 26TH NOVEMBER 1949

Jimmy Stephen, Jimmy Elder and Dan Ekner all made their Pompey debuts in a 2-2 draw with Sunderland in front of 36,707 at Fratton Park. The match started ten minutes early due to bad light.

SATURDAY 26TH NOVEMBER 1977

Third Division Pompey had to work hard to see off Western League side Bideford Town in the FA Cup first round at Fratton Park, eventually beating them 3-1. Bobby Stokes, scorer of the goal that won the 1976 FA Cup Final for Southampton, notched his first goal for his hometown club.

SATURDAY 27TH NOVEMBER 1948

Pompey celebrated their Golden Jubilee in magnificent fashion as a crowd of 42,687 saw them waltz to a thrilling 4-1 victory over Arsenal at Fratton Park. Jack Froggatt, Ike Clarke, Len Phillips and Bert Barlow were the Pompey goalscorers. Before the game both teams were introduced to former Pompey players, some of whom played in the club's first fixture in 1899.

SATURDAY 27TH NOVEMBER 2004

Arjan De Zeeuw's headed goal on the stroke of half-time ensured Velimir Zajec's first game in charge of Pompey ended in their first Premiership away victory of the season against Bolton Wanderers in front of 25,008. This was Pompey's first victory at the Reebok Stadium and their first at Bolton since they won 1-0 at Burnden Park in September 1969.

THURSDAY 27TH NOVEMBER 2008

Fratton Park staged one of its greatest ever matches with Pompey keeping their UEFA Cup hopes alive against seven-times European champions AC Milan with a superb display that brought a 2-2 draw. Younes Kaboul and Kanu gave Pompey a 2-0 lead but two goals in the last six minutes by Ronaldinho and Filippo Inzaghi brought the scores level.

FRIDAY 27TH NOVEMBER 2009

Avram Grant was appointed Pompey manager three days after the club parted company with Tony Adams. The Israeli failed to keep Pompey in the top flight but managed to lead the team to the 2010 FA Cup Final.

SATURDAY 28TH NOVEMBER 1970

Nick Jennings scored twice to earn Pompey a 2-2 draw with Hull City at Fratton Park after the Tigers had led 2-0.

WEDNESDAY 28TH NOVEMBER 2007

Pompey manager Harry Redknapp, chief executive Peter Storrie and former chairman Milan Mandaric were among five men arrested by police investigating claims of corruption in football.

SATURDAY 28TH NOVEMBER 2009

Wayne Rooney scored a hat-trick, including two goals from the penalty spot in a 4-1 win for Manchester United over Pompey at Fratton Park. United's other goal came from Ryan Giggs – his 100th in the Premier League. This was manager Avram Grant's first match in charge, having been appointed manager following the recent sacking of Paul Hart.

SATURDAY 29TH NOVEMBER 1952

A first-half goal by George Robledo was enough to give Newcastle United victory over Pompey at St James' Park in front of a crowd of 47,680. Maurice Leather was in inspired form in the Pompey goal and had it not been for him the Magpies would have won by a bigger margin.

SATURDAY 29TH NOVEMBER 1975

Mick Tait, aged 18, netted twice as Oxford United claimed their first win at Fratton Park in a Second Division relegation clash. Pompey were rooted at the bottom of the table and still in search of their first home win.

SATURDAY 29TH NOVEMBER 1997

Two goals by Paul Furlong for Birmingham City at St Andrews sent Pompey crashing to the bottom of the First Division. Paul Hall put Pompey ahead but Furlong struck twice to give Birmingham a 2-1 win.

TUESDAY 29TH NOVEMBER 2011

Portsmouth Football Club was put up for sale as owners Convers Sports Initiatives went into administration. Vladimir Antonov, who was arrested for alleged fraud and money laundering the previous day, resigned as club chairman.

SATURDAY 30TH NOVEMBER 1974

Pompey won for the first time in thirteen matches, Andy Stewart grabbing the only goal in a home clash with fellow Second Division strugglers Sheffield Wednesday. George Graham was making his Pompey debut on his 30th birthday but limped off after half an hour.

TUESDAY 30TH NOVEMBER 2004

Milan Mandaric absolved former boss Harry Redknapp from any wrong doing in his transfer deals. At a specially convened news conference, Mr. Mandaric clarified his revelation that £3m had been paid to agents during Redknapp's reign. Mandaric said, "At no time did I imply there was any wrong doing. I was simply saying that agents take too much money from the game. All transactions and fees have been registered with the FA."

PORTSMOUTH
On This Day & Miscellany

DECEMBER

SATURDAY 1st DECEMBER 1962

A crowd of 15,519 was treated to a shared six-goal thriller between Leeds United and Pompey at Fratton Park at fog-shrouded Elland Road.

SATURDAY 1st DECEMBER 1984

Blackburn Rovers had scored in every match before they drew 2-2 at Fratton Park in a Second Division fixture on 1 December 1984 but they had to rely on Pompey to keep the run going. The ball rebounded in off Noel Blake after hitting the post and then Mick Tait sliced the ball out of Alan Knight's hands to give Rovers a 2-0 half-time lead. Kevin Dillon pulled a goal back from the penalty spot before Vince Hilaire crowned his Pompey debut by equalising with a spectacular diving header.

FRIDAY 1st DECEMBER 2000

Andy Awford was appointed chief scout and at 28 was the youngest to be appointed in the club's history. Awford, who was only 16 when he made the first of 372 Pompey appearances, had suffered two broken legs during his career and decided to retire from the game.

SATURDAY 2nd DECEMBER 1967

Pompey sat top of the Second Division, two points above Blackpool after beating the Seasiders 3-1 at Fratton Park. The crowd of 35,038 is Pompey's largest attendance for a league game outside the top flight. Cliff Portwood headed Pompey in front on 26 minutes but 'Pool drew level right on half-time through Alan Skirton. Pompey suffered a blow when Nicky Jennings left the field with a broken ankle but substitute Mick Travers slammed the ball home to make it 2-1 and with a minute remaining Ray Pointer made certain of victory with a glorious angled drive.

SATURDAY 2nd DECEMBER 1978

A week after defeating Northampton Town 2-0 in the FA Cup at Fratton Park, Pompey beat the Cobblers by the same scoreline in a Fourth Division clash at the County Ground before 3,592. Colin Garwood and Jeff Hemmerman were on target for Pompey.

TUESDAY 2nd DECEMBER 2003

Pompey went to neighbours Southampton in the League Cup for the first time. Saints won 2-0 in the fourth round before a crowd of 29,201.

SATURDAY 3RD DECEMBER 1949

A crowd of 44,851 at Anfield saw leaders Liverpool preserve their unbeaten record by drawing 2-2 with Pompey on a muddy waterlogged pitch. After Ike Clarke had notched Pompey's equaliser both sides pressed for the winner in a match played out in semi-darkness.

TUESDAY 3RD DECEMBER 1985

Pompey were denied a last-gasp equaliser against Bradford City at Odsal Stadium for as Tommy Christensen's shot entered the net, referee Joe Worrall blew for full-time. It seemed that Christensen's low shot had earned Pompey a 2-2 draw but as the players celebrated Mr. Worrall signalled that he had blown the whistle before the ball crossed the line.

SATURDAY 3RD DECEMBER 1994

Pompey were thrashed by Middlesbrough at Ayresome Park in front of 17,185 and the sending-off of Gerry Creaney only added to the gloom.

TUESDAY 4TH DECEMBER 1954

FA Cup holders West Bromwich Albion were thrashed 6-1 by Pompey in front of 28,027 at Fratton Park. The Pompey goalscorers were Peter Harris (2), Jackie Henderson, Mike Barnard, Johnny Gordon and Len Millard (own goal) with Ronnie Allen netting a consolation for the visitors.

TUESDAY 4TH DECEMBER 1973

A crowd of 17,226 attended Fratton Park to watch Pompey draw 1-1 with Manchester United in a friendly match to celebrate the club's 75th anniversary. Norman Piper headed Pompey in front and United's equaliser was scored by Mick Martin. Notable members of the Reds' team were George Best, who was making his only Fratton Park appearance, Alex Stepney, Brian Kidd, Martin Buchan and Willie Morgan.

SATURDAY 4TH DECEMBER 2004

Lomana LuaLua's late winner gave Pompey a 3-2 victory over West Bromwich Albion in a remarkable match before 20,110 at Fratton Park. The visitors were leading 2-1 with five minutes left, but after an inspired substitution in which Nigel Quashie was replaced by Eyal Berkovic, skipper Arjan de Zeeuw equalised with a powerful header and LuaLua snatched all three points with a thunderous strike.

THURSDAY 4TH DECEMBER 2008

Pompey's UEFA Cup dream ended in Germany as they were defeated 3-2 by Wolfsburg at the Volkswagen Arena. The Blues' elimination had been settled with one game still to play.

SATURDAY 5TH DECEMBER 1931

Newcastle United and Pompey played out a goalless draw at St James' Park. It is believed to be the only Football League match that failed to produce a corner kick.

WEDNESDAY 5TH DECEMBER 1956

Jimmy Dickinson won the last of his 48 England caps in a 5-2 victory over Denmark. Tommy Taylor scored a hat-trick and his Manchester United team-mate Duncan Edwards netted twice in the World Cup qualifier at Molineux, Wolverhampton.

SATURDAY 5TH DECEMBER 1992

Pompey were the visitors when Charlton Athletic played their first match at The Valley after an absence of over seven years. The home side celebrated with a 1-0 victory over the Blues, the decisive goal coming from Colin Walsh after only seven minutes.

SATURDAY 5TH DECEMBER 2009

Goals by Hermann Hreidarsson and Aruna Dindane brought Pompey their first win under Avram Grant – a 2-0 home victory over Burnley. The club still remained bottom of the Premiership with ten points.

SATURDAY 6TH DECEMBER 1969

Goals by Ray Hiron, seconds either side of the break, set up a win for Pompey over Preston North End at Fratton Park in front of 11,121. Pompey led 1-0 at the end of a scrappy, disjointed first half but a second goal by Hiron and strikes from Brian Bromley and Nick Jennings secured a 4-0 victory for their team.

THURSDAY 6TH DECEMBER 1973

Paul Went became the costliest player in Pompey history when he moved from Fulham for £154,000. His transfer followed that of fellow central-defender Malcolm Manley from Leicester City the previous day.

SATURDAY 7TH DECEMBER 1946

Pompey's First Division clash with Sheffield United at Bramall Lane was postponed due to a waterlogged pitch.

SATURDAY 7TH DECEMBER 1985

Pompey desperately needed a victory after losing their four previous matches and they achieved a rare win at Roker Park, beating Sunderland 3-1 to stay top of the Second Division. Tommy Christensen, Mick Tait and Paul Wood gave the Blues a 3-0 lead before Sunderland, who had Gary Bennett sent off late in the game, pulled a goal back through Eric Gates with two minutes remaining.

SATURDAY 7TH DECEMBER 2005

Harry Redknapp made a sensational return to become Pompey manager for a second spell little more than a year after he had left.

SATURDAY 8TH DECEMBER 1928

Two days after signing for Pompey from Hearts, goalkeeper Jock Gilfillan made his debut in the 1-0 home defeat by Cardiff City. Only Alan Knight and John Milkins have appeared in goal more often than Gilfillan, who represented the club in two FA Cup Finals.

SATURDAY 8TH DECEMBER 1973

Defenders Malcolm Manley and Paul Went, who had cost Pompey £200,000, made their debuts as their new team defeated Bristol City 1-0 at Fratton Park through an out of the blue long range shot by Ron Davies.

SATURDAY 8TH DECEMBER 2007

Pompey claimed their seventh consecutive away victory – their sixth in the Premier League – beating Aston Villa 3-1. Craig Gardner put Pompey ahead with an own goal and Sulley Muntari scored twice before Gareth Barry replied for Villa with a penalty.

SATURDAY 9TH DECEMBER 1967

Pompey extended their lead at the top of the Second Division with a brilliant 2-1 win over promotion rivals Ipswich Town watched by 14,983 at Portman Road. Pompey went ahead in the opening minute through Ray Pointer. Albert McCann made it 2-0 after the interval, but Ipswich hit back with a goal by Danny Hegan. Pompey 'keeper John Milkins saved brilliantly from Colin Viljoen late on as Pompey ended Ipswich's unbeaten home record.

SATURDAY 9TH DECEMBER 1967

Pompey led Sunderland 2-1 with three minutes to go in a Second Division bottom of the table tussle but ended up losing 3-2. The crowd of 5,783 was the lowest at Fratton Park for a league game since the war but that was "beaten" just one week later.

SATURDAY 9TH DECEMBER 2006

A spectacular 45-yard volley by Matt Taylor set up a comfortable 2-0 win for Pompey against a disappointing Everton side in front of 19,528 at Fratton Park. Taylor's amazing long range strike was followed by a goal from Kanu and despite an improvement by Everton after the interval there was never any doubt that Pompey would record their first home victory over the Toffees since November 1957.

FRIDAY 9TH DECEMBER 2011

Former Pompey and England inside-left and wing-half Len Phillips died aged 89. Phillips was the last survivor of the regular players who won the Football League championship for the Club in 1949 and 1950. He won three caps for England before being forced to retire from the first-class game in 1956 through injury.

MONDAY 9TH DECEMBER 2013

Richie Barker was appointed manager of Pompey following the recent sacking of Guy Whittingham while former Manchester United and England winger Steve Coppell was unveiled as the club's Director of Football. The new boss promised to entertain the Fratton faithful with an exciting brand of football but results and performances failed to improve and he was dismissed before the end of March with relegation from League Two looking more than possible.

SATURDAY 10TH DECEMBER 1955

Pompey produced two late goals to earn victory over Manchester United at Fratton Park before 24,594 thus knocking the Busby Babes off the top of the First Division. With five minutes to go, and the score at 2-1 to United,

Jimmy Dickinson's shot took a deflection and sailed past Ray Wood. Mark Jones then blasted Jackie Henderson's cross into his own net.

TUESDAY 10TH DECEMBER 1985

A Noel Blake header put Pompey into the League Cup quarter-finals for the first time as Alan Ball's men beat Tottenham Hotspur at Fratton Park in front of 26,306. After a 0-0 draw at White Hart Lane and another goalless battle at Fratton that went to extra time, Blake rose at the far post a minute before the interval to power a header past Ray Clemence in the second, and conclusive, replay.

SATURDAY 10TH DECEMBER 1988

Pompey shared six goals with Second Division title-chasing Chelsea in a thriller watched by 20,221 at Stamford Bridge.

SATURDAY 10TH DECEMBER 2011

David Norris scored deep into stoppage time to give Pompey a 1-0 victory over Burnley at Turf Moor. This was Pompey's first away triumph of the season and their first win under new manager Michael Appleton.

SATURDAY 11TH DECEMBER 1971

Forty four years after their first visit to Burnley, Pompey won at Turf Moor for the first time. The side that recorded a 3-1 victory included three former Burnley players, Ray Pointer, Fred Smith and Colin Blant.

SATURDAY 11TH DECEMBER 1976

Pompey defeated Southern League Minehead 2-1 in the FA Cup second round at Fratton Park watched by a crowd of 14,089. Dave Kemp and Chris Kamara scored for Ian St John's young side. Both clubs were happy with the result of the afternoon – Pompey for earning their passage into the next round and Minehead for collecting enough gate money to clear their £2,500 overdraft.

SATURDAY 11TH DECEMBER 2004

Pompey held Newcastle United to a 1-1 draw at St James' Park before 51,480 despite surrendering most of the possession and an early lead. Lee Bowyer put Newcastle ahead in only the third minute but Steve Stone equalised on the half-hour mark.

SATURDAY 12TH DECEMBER 1970

Ray Hiron's first-half header was enough to give Pompey victory over Oxford United in a Second Division fixture at Fratton Park.

SATURDAY 12TH DECEMBER 1998

About 20 Pompey fans demonstrated outside Martin Gregory's Surrey home, venting their anger at the club crisis. They held banners protesting at Gregory's handling of the financial crisis and called for his resignation.

SATURDAY 12TH DECEMBER 2009

Younes Kaboul poked home a last minute equaliser for Pompey away to Sunderland. The defender, having been yellow-carded earlier in the match, was immediately sent off for removing his shirt in the celebrations.

SATURDAY 13TH DECEMBER 1924

Sheffield Wednesday's Jimmy Trotter became the first player to score five goals against Pompey in a Football League match when his side beat Pompey 5-2 in a Second Division clash at Hillsborough.

SATURDAY 13TH DECEMBER 1986

Three Pompey players were sent off in a Second Division match against Sheffield United at Bramall Lane. Billy Gilbert saw red for dissent, Kevin Dillon was sent off for two bookings and Mick Tait received his marching orders for an off-the-ball incident involving Blades' Peter Beagrie who was also ordered off. The home side won the match 1-0.

SATURDAY 14TH DECEMBER 1996

Swedish striker Mathias Svensson exploded into Pompey life by firing two goals in a 3-1 home win over Huddersfield Town. Fitzroy Simpson scored Pompey's first goal from the penalty spot.

TUESDAY 14TH DECEMBER 2004

Lomana LuaLua equalised in the final minute to earn Pompey a 1-1 draw against Liverpool at Anfield after Steven Gerrard had put the Reds in front from 30 yards.

SATURDAY 15TH DECEMBER 1962

Two goals in the last two minutes earned Pompey a 5-3 victory at Walsall in Division Two. They fell behind to a goal by Colin Taylor but stormed into a 3-1 lead through goals by Johnny Gordon, Ron Saunders and David Dodson. Jimmy O'Neill and Taylor scored for the Saddlers to make the score 3-3, then a minute from time Dodson netted for Pompey before Tony Barton netted with the last kick of the game.

SATURDAY 16TH DECEMBER 1961

Dave Dodson scored the fastest goal by a player making his Pompey debut. Three days after signing from Swansea, he played at outside-left in a Second Division home fixture against Swindon Town and headed Pompey into the lead after only 19 seconds. The match ended 2-2.

SATURDAY 16TH DECEMBER 2006

Arsenal came from two goals down to deny Pompey victory on their first visit to the Emirates Stadium in front of 60,037. Noe Pamarot headed his first Pompey goal seconds before half-time and Matt Taylor doubled Pompey's lead two minutes after the break. Frustrated Gunners' boss Arsene Wenger was sent from the dug-out but his mood improved when substitute Emmanuel Adebayor pulled a goal back after 58 minutes and Arsenal's comeback was completed when Gilberto Silva equalised on the hour.

SATURDAY 17TH DECEMBER 1927

Playing in their first season in Division One, Pompey beat the reigning champions Newcastle United on their first visit to St James' Park. Goals from Dave Watson, Fred Forward and Freddie Cook eased Pompey to a 3-1 victory.

SATURDAY 17TH DECEMBER 1966

Pompey fought back to score three goals – as well as have two disallowed – to draw 3-3 with Norwich City at Fratton Park before 12,431. Two minutes from time, Hiron grabbed the equaliser following a free-kick by Brian Lewis and crowds swarmed onto the pitch in celebration of Pompey's amazing fight back.

FRIDAY 17TH DECEMBER 1982

Mrs Joan Deacon, wife of the Pompey chairman, was made a director of Portsmouth Football Club. So far, she has been the club's only lady director.

SATURDAY 17TH DECEMBER 2005

Svetoslav Todorov scored his first goal in two and a half years to deliver Pompey a first home win of the season against West Bromwich Albion in a Premiership bottom of the table clash at Fratton Park.

SATURDAY 18TH DECEMBER 1948

Pompey strolled comfortably to a 3-1 win over lowly Preston North End at Fratton Park before 26,545 thanks to goals by Peter Harris, Len Phillips and a Bert Barlow penalty.

SATURDAY 18TH DECEMBER 1976

Matt Pollock scored twice as Pompey outclassed fellow Third Division strugglers York City at Bootham Crescent in front of 2,058 to win 4-1.

SATURDAY 18TH DECEMBER 1982

A scrambled goal by Mick Tait immediately after half-time earned Pompey a 1-0 victory over Chesterfield in a scrappy match at Saltergate watched by 2,440. On a partially frozen pitch, Bobby Campbell's men always looked several classes above their opponents and goalkeeper Alan Knight must have been close to becoming a frostbite victim for the home team failed to produce a single shot on target in the entire match.

SUNDAY 18TH DECEMBER 2011

Joel Ward scored a late equaliser for Pompey against Southampton at Fratton Park in the first League meeting between the two clubs since 2005. The Saints goalscorer was Rickie Lambert.

SATURDAY 19TH DECEMBER 1964

Johnny Gordon completed his century of goals for Pompey when he scored the second in a 3-3 draw against Charlton Athletic at The Valley.

SATURDAY 19TH DECEMBER 1970

Ray Pointer gave Pompey a 37th minute lead against Bolton Wanderers at Burnden Park but John Manning equalised to leave the Blues awaiting their first away win of the campaign.

SATURDAY 19TH DECEMBER 1998

Martin Gregory announced that he had cut financial support to Pompey after receiving death threats. The move followed his decision to step down as chairman. Fears were growing that his resignation would spark a winding-up order from his mother who was owed £2.1m of the club's £5.5m debts.

SATURDAY 19TH DECEMBER 2009

Pompey kept their hopes of Premiership survival alive by pulling off a deserved victory over Liverpool at Fratton Park. Goals by Nadir Belhadj and Frederic Piquionne brought the Blues a 2-0 win. Pompey were still bottom of the table but had pulled level on points with West Ham United.

SATURDAY 20TH DECEMBER 1975

Without a home victory all season, Pompey hosted York City, who were yet to win away, in a Second Division relegation clash. Jim Hinch netted the only goal to give the visitors the points and leave Pompey rooted at the bottom of the table.

SATURDAY 20TH DECEMBER 1980

Centre-forward Billy Rafferty made his Pompey debut following his £85,000 move from Newcastle United but couldn't mark his first match with a goal. His new side were held to a goalless draw by Huddersfield Town who were top of the Third Division. The draw kept Pompey well in the promotion race as they were still in third place and only one point behind the leaders.

SATURDAY 20TH DECEMBER 2008

Pompey were 2-0 down inside three minutes against Bolton Wanderers at the Reebok Stadium. Former Fratton favourite Matt Taylor smashed home the opener after 48 seconds with Ricardo Gardner netting a second for the Trotters within two minutes and 46 seconds of the kick-off. The final score was 2-1, Peter Crouch grabbing Pompey's goal.

WEDNESDAY 21st DECEMBER 1994

Following Whitehall's decision to turn down Pompey's planning application for a new home at Farlington, Mick Channon called for Pompey and Southampton to break new ground by sharing a new super stadium. The Saints legend who also spent a season at Fratton Park during the mid-1980s said, "The good old days are gone. We have to look to the future."

SUNDAY 21st DECEMBER 2003

Pompey were beaten 3-0 by an ordinary-looking Southampton side at St Mary's. After what was Pompey's ninth Premiership defeat manager Harry Redknapp confessed, "I'm not bothering with Christmas this year."

SATURDAY 21st DECEMBER 2004

Velimir Zajec was unveiled as Pompey's permanent boss after Milan Mandaric finally convinced him to take the job. Mandaric said, "Velimir is our manager for the foreseeable future and I want to end speculation that another manager is coming in."

SATURDAY 22nd DECEMBER 1984

Pompey beat Oxford United 2-1 at Fratton Park in a Second Division top-of-the-table clash. With time running out and Pompey 1-0 down, a fan dressed as Father Christmas ran onto the pitch and in the time added on, Alan Biley headed two goals for the Blues. The victory put Pompey in second place with Oxford dropping to fourth.

SATURDAY 22nd DECEMBER 2007

Liverpool bounced back from their disappointing Carling Cup semi-final exit with a slick display that produced a 4-1 victory at Anfield, ending Pompey's six-match winning run on their travels.

SATURDAY 23rd DECEMBER 1933

Outside-left Cliff Parker made his debut in a 2-2 draw at home to West Bromwich Albion in Division One. Parker was the scorer of two goals in Pompey's 1939 FA Cup final triumph against Wolverhampton Wanderers and he also starred for the club after the war.

SATURDAY 23RD DECEMBER 1995

John Durnin's second-half strike was enough to earn Pompey victory over Norwich City at Fratton Park and chalk up their fourth straight win.

SATURDAY 23RD DECEMBER 2006

Pompey produced a Jekyll and Hyde performance to come from behind to beat Sheffield United 3-1 at Fratton Park before a crowd of 20,164. Sol Campbell headed his first goal for Pompey midway through the second half.

SATURDAY 24TH DECEMBER 1955

Pompey recorded their first victory at Blackpool since the war, winning 3-2 with two goals by Peter Harris and one from Jack Mansell.

MONDAY 24TH DECEMBER 1979

Pompey and Wimbledon shared six goals in a thrilling FA Cup second round replay at Fratton Park. After the match the Dons won the toss to decide the venue for a second replay – won 1-0 by Pompey.

MONDAY 25TH DECEMBER 1922

Pompey suffered their (then) heaviest Football League defeat, going down 7-1 to Brighton & Hove Albion at The Goldstone Ground.

SATURDAY 25TH DECEMBER 1948

Pompey returned to the top of Division One by beating Chelsea 2-1 at home with Peter Harris scoring both goals. The attendance was 42,153.

WEDNESDAY 25TH DECEMBER 1957

Jimmy Greaves scored a hat-trick for Chelsea as the Londoners won 7-4 at Stamford Bridge in what was the last match in which Pompey played on Christmas Day. Greaves, who was aged 17 years 308 days, was then the youngest player to notch a treble in the top flight.

MONDAY 26TH DECEMBER 1955

Jimmy Dickinson became Pompey's record appearance holder by playing his 397th league and cup match in a 3-1 victory away to Aston Villa. The record was previously held by Johnny Weddle. Dickinson went on to play more than double that number of games for the club and it is almost impossible to imagine that his appearance tally will ever be surpassed.

SATURDAY 26TH DECEMBER 1992

Guy Whittingham scored all four goals in Pompey's 4-1 win at home to Bristol Rovers.

WEDNESDAY 26TH DECEMBER 2007

Pompey failed to score at home for the fifth successive match – their goalless draw with Arsenal before 20,566 at Fratton Park denying the Gunners the chance to reclaim first place after Manchester United had beaten Sunderland to go top earlier in the day.

SATURDAY 27TH DECEMBER 1969

A first minute strike by Jim Storrie and two goals from Mike Trebilcock gave Pompey an unexpected 3-0 win against Second Division leaders Blackburn Rovers at Ewood Park.

WEDNESDAY 27TH DECEMBER 1972

Southampton-based John Deacon was elected to the board. He became chairman five months later and remained at the helm until 1988.

MONDAY 27TH DECEMBER 1976

A crowd of 32,368 saw Pompey defeat Brighton and Hove Albion 1-0 at Fratton Park in a Third Division fixture. Dave Kemp netted after only three minutes and Pompey goalkeeper Grahame Lloyd kept the lead intact when he saved a penalty from Brian Horton.

SATURDAY 28TH DECEMBER 1991

Pompey blew away promotion favourites Middlesbrough, thrashing them 4-0 with a devastating performance in front of 12,324 at Fratton Park. They were 3-0 ahead after half an hour through goals by Guy Whittingham, John Beresford (penalty) and Darryl Powell and Martin Kuhl added another in the second half.

SATURDAY 29TH DECEMBER 1956

Despite taking the lead through Jackie Henderson, Pompey were well beaten 3-1 by First Division leaders Manchester United in front of 32,147 at Fratton Park. David Pegg's shot was deflected into the net by Jack Mansell for the visitors' first goal and United's other scorers were Duncan Edwards and Dennis Viollet.

SATURDAY 29TH DECEMBER 1990

Pompey failed to win for the thirteenth match in a row, this time losing 2-1 to Sheffield Wednesday at Hillsborough. Guy Whittingham's goal was cancelled out by two from David Hirst, leaving Pompey joint bottom of Division Two after a match that saw Colin Clarke forced to take over in goal from the injured Alan Knight.

SATURDAY 30TH DECEMBER 1989

Guy Whittingham notched his first hat-trick of his career to give Pompey a 3-3 draw against Oldham Athletic at Boundary Park. His treble was nearly enough to end the Latics' 26-match unbeaten home run but Mike Milligan grabbed a late equaliser.

SATURDAY 30TH DECEMBER 1995

Jimmy Carter and Deon Burton scored to earn Pompey a 2-2 draw after they trailed 2-0 against Wolverhampton Wanderers at snowy Molineux. Much of the game was fought out in a heavy snowstorm but the under-soil heating at the Wolves' stadium ensured that the match beat the weather.

SATURDAY 31ST DECEMBER 1960

A crowd of 31,059 saw Pompey and Southampton draw 1-1 at Fratton Park. Sammy Chapman put Pompey ahead but Tommy Mulgrew equalised in the last minute after Pompey 'keeper Dick Beattie had saved a penalty from John Page. Saints goalkeeper Ron Reynolds left the field injured early in the game and throughout the 26 minutes that Terry Paine was wearing the jersey, Pompey failed to manage a single shot on target.

SATURDAY 31ST DECEMBER 2005

Gary O'Neil's 43rd minute strike gave Pompey a 1-0 win at Fratton Park to preserve their unbeaten home record since Harry Redknapp returned as manager.

THURSDAY 31ST DECEMBER 2009

Lens called on FIFA and UEFA to step in and put Pompey out of business for failing to pay their debts. The French club insisted they had been cheated over millions in alleged unpaid transfer fees for Aruna

Dindane and Nadir Belhadj. President Gervais Martel fumed: "They don't pay, they get shut down. That's it." Lens claimed Pompey reneged on a deal to buy £4m rated striker Dindane once he played eleven games and also insisted they failed to keep up instalments for £4.2m defender Belhadj.

PORTSMOUTH
On This Day & Miscellany

MISCELLANY

FORMATION OF PORTSMOUTH FOOTBALL CLUB

Portsmouth Football Club was formed on 5 April 1898, when a group of businessmen and legal people formed a syndicate. Fratton Park was purchased for £4,950, and a limited company was registered. The ground was farmland, used largely as a market garden. The prospectus of the new company was prepared and advertised, with a capital of £8,000 divided into £1 shares. The prospectus set forth that, "the company was formed for the purpose of acquiring and laying out of a piece of land with an acreage of four-and-a-half acres situated at Goldsmith Avenue, Fratton to be used primarily for the game of football and also for other games and exercises as shall be decided on by the directors from time to time."

THE FIRST SUBSTITUTES

Tony Barton was the first ever used Pompey substitute. He replaced injured Vince Radcliffe during a 2-2 draw with Southampton at The Dell on 28 August 1965. The first Pompey sub to score was Mick Travers, who netted in a 3-1 home win over Blackpool on 2 December 1967.

MATCH OF THE DAY

Pompey's first appearance on BBC *Match of the Day* was on 25 February 1967. They lost a Second Division clash 3-2 at home to promotion-chasing Wolverhampton Wanderers after leading 2-0 at half-time, with Cliff Portwood scoring both goals.

LONG THROW

Roy Lunniss, a Pompey full-back between 1963 and 1966, was known for taking long throw-ins. His throw was measured at 37yds 2ft 6ins (34.6m).

LOCAL BOY MAKES GOOD

On 19 April 1939, 18-year-old Reg Flewin was the first Portsmouth-born player to appear in Pompey's League side since the club became members of the Football League in 1920. He played at centre-half in a 2-1 victory at home to Grimsby Town. This was his only league outing before war broke out, and he is the last surviving first-team player from Pompey's pre-war days.

RECORD TRANSFERS

Pompey broke their transfer record four times within 12 months. On 27 December 1972, Bobby Kellard rejoined the club from Crystal Palace for £42,000. In May 1973, Phil Roberts switched from Bristol Rovers for £55,000, and within days Pompey made their first £100,000 signing when Peter Marinello moved from Arsenal. The record transfer fee was shattered again on 6 December 1973, with Paul Went leaving Fulham for £154,000. This fee remained the club's highest transfer fee paid for the best part of ten years – it was broken when Mark Hateley signed from Coventry City for £190,000 in May 1983.

HOLDING THE CUP

The late Mrs Gladys Smith claimed she held the FA Cup more than anybody else in the history of the competition! She joined the Fratton Park staff in 1930 as matchday hostess, and worked at the ground during the week as a cleaner and laundry woman. During the Second World War, one of her jobs was to polish the FA Cup trophy, which was won by Pompey in 1939. As the competition was suspended until 1946, the cup remained at Fratton Park throughout the hostilities, and so Mrs Smith's claim is almost certain to be true. She was still working for the club when she died in 1978.

HIGHEST RESERVE ATTENDANCE

On 1 March 1952 at Fratton Park, a record reserve crowd of 30,289 watched Pompey Reserves thrash Charlton Athletic's second string 5-1 in a London Combination fixture. The reason for this huge attendance was that tickets for the following week's FA Cup quarter-final clash at home to Newcastle United were on sale.

PROUD HOME RECORD

Pompey dropped only three points as they remained unbeaten at Fratton Park throughout the 1948/49 campaign. They triumphed in 18 of the 21 league fixtures at Fratton Park, and won all four of their FA Cup-ties. Blackpool, Bolton Wanderers, and Manchester United were the three teams to return home with a point.

POMPEY KNOCK OUT SAINTS

After many years of waiting Pompey have finally beaten south coast rivals Southampton in a major Cup competition. A 4-1 win at the St Mary's Stadium in February 2010 saw Pompey knock Saints out of the FA Cup in the fifth round. They were first drawn together in the first round of the FA Cup in 1906, when Saints won 5-1 at The Dell. Remarkably, they didn't meet again until 1984 when, at Fratton Park, a last-minute goal by Steve Moran was enough to knock Pompey out of the cup in the fourth round. In 1996, Saints won an FA Cup third round tie 3-0 at The Dell, and they also won 2-1 at St. Mary's in the fourth round in January 2005. So far, the two clubs have met just once in the League Cup – in December 2003, when Southampton won the fourth round tie 2-0.

FIRST TIME AT THE TOP

Pompey went top of Division One for the first time on 10 September 1932 by beating Wolverhampton Wanderers 2-0 at Fratton Park. Jack Smith scored with seven minutes to go, then Jimmy Allen made sure of victory with a header.

THREE POINTS

Three points, instead of two, for a win was introduced at the start of the 1981/82 season to encourage more attacking football. Pompey had to wait until their sixth league match to collect their first three points, winning 2-0 away to Oxford United in a Division Three fixture.

FIRST LEAGUE HAT-TRICK

The first Pompey player to score a hat-trick in the Football League was Percy Cherrett; he netted three times in the 4-1 home win over Gillingham in October 1921 in a Division Three (South) fixture.

TOP MARKSMEN

Two Pompey players have led their divisional goalscoring charts. Ron Saunders topped the Second Division with 33 league goals in 1963/64 and the 1992/93 campaign saw Guy Whittingham lead the First Division scoring charts with 42.

THE SHANKLY CONNECTION

Robert Blyth, the uncle of legendary Liverpool manager Bill Shankly, served Portsmouth Football Club as player, captain, manager, director, vice-chairman, and chairman. He captained Pompey in their very first competitive match, and made 175 appearances before becoming manager in 1901, guiding the team to the Southern League championship in his first year. He joined the board of directors in 1909, and was chairman from September 1924 until August 1934. The family connection continued when his son Bob scored twice in eight league appearances during the 1921/22 campaign before moving to Southampton. Two of Bill Shankly's four brothers, John and Jimmy, were also on Pompey's books, and played regularly for the reserves, but only John played in the first team, making three appearances in 1923.

NOT EVEN A CORNER

On 5 December 1931, Newcastle United and Pompey played out a goalless draw at St James' Park. It is believed to be the only Football League match that failed to produce a corner kick.

TOP FIVE FA CUP GOALSCORERS

The top five Pompey goalscorers in the FA Cup are:

Peter Harris 15
Johnny Weddle 12
Guy Whittingham.... 10
Ron Saunders............ 9
Billy Haines 8

FIRST LEAGUE CUP GOAL

Tony Priscott scored Pompey's first goal in the Football League Cup competition. He netted in a 2-0 win at home to Coventry City on 2 November 1960.

RECORD CUP VICTORY

The 10-0 thrashing of Ryde in their first FA Cup tie on 30 September 1899 remains Pompey's biggest victory in the competition. Pompey were at that time obliged to play through the qualifying stages of the English Cup, as it was then known, and they defeated Cowes, Swindon, Bristol Rovers, and Bedminster before meeting Blackburn Rovers in the first round. They drew twice with the Lancashire club before losing 5-0 in the second replay.

BIGGEST POST-WAR VICTORIES

On 8 January 1949 Stockport County were dumped out of the FA Cup at Fratton Park with Peter Harris scoring a hat-trick and Len Phillips and Ike Clarke both netting twice in a 7-0 victory. The team was: Ernie Butler, Phil Rookes, Harry Ferrier, Jimmy Scoular, Reg Flewin, Jimmy Dickinson, Peter Harris, Bert Barlow, Ike Clarke, Len Phillips, Jack Froggatt. Eight months later, on 10 September 1949, Everton were thrashed by the same scoreline in a First Division fixture at Fratton Park. The Pompey team was: Ernie Butler, Bill Hindmarsh, Harry Ferrier, Jimmy Scoular, Reg Flewin, Jimmy Dickinson, Peter Harris, Duggie Reid, Ike Clarke, Len Phillips, Jack Froggatt. Duggie Reid grabbed a hat-trick, and his fellow forwards Harris, Clarke, Phillips, and Froggatt all scored a goal apiece.

ABERDARE ATHLETIC

Pompey were Aberdare Athletic's first Football League opponents. The Welsh club became members of Division Three (South) in 1921 but only lasted in the league for six years. That first match was played at their Ywys Field ground in front of 9,722 people on 27 August 1921, and the sides fought out a goalless draw.

FIRST LOAN PLAYER

The first player to play for Pompey on loan was York City goalkeeper Bob Widdowson, who made four appearances during the 1969/70 season. First-choice keeper John Milkins fractured a cheekbone in a 4-0 defeat at Watford on 18 October, so Ray Potter stepped up to replace him. Potter broke two fingers in only his second game – a 3-3 draw at Carlisle – and so Widdowson kept goal for the next four matches before Milkins returned from injury.

THREE DIVISIONS

David Pullar played for Pompey in three divisions while still a teenager. He made his debut in Division Two as a substitute in Pompey's 2-1 win at home to Orient in April 1976, but relegation at that time was already assured. He played on the wing as Pompey spent two years in Division Three, and in August 1979 he appeared in the club's first match in the Fourth Division, six months before his 20th birthday.

FOUR DIVISIONS

Goalkeeper Alan Knight is the only player to have represented Pompey in all four divisions of the Football League. He made his debut in Pompey's 1-0 win at Rotherham in Division Three on the final day of their 1977/78 relegation season, and made a handful of appearances over the next two campaigns while the club were in Division Four. He became first-choice goalkeeper as Pompey climbed up through divisions Three and Two, and completed his full set on 15 August 1987, when Pompey played their first top-flight fixture since 1959, losing 4-2 away to Oxford United. The number of League appearances Knight made in each division is set out below:

Division One................36
Division Two.............546
Division Three 93
Division Four................8
TOTAL 683

GOALKEEPER SCORED THE WINNER

Pompey and Northern Ireland goalkeeper Norman Uprichard was a more than useful outfield player, and had he not been such a capable custodian, could well have earned his living "out in the field". On 3 January 1959, while playing in goal for Pompey Reserves against Nottingham Forest, he injured his wrist. This was before substitutes were allowed, so Uprichard moved to outside-right...and scored the winning goal.

THREE BROTHERS

The only occasion in which three brothers took part in an FA Cup semi-final was in 1934, when Pompey and Leicester City met at Highbury. Willie and Jack Smith were in the Pompey line-up, facing their younger brother Sep, who played at right-half for Leicester.

YOUNGEST GOALSCORER

Pompey's youngest goalscorer is Jimmy White, who was only 16 years 291 days when he scored on his debut in a First Division home match against Birmingham City on 21 March 1959.

POMPEY'S HISTORICAL LEAGUE STATUS

1899-1911.......... Southern League Division One
1911-12.............. Southern League Division Two
1912-15 .... Southern League Division One
1915-16 .... South Western Combination
1916-17.............. London Combination
1917-19 .... South Hants War League
1919-20 .... Southern League Division One
1920-21 .... Division Three
1921-24 .... Division Three (South)
1924-27 .... Division Two
1927-39.............. Division One
1939-40.............. Regional League South 'B' and 'C'
1940-41 .... Football League South
1941-42 .... London War League
1942-46............. League South
1946-59 .... Division One
1959-61 .... Division Two
1961-62 .... Division Three
1962-76 .... Division Two
1976-78 .... Division Three
1978-80............. Division Four
1980-83............. Division Three
1983-87 .... Division Two
1987-88 .... Division One
1988-92............. Division Two
1992-2003......... Division One
2003-2010......... FA Premier League
2010-2011 .... Football League Championship
2011-2013 .... Football League One
2013-.................. Football League Two

A.E. KNIGHT

Arthur Egerton Knight was an England amateur international during his spell with Pompey from 1908 until 1922, and also won a cap for the full England side, against Northern Ireland in 1920. Always referred to in the press as A.E. Knight, he played for Surrey as a schoolboy, and joined Godalming after leaving school. He began working for an insurance company and, through his job, moved to Portsmouth. Pompey snapped up the left-back, and he spent a season in the reserves before making his first-team debut in Southern League Division One. He enjoyed an eventful career, winning 30 amateur international caps, and he also represented Great Britain in the 1912 Olympics in Stockholm. He captained the Pompey side that won the 1920 Southern League championship, and but for injury would have led the side in their first Football League fixture. Knight, who played county cricket for Hampshire over a period of ten years, left Pompey in 1922, and played out the remainder of his football career with the legendary Corinthians amateur club, who granted him life membership.

UP FOR THE CUP

FA Cup Final
v Bolton Wanderers. 27 April 1929,
Wembley Stadium. Attendance 96,576

Pompey played in their first FA Cup Final in 1929, but Bolton were making their third visit to Wembley in seven years, having won the trophy in 1923 and 1926. Pompey were forced to reshuffle their side when left-back Tommy Bell was injured close on half-time – he moved to outside-left with both legs bandaged. Billy Butler scored Bolton's first goal with 12 minutes left, then Harold Blackmore made certain with a terrific shot three minutes from time. **Pompey**: Jock Gilfillan, Alex Mackie, Tommy Bell, Jimmy Nichol, John McIlwaine, Dave Thackeray, Fred Forward, Jack Smith, Johnny Weddle, Dave Watson, Freddie Cook.

POINTER INSPIRES FIRST WIN

Pompey's first win at Burnley, in December 1971, was inspired by former Turf Moor legend Ray Pointer. Manager Ron Tindall had recalled the 35-year-old to his struggling side to "show them what spirit is all about". Pompey were not expected to get much from the Second Division clash with the high-riding Clarets, but Pointer led them to a well-deserved 3-1 victory. Also in the Pompey side were former Burnley players Fred Smith and Colin Blant.

FIRST £100,000 DEPARTURE

The first player to be sold by Pompey for a six-figure sum was Steve Foster, who moved to Brighton & Hove Albion for £150,000 in June 1979. A product of Pompey's youth policy, Foster began his career as a centre forward, but was converted to centre-half. At the time of his transfer, Pompey were a Fourth Division club, and his new team had recently won promotion to the First Division.

BRAVE TILSED

Goalkeeper Ron Tilsed played the last 20 minutes of Pompey's 3-3 draw away to Luton Town in September 1973 with a broken arm. Centre-forward Ron Davies, back helping out the defence, struck Tilsed's arm while attempting to clear the ball. Tilsed, obviously in severe pain, defiantly refused to leave the field and helped Pompey to a point.

GENEROUS CLIFF

A Portsmouth tailor promised to donate a suit to any player who scored in the 1939 FA Cup Final against Wolves. Cliff Parker scored twice, so he shared the value of the second suit between the two reserves, Abe Smith and Bill Bagley.

BIGGEST LEAGUE WIN

Pompey recorded their biggest Football League victory on 9 April 1927, by beating Notts County 9-1 at Fratton Park in a Second Division clash. The goalscorers were Billy Haines (3), Jerry Mackie (2), Fred Cook (2), Reg Davies and Fred Forward. The Pompey team was: Dan McPhail, George Clifford, Ted Smith, Reg Davies, Harry Foxall, Billy Moffat, Fred Forward, Jerry Mackie, Billy Haines, Dave Watson, Freddie Cook.

WHEN WAR BROKE OUT

When war was declared on 3 September 1939, League football was suspended, with Pompey having played three First Division fixtures. The aborted season's record was:

26/08/1939......... Blackburn Rovers (h) 2-1
30/08/1939......... Derby County (a) 0-2
02/09/1939......... Bolton Wanderers (a) 1-2

The Pompey line-up in all three matches was: Harry Walker, Lew Morgan, Bill Rochford, Abe Smith, Tommy Rowe, Guy Wharton, Fred Worrall, Jimmy McAlinden, Jock Anderson, Bert Barlow, Cliff Parker.

PLAYED IT AT LAST

On 16 October 1946, Fratton Park staged a friendly between Pompey and Clyde, which the home side won 3-1. The match was originally arranged in 1939, but when war broke out the two clubs agreed to play it as soon as was possible. During the morning of the game, the Clyde party was received by the Lord Mayor of Portsmouth, and given a tour of HMS *Victory*.

WEDDLE TOP MAN

When football was suspended due to the outbreak of war in 1939, Johnny Weddle held the club's appearance and goalscoring record. He scored 168 League goals in 368 appearances, and added another 13 goals from 28 FA Cup games.

HIRON'S SHORTENED RETURN

Ray Hiron spent 11 years with Pompey before his transfer to Reading in 1975, so when the Royals visited Fratton Park for the first time after his move to Elm Park, he was desperate to play, even though he was suffering from a leg injury. He started the match, but was forced to limp off after only three minutes.

EUROPEAN CUP AT FRATTON PARK

The European Cup was paraded round Fratton Park in August 1982, when holders Aston Villa played Pompey in a testimonial match for Alex Cropley, a former player of both clubs.

GEORGE BEST

George Best was arguably the greatest player ever to grace the English game, but he only played at Fratton Park on one occasion – and that was a friendly. In December 1973, Pompey drew 1-1 with Manchester United in one of two friendly matches against major sides staged to celebrate the club's 75th anniversary. Northern Ireland international Best played the full 90 minutes. The only other match in which he faced Pompey was on 7 October 1970, when United beat Pompey 1-0 in a third round League Cup tie at Old Trafford.

CHARITY SHIELD

Pompey have appeared in two Charity Shield finals. As 1949 Football League champions they played Wolverhampton Wanderers at Highbury on 19 October of that year and drew 1-1 which meant the sides kept the shield for six months each. Duggie Reid was the Pompey goalscorer and the team lined up as follows: Ernie Butler, Bill Hindmarsh, Harry Ferrier,

Jimmy Scoular, Bill Thompson, Jimmy Dickinson, Peter Harris, Duggie Reid, Ike Clarke, Bert Barlow, Jack Froggatt. As 2008 FA Cup winners they faced Premier League champions Manchester United at Wembley on 10 August and lost 3-1 on penalties after the two sides played out a goalless ninety minutes. The Pompey team was: David James, Glen Johnson, Sol Campbell, Sylvain Distin, Hermann Hreidarsson (Lauren), Papa Bouba Diop, Lassana Diarra, Pedro Mendes (Arnold Mvuemba), Niko Kranjcar (John Utaka), Peter Crouch, Jermain Defoe.

JOHN DEACON

John Deacon is, at 15 years, Pompey's longest-serving chairman. A Southampton-based property developer, he became a director in December 1972, with the promise of vast sums of money to buy new players. Taking over as chairman in May 1973, he promised success would return to Fratton Park in three years, but after spending a fortune on players the club was relegated to the Third Division in 1976, and plunged into a severe financial crisis. More heartache followed, with relegation to Division Four in 1978, but the club's fortunes slowly turned, and promotion from the basement was attained in 1980, followed by the Third Division title in 1983. Mr Deacon maintained that his aim had always been to bring First Division football to Fratton Park, and his dream was fulfilled in 1987, when Pompey finished Second Division runners-up. But the team was relegated after just one year in the top flight, and with the club once again struggling financially, Mr Deacon sold out to Jim Gregory for £2m. He died in April 1995.

ONLY ONE DEPARTED

In December 1973, Pompey put 11 players on the transfer list in an effort to reduce the wage bill – only one player left: David Munks to Swindon Town.

THE CUP GOES BACK

After winning the FA Cup in 1939, Pompey held it throughout the War, and their first FA Cup tie after the hostilities ended was away to Birmingham City in the first match of a two-legged third round. Reg Flewin scored an own goal: the only goal of the game. The second leg ended goalless, meaning the cup's long stay on the south coast would soon be at an end.

GORDON AND WILSON TESTIMONIAL

Long serving Pompey players Johnny Gordon and Alex Wilson retired at the end of the 1966-67 season and were both promised a benefit match. As it was inevitable that one match would bring in a larger amount of money than the other, it was decided to organise two matches on a joint basis.

SOUTHEND CELEBRATE LANDMARK

Southend United celebrated their 1,000th match at Roots Hall on 12 March 1994 by beating Pompey 2-1. Gerry Creaney put Pompey ahead, but goals by Peter Beadle and Andy Sussex earned a win for the Essex club.

WHEN MATTHEWS PLAYED AT FRATTON

Stanley Matthews has played against Pompey at Fratton Park more than any other player. His first appearance was as a 19-year-old for Stoke City, when he scored his only goal on Pompey's ground in his side's 3-1 defeat. The results from matches he played at Fratton Park for Stoke City and Blackpool are set out below:

20/01/1934.........Pompey 3 Stoke City 1 .... Division One
13/10/1934.........Pompey 0 Stoke City 1 .... Division One
28/03/1936.........Pompey 2 Stoke City 0 .... Division One
10/10/1936.........Pompey 1 Stoke City 0 .... Division One
29/01/1938.........Pompey 2 Stoke City 0 .... Division One
16/11/1946.........Pompey 1 Stoke City 3 .... Division One
06/03/1948.........Pompey 1 Blackpool 1 .... Division One
13/11/1948.........Pompey 1 Blackpool 1 .... Division One
27/08/1949.........Pompey 2 Blackpool 3 .... Division One
14/10/1950.........Pompey 2 Blackpool 0 .... Division One
22/08/1951.........Pompey 1 Blackpool 3 .... Division One
23/08/1952.........Pompey 0 Blackpool 2 .... Division One
27/08/1955.........Pompey 3 Blackpool 3 .... Division One
06/04/1963.........Pompey 0 Stoke City 3 .... Division Two

TRIPLE PENALTY SAVE

On 22 September 1973, in a home match against Notts County, John Milkins saved a penalty three times – from three different players. Firstly, Kevin Randall's spot-kick was saved by Milkins, but the referee ruled that Milkins had moved. Up stepped Don Masson, and the keeper deflected his shot against the crossbar. Again, the referee decided Milkins had moved. Next Brian Stubbs took the shot, which Milkins turned over the bar.

OLDEST PROGRAMME

The Pompey programme believed to be the oldest in existence dates back to 13 February 1901 – shortly after the death of Queen Victoria. The match was a Western League fixture between Pompey and Bristol Rovers. The hosts won 3-0, with the goals from Bob Marshall, Frank Bedingfield and John Lewis.

YOUNG AWFORD

Andy Awford was Pompey's youngest player at 16 years 275 days when he played in an away game against Crystal Palace on 15 April 1989. He had by then already claimed the record for being the youngest player to play in the FA Cup competition. On 10 October 1987, he came on as substitute for Worcester City, against Boreham Wood in a qualifying round, aged 15 years 88 days.

DRESSING-ROOM RUMPUS

When the Pompey players reached the dressing-room prior to the 1942 Wartime Cup Final with Brentford, skipper Jimmy Guthrie informed manager Jack Tinn that the players would not turn out unless they were paid money they'd been owed since September 1939. All contracts had been cancelled due to the outbreak of war, and as the players were paid fortnightly they were still owed a week's money. All the directors were called to the dressing-room, and the players were told that they would never kick a ball in England again unless they went onto the field. The players held firm, and the directors reluctantly surrendered with only eight minutes left before the start of play.

SEASON'S TOP MARKSMEN

Pompey's eight highest league scorers in a season are:

Guy Whittingham (1992-93) 42
Billy Haines (1926-27) 40
Ron Saunders (1963-64) 33
Jimmy Easson (1930-31) 29
Duggie Reid (1946-47) 29
Billy Haines (1923-24) 28
Ron Saunders (1961-62) 26
Johnny Weddle (1934-35) 25

TOP SCORER FOR TWO TEAMS

Colin Garwood topped Pompey's goalscoring chart in 1979/80 – despite being sold to Aldershot midway through the campaign. He continued in goalscoring vein at the Recreation Ground, and ended the season with a total of ten goals for the Shots, thus making him leading scorer for two different teams in the same season.

HUGHIE GALLACHER

Hughie Gallacher was the only player to visit Fratton Park in the First Division with four different clubs. He turned out for Newcastle United, Chelsea, Derby County, and Grimsby Town.

SUPERSTITIOUS WORRALL

Pompey and England outside-right Freddie Worrall must go down as the most superstitious footballer of all time. He went into every cup-tie with a small horseshoe in his pocket, a sprig of white heather pushed down each sock, and a small white elephant tied to one of his garters. He died in April 1979 – almost inevitably, on Friday 13th.

LUCKY ESCAPE

Returning home by coach from a 1-0 defeat at Bolton Wanderers in September 1946, the Pompey party were involved in an accident at Wickham at 3.30 on Sunday morning, when the driver was unable to avoid the obstruction of an American service vehicle. Manager Jack Tinn and trainer Jimmy Stewart, who occupied the front seats, were badly bruised, but fortunately none of the players were injured.

NEUTRAL GROUNDS

Other than their Wembley appearances, Pompey have played on neutral grounds on the following occasions:

09/02/1925	Blackburn Rovers	Highbury	FAC2	0-1
18/01/1926	Derby County	Filbert Street	FAC3	0-2
23/03/1929	Aston Villa	Highbury	FAC SF	1-0
17/03/1934	Leicester City	St Andrew's	FAC SF	4-1
25/03/1939	Huddersfield T	Highbury	FAC SF	2-1
26/03/1949	Leicester City	Highbury	FAC SF	1-3
19/10/1949	Wolverhampton W	Highbury	CS	1-1
08/02/1954	Scunthorpe United	Highbury	FAC4	4-0
19/03/1963	Coventry City	White Hart Lane	FAC4	1-2
19/03/1967	Hull City	Highfield Road	FAC4	1-2
05/02/1974	Orient	Selhurst Park	FAC4	2-0
05/04/1992	Liverpool	Highbury	FAC SF	1-1
13/04/1992	Liverpool	Villa Park	FAC SFR	0-0

TRIBUTE TO AARON FLAHAVAN

Pompey's first home match of the 2001/02 season against Bradford City was preceded by a tribute to goalkeeper Aaron Flahavan, who was killed in a car accident a fortnight earlier. There was a moving address by club chaplain Andy Rimmer before the singing of 'Abide With Me'. Flahavan's girlfriend then laid a wreath in the Fratton End goalmouth, and this was followed by a minute's silence.

GORDON NEAVE

Gordon Neave was one of Pompey's unsung heroes, working in various roles over a period of 51 years. He arrived at Fratton Park as a player in 1948, and while Pompey were winning the first of their two successive First Division titles, he played regularly at right-half for the reserve team. He was transferred to Bournemouth in 1950, and later moved to Aldershot, but returned to Fratton Park in 1959. For the next 40 years, he worked for the club variously as a coach, trainer, physiotherapist, and kit man. He was awarded a testimonial in 1974, and another when he retired in 1999.

LONG WAIT

Milan Mandaric waited five years to see Pompey win an FA Cup tie. Efforts during the first four years of his ownership ended in failure at the first hurdle, but on 3 January 2004, a last-minute goal by Yakubu Ayegbeni gave Pompey a 2-1 home win over Second Division Blackpool.

LADIES' DAY

It was Ladies' Day at Fratton Park when Pompey entertained Manchester City on 8 January 1966. To encourage wives and girlfriends to become Fratton regulars, they were made guests of the club in the centre section of the North Stand.

BIGGEST LEAGUE DEFEAT

Pompey's heaviest Football League defeat occurred on 20 October 1928 at Filbert Street, where Leicester City beat them 10-0. The Pompey team was: Dan McPhail, George Clifford, Jock McColgan, Jimmy Nichol, John McIlwaine, Dave Thackeray, Fred Forward, Bobby Irvine, Johnny Weddle, Dave Watson, Freddie Cook.

PRAISE FROM CHARLTON

Pompey earned praise from Bobby Charlton after they lost to Manchester United in the third round of the League Cup at Old Trafford on 7 October 1970. Charlton, who scored the only goal of the game, said, "I thought Pompey were unlucky to lose and it was a treat to play against a team who at no time tried to kick anyone up in the air."

NEW MILLENNIUM

Pompey's first match of the new Millennium was a First Division clash away to Norwich City, which ended in a 2-1 defeat. Pompey's scorer was Lee Bradbury.

LIFE OF REILLY

Matt Reilly was the regular goalkeeper in the Southern League for the Royal Artillery team, and with their demise in 1898, he became Pompey's first goalkeeper. He was capped twice for Ireland, and helped Pompey win the Southern League championship in 1901/02. He was responsible for an alteration in the laws of the game. At Donnybrook in his youth, he played Gaelic football, and his habit of bouncing the ball as he dodged opponents caused the Football Association to prohibit the handling of the ball by goalkeepers outside the penalty area.

FIRST IN THE FIRST

Freddie Cook scored Pompey's first goal in the First Division after five minutes of the 3-3 draw at Sunderland on 27 August 1927. Four days later, Fratton Park staged its first Division One match, and Cook gave his team an early lead in the 3-1 victory over Aston Villa.

COUSINS PLAYING FOR ENGLAND

Jack Froggatt and his cousin, Redfern Froggatt of Sheffield Wednesday, played together in the same England side. In November 1952, they were in the team that beat Belgium 5-0 at Wembley, and in April 1953 both appeared in a 2-2 draw with Scotland, also at Wembley. Their third and last match together for the national side came in June 1953 in New York, where England beat the USA 6-3.

THE TRAINER TREATED HIMSELF

In October 1946, Pompey were drawing 1-1 at Aston Villa when, with eight minutes to go, Pompey inside-forward Bert Barlow went down injured. Trainer Jimmy Stewart grabbed his bucket and sponge, but collapsed with a twisted knee after running onto the pitch. Duggie Reid carried Stewart to treat Barlow, who admitted he was not injured at all but was just playing for time. The trainer was then carried off the field to treat himself. Afterwards, he was advised to do no more running, so in order to retain his services, the directors appointed him Training Supervisor, and promoted reserve team trainer Jimmy Easson to the senior team.

FIVE-MINUTE HAT-TRICK

In February 1981, Mick Tait scored a hat-trick in five minutes. With Pompey leading Exeter City 1-0 in a Third Division home clash at Fratton Park, Tait fired home two shots from outside the box, then completed his hat-trick with a header. Pompey won the match 5-0.

CHRISTMAS DAY

Time was when Christmas Day was part of the Football League calendar, but Pompey have not been in action on 25 December since they were beaten 7-4 by Chelsea at Stamford Bridge in 1957. Pompey's Football League results from matches played on Christmas Day are:

1920....... Watford 3 Pompey 2	....	Division Three (South)
1922....... Brighton 7 Pompey 1	....	Division Three (South)
1923....... Millwall 2 Pompey 0	....	Division Three (South)
1924....... Pompey 0 Crystal Palace 0	....	Division Two
1925....... Stockport County 3 Pompey 3	....	Division Two
1926....... Pompey 0 Nottingham Forest 0	....	Division Two
1928....... Pompey 3 Aston Villa 2	....	Division One
1929....... Pompey 0 Arsenal 1	....	Division One
1930....... West Ham 4 Pompey 3	....	Division One
1933....... Liverpool 3 Pompey 3	....	Division One
1934....... Blackburn Rovers 0 Pompey 0	....	Division One
1935....... Pompey 3 Derby County 0	....	Division One
1936....... Charlton Athletic 0 Pompey 0	....	Division One
1937....... Pompey 3 Preston North End 2	....	Division One
1946....... Pompey 0 Arsenal 2	....	Division One
1947....... Manchester United 3 Pompey 2	....	Division One
1948....... Chelsea 1 Pompey 2	....	Division One
1950....... Pompey 1 Chelsea 3	....	Division One
1951....... Arsenal 4 Pompey 1	....	Division One
1953....... Tottenham Hotspur 1 Pompey 1	....	Division One
1954....... Blackpool 2 Pompey 2	....	Division One
1957....... Chelsea 7 Pompey 4	....	Division One

A MIRACLE HAPPENED

On the day Pompey beat Wolverhampton Wanderers in the 1939 FA Cup Final, Mr Will Harmer lay, as he had for over a year, stiff in bed suffering from rheumatism. With the help of his wife and mother-in-law, he struggled downstairs to hear the match commentary on the wireless. When Pompey scored their first goal, Mr Harmer jumped out of his chair, and by the time Cliff Parker grabbed the third, he could walk without any assistance. After that day, Mr Harmer was able to return to work, and although he required a stick to help him walk, he maintained that Pompey's triumph put him back on his feet and gave him the determination to get really well again.

FIRST VISIT TO ANFIELD

Pompey's first-ever visit to Anfield, to tackle Liverpool in October 1927, could hardly have turned out worse. Goalkeeper Dan McPhail was declared unfit, so John Jarvie was called up for only his second first-team game. He conceded two goals in the first six minutes, and by half-time Pompey were 6-0 down. They hit back with two goals in the second half, but the home side added two more to make the final score Liverpool 8 Pompey 2.

POMPEY V EVERTON

Pompey enjoyed a run of nine successive home wins over Everton from 1946/47 to 1957/58. The Toffees were relegated from the First Division in 1951, and up to that time Pompey had beaten them at Fratton Park on five consecutive occasions since the war. After Everton's return to the top flight in 1954, Pompey won the next four Fratton duels, until in April 1959 the visitors triumphed 3-2.

FOUR POINTS FROM FORTY-EIGHT

After Burnley were beaten 4-2 in Division One at Fratton Park on 22 November 1958, Pompey only picked up one point at home during the rest of the season. They managed to scrape three draws away to bring their points tally to four from 24 matches. Needless to say, they were relegated.

HAPPY BIRTHDAY ALAN

Alan Ball took charge of Pompey for the first time on his 39th birthday. Pompey were playing hosts to Swansea City in Division Two, and Ball was in temporary charge following the recent sacking of Bobby Campbell. The final score was 5-0 to Pompey, and Ball was soon handed the manager's position on a permanent basis.

CONSECUTIVE RUN FOR SANDY KANE

Goalkeeper Sandy Kane played 104 league and cup matches for Pompey – all consecutive. He made his debut on the opening day of the 1923/24 campaign, and didn't miss a game before playing his last match for the club in a 5-1 defeat away to South Shields in October 1925.

A GOAL FOR BOTH SIDES

In February 1978, Pompey drew 1-1 at home to Exeter City in a Third Division tussle. In the second half, Pompey defender Paul Cahill gave the visitors the lead by heading into his own net, but then scored in the opposite end to atone for his mistake.

BAD START FOR YOSHI

Goalkeeper Yoshikatsu Kawaguchi had a bad start to his Pompey career, conceding a goal after only 26 seconds of his debut in a First Division clash away to Sheffield Wednesday on 3 November 2001. At least he finished up on the winning side, as Pompey won 3-2.

NAMED AFTER LINDBERGH

Lindy Delapenha made eight appearances for Pompey before moving to Middlesbrough in April 1950. His full name was Lloyd Lindbergh Delapenha, and he was born in Kingston, Jamaica on 20 May 1927, the day Charles Lindbergh flew the Atlantic – hence his middle name.

KANU NEARLY DID IT

No Pompey player has scored a hat-trick on his debut, neither has a Pompey player scored a hat-trick after coming on as a substitute, but Kanu nearly did both in the same match on the opening day of the 2006-07 campaign. Entering the action in the second half with Pompey leading Blackburn Rovers 1-0 at Fratton Park, he headed two goals before being brought down in the penalty-area in the last minute. He took the spot-kick himself but Brad Friedel made a save to deny him those two feats.

TWO RECORDS FOR JAMES

On 22 April 2007, David James produced a superlative display to ensure Pompey came away from Villa Park with a point to bolster their bid for European qualification. James' display ensured he set a new record of Premiership clean sheets – 143 – to surpass David Seaman. James also created a Premiership appearance record (subsequently beaten by Ryan Giggs) while with Pompey. He played his 536th Premiership game on 14 February 2009 at Fratton Park and celebrated the occasion by keeping a clean sheet against his former club Manchester City. Goals by Glen Johnson and Hermann Hreidarsson gave Pompey a 2-0 victory in the team's first match since Tony Adams was sacked as manager.

ELEVEN GOALS

When Pompey beat Reading 7-4 in the Premier League on 29 September 2007, it was the first time eleven goals had been scored in a competitive match at Fratton Park. Ironically the previous game at Fratton produced a goalless draw, as did Pompey's next three home fixtures.

PROMOTION

Pompey won the Division Three (South) championship in 1923/24. They clinched the title by beating Swindon Town 4-1 at Fratton Park in the penultimate match of the season and wound up the campaign by winning 2-0 at Gillingham, thanks to two goals by Steve Dearn, on his club debut.

Football League Division Three (South) 1923/24

	Pl	W	D	L	F	A	W	D	L	F	A	Pts
1 POMPEY	42	15	3	3	57	11	9	8	4	30	19	59
2 Plymouth Argyle	42	13	6	2	46	15	10	3	8	24	19	55
3 Millwall	42	17	3	1	45	11	5	7	9	19	27	54
4 Swansea Town	42	18	2	1	39	10	4	6	11	21	38	52
5 Brighton	42	16	4	1	56	12	5	5	11	12	25	51
6 Swindon Town	42	14	5	2	38	11	3	8	10	20	33	47
7 Luton Town	42	11	7	3	35	19	5	7	9	15	25	46
8 Northampton Town	42	14	3	4	40	15	3	8	10	24	32	45
9 Bristol Rovers	42	11	7	3	34	15	4	6	11	18	31	43
10 Newport County	42	15	4	2	39	15	2	5	14	17	49	43
11 Norwich City	42	13	5	3	45	18	3	3	15	15	41	40
12 Aberdare Athletic	42	9	9	3	35	18	3	5	13	10	40	38
13 Merthyr Town	42	11	8	2	33	19	0	8	13	12	46	38
14 Charlton Athletic	42	8	7	6	26	20	3	8	10	12	25	37
15 Gillingham	42	11	6	4	27	15	1	7	13	16	43	37
16 Exeter City	42	14	3	4	33	17	1	4	16	4	35	37
17 Brentford	42	9	8	4	33	21	5	0	16	21	50	36
18 Reading	42	12	2	7	35	20	1	7	13	16	37	35
19 Southend United	42	11	7	3	35	19	1	3	17	18	65	34
20 Watford	42	8	8	5	35	18	1	7	13	10	36	33
21 Bournemouth & BA	42	6	8	7	19	19	5	3	13	21	46	33
22 Queens Park Rangers	42	9	6	6	28	26	2	3	16	9	51	31

FIRST AT THE CITY OF MANCHESTER STADIUM

Pompey were the visitors when Manchester City played their first league fixture at the City of Manchester Stadium. Playing their first away fixture in the Premiership, Pompey went ahead through Yakubu Ayegbeni on 24 minutes, and looked to have wrecked the party. But with only five seconds of normal time remaining, David Sommeil headed an equaliser for City.

PALMER IS SENT OFF TWICE

Carlton Palmer was the first opposition player to be sent off at Fratton Park for two different teams. On 3 December 1988, while playing for West Bromwich Albion in a goalless draw, he was ordered off for retaliating against Barry Horne, and then on 6 April 1991 he was sent off for protesting about a foul that gave Pompey a penalty against Sheffield Wednesday. Pompey won the game 2-0.

HIRON BEATS OWN RECORD

Ray Hiron was Pompey's top scorer in 1968-69 with 17, and the following season he had scored 15 with one fixture of the season remaining. That match was played away to Hull City, and Hiron scored all Pompey's goals in a 3-3 draw to beat his previous season's tally.

BLADES HIT FIVE – THREE TIMES

Sheffield United hit five goals against Pompey in three consecutive league matches. In August 1969, they beat Pompey 5-1 at Fratton Park, and won 5-0 in the return fixture at Bramall Lane. When the two sides met again at Fratton the following season, the Blades recorded another 5-1 victory.

TOP FLIGHT ONLY

Arsenal and Everton are the only two clubs that Pompey have faced in the league, in no other division than the top flight.

BERGER DELIGHT

On 18 October 2003, Pompey met Liverpool for the first time in the Premiership, and they defeated the Reds 1-0. Patrik Berger, who had recently made the move from Anfield, scored the only goal of the game in the fourth minute. This was the first time Pompey had beaten Liverpool since 12 March 1960.

LOW ATTENDANCES

The lowest attendance for a first-team match at Fratton Park was when Pompey beat Liverpool 2-1 on 25 February 1933. Only 4,031 attended the First Division fixture. The lowest post-war crowd – 4,688 – watched Pompey and Middlesbrough fight out a goalless draw in Division Two on 16 December 1972.

CLOCK TOWER

In 1905, Pompey chairman Sir John Brickwood paid for a clock tower to be built as the club spent money on ground improvements for the first time. As part of the facelift, a pavilion was built at the Frogmore Road entrance to the ground and the clock tower was added thanks to Sir John's personal donation. It only lasted 20 years because, in 1925, the new South Stand was erected, and this necessitated the tower's removal.

THE FIRST NAME

Pompey was the first football club to have its name printed on the front cover of the *United Review*, the Manchester United official matchday programme. The programme in question was for a First Division fixture which took place at Old Trafford on 21 October 1951. For the record, the match ended goalless.

THIRD TIME LUCKY

It was third time lucky for George Smith when he signed Bobby Kellard for Pompey in March 1966. He first tried to sign the player when he was a teenager at Southend United, but felt the price was too high, and Kellard moved to Crystal Palace instead. Smith tried for Kellard again the following November, and agreed to pay Palace £15,000, but this time Ipswich Town won the race for his signature. When Smith heard that Kellard was not too happy at Portman Road, he contacted Ipswich boss Bill McGarry, a £15,000 deal was struck, and the Pompey manager at last got his man.

BILL PROBERT

Bill Probert was the automatic choice for the right-back berth in the club's early Football League days. Joining the club in 1911 as a 16-year-old, he made his debut away to Southampton in September 1913. He played regularly during World War I, while employed at Portsmouth Dockyard, and featured in every match of the 1919/20 season when Pompey won the Southern League championship. He was also ever-present throughout the subsequent campaign in Division Three, and continued to be a regular in the side over the next few years, only missing matches through illness or injury, and winning a Third Division championship medal in 1923/24. Midway through the 1924/25 season he was transferred to Fulham, and after his retirement from football he became licensee of the Milton Arms, close to Fratton Park. Sadly, he committed suicide on 31 August 1948.

MRS DEACON

So far, Portsmouth Football Club have only had one lady director. Mrs Joan Deacon, wife of chairman John, joined the board on 17 December 1982, and left the club in May 1988, when her husband sold out to Jim Gregory.

WHERE'S MY MONEY?

The most embarrassing of the club's debts, if by no means the biggest, when the SOS appeal was launched in 1976 was money owed to former player Albert McCann. His testimonial match against West Ham at Fratton Park in May 1973 attracted a crowd of 22,000, but three years later McCann was owed the balance – over £2,000 plus interest – of his testimonial fund of £10,300.

UNITED'S YOUNGEST PLAYER

The youngest player to appear in Manchester United's first team is Jeff Whitefoot, who made his debut aged 16 years 105 days against Pompey at Old Trafford on 15 April 1950. It was a curious decision by Matt Busby to select the youngster, considering the importance of the match. Before the game, United led the First Division with 48 points from 39 matches, while Pompey were lying third, having collected 47 points from 38 matches. Late goals by Duggie Reid and Jack Froggatt gave Pompey a 2-0 victory, and they went top of the table while United dropped to third. When the season ended three weeks later, Pompey were crowned champions, and Manchester United finished runners-up.

HIGH FIVES

The last time Pompey scored five goals in the first half was at home to Swindon Town on 19 September 1964. They led 5-0 at the break after John McClelland and Cliff Portwood scored two each with the other goal coming from Albert McCann. There was no further scoring in the second half. Ironically, Pompey had failed to score in their previous three matches.

MRS WORRALL'S DREAM

A few nights before the 1939 FA Cup Final, Mrs Worrall, wife of outside-right Fred, dreamt Pompey beat Wolverhampton Wanderers 2-0. The result was 4-1 to Pompey and they led 2-0 at the interval. Worrall joked that his wife must have woken up at half-time.

HAPPY RETURN FOR SHOWERS

On 8 September 1979, Derek Showers sustained a knee injury that seriously threatened his career during Pompey's 1-0 home win over Stockport County in a Fourth Division clash. He didn't play again all season, but was named as substitute for the first four matches of the 1980/81 campaign without getting on the pitch. In a Third Division home fixture with Rotherham United, he came on for the second half and headed Pompey into a 2-1 lead. They eventually won the game 3-1. The following week, in a 2-0 victory at Blackpool, Showers celebrated his first start in almost a year with another goal.

OFF TO A BAD START

The heaviest defeats Pompey have suffered on the opening day of the season are:
29 August 1925......Pompey 1 Middlesbrough 5
31 August 1929......Pompey 0 Sheffield Wednesday 4
17 August 2008 .....Chelsea 4 Pompey 0

HIGHEST POSITION

Pompey's highest league position since back-to-back championship successes in 1948/49 and 1949/50 is third in Division One. Achieved in the 1954/55 season, Pompey still had a chance of winning the title when Chelsea visited on 16 April 1955. The match, watched by a crowd of 40,230, finished 0-0, and Chelsea went on to clinch their first championship.

WRIT COULD HAVE KILLED OFF HEREFORD

Pompey issued Hereford United with a writ in May 1982, as they owed Pompey £27,000 18 months after Derek Showers and Joe Laidlaw moved to Edgar Street. Pompey were willing to take defender Chris Price to liquidate the debt, but Hereford would not agree. The money was eventually paid, and Price became a Pompey player 11 years later.

THE MORTIMORE BROTHERS

John Mortimore managed Pompey from July 1973 to September 1974. His brother Charlie made one appearance for the club as an amateur, on 25th December 1953, in a 1-1 draw with Tottenham Hotspur at White Hart Lane.

LAST DAY ESCAPE

24 April 1965, Division Two: Northampton Town 1 Pompey 1

This vital match was played on a Saturday evening, and Pompey knew that a point would see them safe. Northampton Town were already promoted, and were unbeaten at home, so it would be no easy task. The match was also the last of Jimmy Dickinson's magnificent career, and he was applauded onto the pitch by both teams on what was his 40th birthday. Pompey started well, and Dennis Edwards, Cliff Portwood and John McClelland all had chances to put them ahead. In the 77th minute, a free-kick was lobbed into the Pompey goalmouth, and Johnny Gordon headed past his own goalkeeper John Armstrong. Pompey piled forward, and got their reward when Harry Harris headed on John McClelland's corner, allowing Alex Wilson to slam the ball home from ten yards and secure survival. **Pompey**: John Armstrong, Alex Wilson, Ron Tindall, Johnny Gordon, Jimmy Dickinson, Harry Harris, John McClelland, Cliff Portwood, Dennis Edwards, Albert McCann, Tony Barton.

NICHOL AND THACKERAY

Jimmy Nichol and Dave Thackeray formed a wing-half partnership that served Pompey for eight years. Nichol was Jack Tinn's first major signing in November 1927, and Thackeray joined the club from Alloa Athletic in the summer of 1928. He was a tough competitor and played a defensive role, whereas Nichol was the more artistic, often setting up attacks. The pair played in the 1929 FA Cup Final, which Pompey lost 2-0 to Bolton Wanderers, and they returned to Wembley in 1934 to face Manchester City, finding themselves on the losing side again, as City won 2-1. Thackeray captained the side that day, having been appointed skipper in 1930. He made his final appearance in September 1935, and retired from the game at the end of that season, but Nichol was still a fixture in the side until December 1936, playing his final game for Pompey in a 5-1 home defeat by Arsenal. This was his 351st League outing in a Pompey shirt, at the time a club record. But this was not the end of their links with Pompey. Thackeray returned in 1950 to become assistant groundsman to Harold Reed, and he took charge of the 'A' team on match days. Sadly, he died in July 1954, shortly after Nichol returned to take up the position of head trainer. Tragically, in November of that year, he too died. Like Thackeray, he was only in his early 50s. A testimonial match was played in May 1955 between a Pompey XI and a team made up of former players, and the proceeds were divided between the dependants of two of the club's finest wing-halves.

AT LAST: A WIN AT ST JAMES' PARK

When Pompey defeated Newcastle United 4-1 in the Premier League on 3 November 2007, it was the first time they had won at St James' Park since August 1949. It was also the quickest any Pompey side had taken a 3-0 lead, for they were three goals to the good after only eleven minutes' play.

MESSAGE FROM MONTY

In 1949, at the start of their Golden Jubilee, Portsmouth Football Club received the following letter of congratulations from their President Field Marshal The Viscount Montgomery of Alamein, KG, GCB, DSO: *I am very glad to send this message of goodwill to the Portsmouth Football Club for its Golden Jubilee. The Club has a very fine record and I am sure all its supporters will join me in sending its members congratulations and best wishes for future successes.*

FRATTON ATTENDANCE RECORDS

The Southern League Division One clash between Pompey and Southampton on 10 January 1903 was the first match that drew a crowd of over 20,000 to Fratton Park – the official attendance being recorded at 20,447. The list below shows when new ground records were set.

12/01/1906... Pompey 2 Manchester Utd 2 ....FA Cup 1st rnd... 24,329
06/02/1909... Pompey 2 Sheffield Wed 2 ....FA Cup 2nd rnd ..27,853
31/08/1927... Pompey 3 Aston Villa 1 ....Division One 32,050
25/08/1928... Pompey 1 Huddersfield Town 0 ..Division One 33,475
02/03/1929... Pompey 3 West Ham United 2....FA Cup 6th rnd ...39,088
25/08/1934... Pompey 3 Arsenal 3 ....Division One 39,710
26/02/1938... Pompey 0 Arsenal 0 ....Division One 43,741
11/02/1939... Pompey 2 West Ham United 0....Division One 47,614
12/02/1949... Pompey 3 Newport County 2......FA Cup 5th rnd ...48,581
26/02/1949... Pompey 2 Derby County 1 ....FA Cup 6th rnd ...51,385

KELLY AT SPURS

In November 1990 Mark Kelly joined Spurs on a month's loan. Kelly was not a regular in Pompey's Second Division side, so his move to a First Division club left fans slightly puzzled. He failed to make a first-team appearance, but did face Pompey in a reserve game at White Hart Lane that Spurs won 2-0.

BOTH SCORERS ON LOAN

When Pompey beat Plymouth Argyle 2-0 at home in Division Two on 14 February 1976, both goalscorers were spending a month on loan at Fratton Park. Martyn Busby of Queens Park Rangers scored the first goal, and the second came from Tony Macken, who was from Derby County.

POMPEY MANAGERS

1898-1901	Frank Brettell
1901-1904	Robert Blyth
1904-1911	Richard Bonney
1911-1920	Robert Brown
1920-1927	John McCartney
1927-1947	Jack Tinn
1947-1952	Bob Jackson
1952-1958	Eddie Lever
1958-1961	Freddie Cox
1961	Bill Thompson (caretaker)
1961-1970	George Smith
1970-1973	Ron Tindall
1973-1974	John Mortimore
1974	Ron Tindall (caretaker)
1974-1977	Ian St John
1977-1979	Jimmy Dickinson
1979-1982	Frank Burrows
1982-1984	Bobby Campbell
1984-1989	Alan Ball
1989-1990	John Gregory
1990-1991	Frank Burrows
1991-1995	Jim Smith
1995-1998	Terry Fenwick
1998	Keith Walden (caretaker)
1998-1999	Alan Ball
1999	Bob McNab (caretaker)
2000	Tony Pulis
2000-2001	Steve Claridge (player-manager)
2001-2002	Graham Rix
2002-2004	Harry Redknapp
2004-2005	Velimir Zajec (caretaker)
2005	Alain Perrin
2005-2008	Harry Redknapp
2008-2009	Tony Adams
2009-	Paul Hart
2009-2010	Avram Grant
2010-11	Steve Cotterill
2011-12	Michael Appleton
2012	Guy Whittingham (caretaker)
2012	Guy Whittingham
2012	Andy Awford (caretaker)
2013-14	Richie Barker
2014	Andy Awford

GORDON ON SONG

Johnny Gordon possessed a fine singing voice, and in 1966 appeared on Southern Television's talent contest *Home Grown*. He was pipped to first place by a singing group from Chatham.

THREE GENERATIONS

When Danny Hinshelwood made his debut for Pompey on 23 March 1996 in a goalless draw away to Crystal Palace, he was the third generation to play League football. His grandfather Wally Hinshelwood played for Fulham immediately after World War II, and went on to serve Chelsea, Reading, Bristol City, Millwall, and Newport County. His sons Martin and Paul both played for Crystal Palace during the 1970s, and Martin became manager of Pompey's youth and reserve teams in the 1990s.

WHARTON OK FOR THE CUP FINAL

On 1 April 1939, four weeks before Pompey were due to meet Wolverhampton Wanderers in the FA Cup Final, Guy Wharton was sent off in a 2-0 defeat against Birmingham City at Fratton Park. As was always the case for a sending-off in those days, the player had to attend an FA inquiry. At the hearing on 12 April, after listening to the evidence, the Commission decided to announce their decision at a later date, enabling Wharton to face his former club in the final.

CURRY TOO HOT FOR POMPEY

Bill Curry scored hat tricks against Pompey for three different clubs. On 11 March 1959, he netted a treble for Newcastle United, who won 5-1 at Fratton Park to push Pompey nearer to relegation from Division One. In July of that year, he was transferred to Brighton & Hove Albion and, on the third Saturday of the new season – 5 September 1959 – scored all three goals for his new club as they beat Pompey 3-1 at the Goldstone Ground in a Second Division fixture. His third hat-trick against Pompey came on 10 May 1963, when he helped Derby County beat Pompey 4-0 at the Baseball Ground in another Second Division clash.

UPHILL FOR UPRICHARD ON DEBUT

Goalkeeper Norman Uprichard marked his Pompey debut with an own goal. With Pompey leading Tottenham Hotspur 2-0 on 8 November 1952, Uprichard made a save from Dennis Uphill. He failed to retain possession, and as he attempted to collect the ball as he lay on the ground, he had the misfortune to scoop it into his own net. There were no further goals in the match.

SAME AGAIN

On 28 January 1976, Pompey were beaten 1-0 at home by Wrexham in Division Three, and the goal was scored by Graham Whittle at the Fratton End after 21 minutes. A year and a week later, Wrexham again visited Fratton Park for a Third Division fixture, and again beat Pompey 1-0. The goal was scored by Graham Whittle – at the Fratton End – after 20 minutes.

LOST IN THE FOG

Full-back Willie Smith brought great amusement to his Pompey team-mates when they travelled to Filbert Street to play Leicester City in a First Division fixture on 19 December 1931. Late out of the tunnel, he found the two teams were lined up ready for kick-off in thick fog. Unable to see the faces of the players and forgetting that Pompey would be playing in red jerseys, he made his way towards the Leicester City team. Not surprisingly, the match was abandoned.

UNHAPPY VALLEY FOR POMPEY

Pompey were the visitors when Charlton Athletic played their first match at The Valley on 5 December 1992 after an absence of over seven years. The home side celebrated with a 1-0 victory over the Blues, the decisive goal coming from Colin Walsh after only seven minutes.

NEW SECRETARY REQUIRED

When goalkeeper Alan Barnett was transferred to Grimsby Town in December 1958, a new manager's secretary was required because the position was held by Barnett's wife Julie.

WHEN THE LIGHTS WENT OUT

On 12 January 1974, the second half of the Second Division clash between Pompey and Luton Town was held up for 24 minutes due to floodlight failure. Because of a power crisis, Pompey and Southampton shared the hire of a generator to power the lights, but in the 71st minute of the game, it broke down, leaving Fratton Park in semi-darkness. Referee Roger Kirkpatrick made an announcement asking the crowd to remain in their places while attempts were being made to restart the generator, and eventually Pompey chairman John Deacon ordered that the lights be plugged into the mains. Although this was, technically, a breach of the emergency lighting regulations, Mr Deacon emphasised that he ordered the switch-over in the interests of public safety. The match ended 0-0.

PROMOTION TO DIVISION ONE

Pompey were promoted to the First Division on 7 May 1927 thanks to a 5-1 victory over Preston North End at Fratton Park on the last day of the season. In those days of goal average rather than goal difference, it was a close run thing: Pompey pipped Manchester City by a 200th part (or 0.005) of a goal. If City had scored one more goal, or Pompey one fewer, the Sky Blues would have gone up instead. Billy Haines was Portsmouth's top scorer with 40 goals.

Football League Division Two 1926/27

	Pl	W	D	L	F	A	W	D	L	F	A	Pts
1 Middlesbrough	42	18	2	1	78	23	9	6	6	44	37	62
2 POMPEY	42	14	4	3	58	17	9	4	8	29	32	54
3 Manchester City	42	15	3	3	65	23	7	7	7	43	38	54
4 Chelsea	42	13	7	1	40	17	7	5	9	22	35	52
5 Nottingham Forest	42	14	6	1	57	23	4	8	9	23	32	50
6 Preston North End	42	14	4	3	54	29	6	5	10	20	43	49
7 Hull City	42	13	4	4	43	19	7	3	11	20	33	47
8 Port Vale	42	11	6	4	50	26	5	7	9	38	52	45
9 Blackpool	42	13	5	3	65	26	5	3	13	30	54	44
10 Oldham Athletic	42	12	3	6	50	37	7	3	11	24	47	44
11 Barnsley	42	13	5	3	56	23	4	4	13	32	64	43
12 Swansea Town	42	13	5	3	44	21	3	6	12	24	51	43
13 Southampton	42	9	8	4	35	22	6	4	11	25	40	42
14 Reading	42	14	1	6	47	20	2	7	12	17	52	40
15 Wolverhampton W	42	10	4	7	54	30	4	3	14	19	45	35
16 Notts County	42	11	4	6	45	24	4	1	16	25	72	35
17 Grimsby Town	42	6	7	8	39	39	5	5	11	35	52	34
18 Fulham	42	11	4	6	39	31	2	4	15	19	61	34
19 South Shields	42	10	8	3	49	25	1	3	17	22	71	33
20 Clapton Orient	42	9	3	9	37	35	3	4	14	23	61	31
21 Darlington	42	10	3	8	53	42	2	3	16	26	56	30
22 Bradford City	42	6	4	11	30	28	1	5	15	20	60	23

POMPEY CHAIRMEN

1899-1912	Sir John Brickwood
1912-1920	George Lewin Oliver
1920-1924	Rev Bruce Cornford
1924-1934	Robert Blyth
1934-1937	Alfred Hooper
1937-1940	William Kiln
1940-1945	Sydney Leverett
1945-1946	Stephen Cribb
1946-1949	Richard Vernon Stokes
1949-1951	James Chinnick
1951-1954	Richard Vernon Stokes
1954-1955	John Privett
1955-1957	Guy Spriggins
1957-1959	Jack Sparshatt
1959-1966	Dr Ian McLachlan
1966-1973	Dennis Collett
1973-1988	John Deacon
1988-1996	Jim Gregory
1996-1997	Martin Gregory
1997-1998	Terry Venables
1998	Martin Gregory
1998-1999	Les Parris
1999-2006	Milan Mandaric
2006-	Sacha Gaydamak
2006-2009 (Oct-July)	Vacant
2009-2010 (Aug-Feb)	Sulaiman Al-Fahim
2010 (Feb-Oct)	In administration
2010-2011 (Nov-May)	Balram Chainrai
2011 (Jun-Nov)	Vladimir Antonov
2011-2012 (Dec-Jan)	Vacant
2012 (Feb-May 2013)	In administration
2013	Iain McInnes

GOAL THAT NEVER WAS

On 22 October 1977, Pompey were beaten 6-1 in their Third Division away match at Shrewsbury Town, but were angered that the Shrews' second goal had been awarded. Brian Hornsby bent a shot goalwards, but it hit the side-netting. Pompey goalkeeper Steve Middleton placed the ball for a goal-kick, only to see Shrewsbury's Chic Bates playfully flick the ball into the net – and referee John Wrennall pointing to the centre-circle! As the Pompey players protested, home fans behind the goal tried to get the referee's attention, as they knew the ball had gone out of play – but to Pompey's anger, the goal stood.

RECORD FEE FOR STEPHEN

In November 1949, Pompey broke their transfer record by paying £15,000 to Bradford Park Avenue for Scottish international full-back Jimmy Stephen. This was, at the time, a British record fee for a full-back.

JACK WARNER

Jack Warner played a vital role in Pompey's rise from the Southern League to the First Division: he was the Pompey trainer from 1919 until 1935. He joined the club from Southampton as a player in 1906, and made 227 appearances in the Southern League. He returned to Fratton Park immediately after World War I, and served under Robert Brown as Pompey won the Southern League championship in 1919/20 and became founder members of the Football League Third Division. He helped Pompey to two promotions in 1924 and 1927 under manager John McCartney, and then visited Wembley for two FA Cup Finals in 1929 and 1934 with Jack Tinn.

SEMI-FINAL HIGH

The crowd of 83,584 that witnessed Pompey's 1-0 victory over West Bromwich Albion at Wembley on 5 April 2008 was then the highest for an FA Cup semi-final. The record was beaten a year later when 88,141 saw Everton defeat Manchester United 4-2 on penalties.

LAST DAY ESCAPE II

5 May 1996, Division One, Huddersfield Town 0 Pompey 1
Pompey needed to win this game and hope Millwall would fail to beat Ipswich Town at Portman Road to avoid the drop. Huddersfield were dealt a blow after only five minutes when striker Andy Booth was carried off. Three minutes later, 19-year-old Deon Burton volleyed home the only goal of the match following a free-kick by Fitzroy Simpson. Alan Knight in the Pompey goal was not tested, and Paul Hall and Alan McLoughlin went close to increasing Pompey's lead. At Portman Road, Ipswich Town and Millwall drew 0-0, so Pompey lived to fight another season in Division One. **Pompey**: Alan Knight, Jason Rees, Andy Awford, Alan McLoughlin, Andy Thomson, Guy Butters, Martin Allen, Fitzroy Simpson, Deon Burton, Paul Hall, Jimmy Carter.

WHEN TED DRAKE LENT A HAND

Ted Drake made one wartime appearance for Pompey – and scored four goals. On Boxing Day 1945, he played at inside-right in Pompey's League South fixture at home to Crystal Palace, and his goals helped Pompey to a 9-1 victory. Three of Drake's goals came in the last seven minutes.

LEAGUE CUP APPEARANCES

Alan Knight played 53 matches for Pompey in the League Cup, and holds the club appearance record in the competition.

PEDRO SPARKS REVIVAL

Pompey made certain of Premiership survival by beating Wigan Athletic 2-1 at the JJB Stadium in April 2006, but it was two goals by Pedro Mendes the previous month that sparked the revival. The club looked certain to be relegated from the Premiership at the time Manchester City visited Fratton Park on 11 March 2006. Mendes gave Pompey the lead with a spectacular effort, but their first win since New Year's Eve looked as far away as ever when Richard Dunne equalised. In the last minute, however, another super strike from the Pompey midfielder earned the much-welcome victory, and a week later he was on the score-sheet again as Pompey beat West Ham United 4-2 to record their first win at Upton Park since October 1929.

GRAY'S "HAT-TRICK"

When Pompey lost 2-1 to Crystal Palace at Selhurst Park on 8 April 1986, Andy Gray scored all three goals. He headed Crystal Palace into the lead on 18 minutes, then a hit-and-hope shot from the touchline gave his side a 2-0 advantage. In the second half, his diving header diverted Mick Kennedy's shot past his own goalkeeper.

SAVED BY THE WHISTLE

Pompey were saved from defeat by the referee's whistle when they met Crystal Palace in a First Division fixture on 23 March 1996. The score was 0-0 when, after five minutes of added-on time, Andy Roberts's shot screamed past Alan Knight for what would have been the winning goal for Palace... but referee Alan Wiley blew for full-time before the ball had crossed the line.

ALL HOME TIES

When Pompey won the FA Cup in 1939 all the ties (except the semi-final and final) were played at Fratton Park:

Round 3........ Lincoln City........................ 4-0
Round 4........ West Bromwich Albion 2-0
Round 5........ West Ham United.............. 2-0
Round 6........ Preston North End............. 1-0

WE ARE THE CHAMPIONS

In season 1948/49, Pompey celebrated their Golden Jubilee year by winning the League Championship. They twice broke the Fratton Park attendance record in FA Cup games, and remained unbeaten at home. The title was clinched on 23 April 1949, when Bolton Wanderers were beaten 2-1 at Burnden Park. Peter Harris and Duggie Reid were the goalscorers.

Football League Division Two 1948/49

	Pl	W	D	L	F	A	W	D	L	F	A	Pts
1 POMPEY	42	18	3	0	52	12	7	5	9	32	30	58
2 Manchester United	42	11	7	3	40	20	10	4	7	37	24	53
3 Derby County	42	17	2	2	48	22	5	7	9	26	33	53
4 Newcastle United	42	12	5	4	35	29	8	8	6	35	27	52
5 Arsenal	42	13	5	3	51	18	5	8	8	23	26	49
6 Wolverhampton W	42	13	5	3	48	19	4	7	10	31	47	46
7 Manchester City	42	10	8	3	28	21	5	7	9	19	30	45
8 Sunderland	42	8	10	3	27	19	5	7	9	22	39	43
9 Charlton Athletic	42	10	5	6	38	31	5	7	9	25	36	42
10 Aston Villa	42	10	6	5	40	36	6	4	11	20	40	42
11 Stoke City	42	14	3	4	43	24	2	6	13	23	44	41
12 Liverpool	42	5	10	6	25	18	8	4	9	28	25	40
13 Chelsea	42	10	6	5	43	27	2	8	11	26	41	38
14 Bolton Wanderers	42	10	4	7	43	32	4	8	11	16	36	38
15 Burnley	42	10	8	5	27	19	2	8	11	16	31	38
16 Blackpool	42	8	8	5	24	25	3	8	10	30	42	38
17 Birmingham City	42	9	7	5	19	10	2	8	11	17	28	38
18 Everton	42	12	5	4	33	25	1	6	14	8	38	37
19 Middlesbrough	42	10	6	5	37	23	1	6	14	9	34	34
20 Huddersfield Town	42	6	7	8	19	24	6	3	12	21	45	34
21 Preston North End	42	8	6	7	36	36	3	5	13	26	39	33
22 Sheffield U	42	8	9	4	32	25	3	2	16	25	53	33

KNIGHT RUNS THE LINE

In February 1931, the appointed referee failed to turn up to officiate Pompey's First Division clash at home to Everton so A.E. Knight took over as one of the linesmen. He generously donated his match fee to the local Royal Hospital.

'POMPEY' WATCHED POMPEY

Pompey outside-right Peter Harris's first wedding anniversary present to wife Sylvia was a pet poodle. The couple named the dog 'Pompey', and Mrs Harris would take him to Fratton Park to watch Peter in action.

POMPEY CRICKETERS

John Atyeo	Wiltshire	1950-51
Mike Barnard	Hampshire	1952-56
Charles Burgess Fry	Hampshire, Sussex, England	1892-1911
Stanley Shute Harris	Surrey, Gloucestershire, Sussex	1900-06
Arthur Egerton Knight	Hampshire	1913-23
Arthur Mounteney	Leicestershire	1911-24
Scot Symon	Perthshire, Hampshire	1935-38
Jim Standen	Worcestershire	1965-72
Ron Tindall	Surrey	1956-66
George Wheldon	Worcestershire, Carmarthenshire	1899-1910

'PLUM THE CARTOONIST'

Alexander Plummer was a Portsmouth-based artist who drew something like 20,000 cartoons in a working life of 70 years. He was best known for his brilliant cartoons relating to Portsmouth Football Club, and his offerings of the ups and downs of life at Fratton Park were featured in the local paper *The Football Mail* from 1920 until 1971. He was born on 9 September 1899 – the day Fratton Park staged Pompey's first home league match – and died on Christmas Day 1987.

HAT-TRICKS AGAINST THEIR FUTURE CLUB

Four players have scored hat-tricks against Pompey and later moved to Fratton Park. Alex Govan netted a treble as Birmingham City won 5-0 at Pompey in October 1955. Ron Davies scored all three goals in 3-0 home win for Norwich City in December 1955. John Lathan hit all three Sunderland goals in a 3-2 win at Roker Park in March 1972; and in September 1975 Mick Channon hit three in Southampton's 4-0 victory at The Dell.

MOST-CAPPED GOALIE

Mart Poom is Pompey's most-capped goalkeeper. He joined Pompey in August 1994 from Swiss club FC Wil, and spent two seasons at Fratton Park. During that time, he represented Estonia on 30 occasions, and yet only made seven appearances for Pompey.

JIM FIXED IT

One of the most important matches in Pompey history occurred on 14 May 1977, when Pompey entertained York City in a Third Division relegation decider at Fratton Park. It was Jimmy Dickinson's first home match in charge, and a win over doomed York City would guarantee Pompey's survival. Two young Pompey supporters, Ian Lindsay and Derek Scott, had made a huge banner displaying the words, "Jim'll Fix It" and it was held up at the Milton End throughout the game. George Hope put York City ahead after half an hour, but two goals by Clive Green and one from David Kemp guaranteed that Third Division football would be played at Fratton Park the following season.

A REMARKABLE SUPPORTER

Mr Jim Scholes was a Pompey supporter for 55 years, and attended matches well into his eighties. What was more remarkable was that for the last 35 years of his life he was totally blind, yet he hardly missed a match at Fratton Park. He didn't "watch" games with the aid of a commentator, but was completely independent. He travelled to and from the ground on his own, and his journey required a long walk before he caught a bus. Mr Scholes always maintained he could follow a game well by the noise of the crowd, and if he needed to check anything then he only had to ask.

FRATTON IS HOME TO MILLWALL

On 1 April 1978, Millwall, banned from their own ground The Den because of crowd violence, played a home game against Bristol Rovers at Fratton Park. Rovers won the Second Division clash 3-1 before a crowd of 3,322. Meanwhile, Pompey lost 1-0 away to Bradford City in Division Three.

CHANGE OF LUCK

In 1967, Pompey abandoned their famous blue and white for an all-blue strip with red and white trimmings. The change seemed to bring the team better results, with seven points gained from their first four matches, and the 1967/68 season was the most exciting for some years.

AFTER THE LORD MAYOR'S SHOW

After taking eventual 1970/71 League and FA Cup double-winners Arsenal to a replay at Highbury and losing only to a late penalty, Pompey came crashing down to earth in their next match. They were beaten in a Second Division fixture 4-1 by Carlisle United, who recorded their first ever victory at Fratton Park. It was also the Cumbrians' first win on their travels since Boxing Day 1969.

SCORED IN ALL COMPETITIONS

Billy Eames scored three goals during the 1975/76 campaign, and each one came in a different competition. He grabbed his first on his debut, after coming on as a substitute in a League Cup second round tie against Leicester City in September 1975. His second came in the FA Cup third round against Birmingham City at Fratton Park in January 1976, and a week later he scored the only goal in the Division Two encounter with Carlisle United. This earned Pompey their first home victory of the season.

NEWTON GOES BACK

One of Alan Ball's first signings after the arrival of Milan Mandaric as the club's new owner in 1999 was midfielder Adam Newton from West Ham United. The intention was for Newton to spend a year on loan at Fratton Park, but after one month the player had only made one start for Pompey, and so Harry Redknapp, then manager of the Hammers, took him back to Upton Park.

POMPEY LINK TO CUP UPSET

In February 1971, Colchester United produced one of the biggest FA Cup shocks of all time when they beat Leeds United 3-2 at Layer Road. The Fourth Division club's side that afternoon contained three players with Pompey links. Former Pompey centre forward Ray Crawford scored the first two goals, Brian Lewis had spent four years at Fratton Park during the 1960s and subsequently returned, while Dave Simmonds, scorer of Colchester United's third goal, was born in Portsmouth.

HOW POMPEY SIGNED HARRY FERRIER

Harry Ferrier guested for Pompey during World War II, and after the war ended, the club paid £1,000 to sign him from Barnsley. He was at the time serving with the Royal Artillery at Woolwich, and Pompey secretary Dan Clarke, complete with signing-on papers, travelled there to meet the player, only to be told he had gone to the cinema. A notice was flashed onto the screen informing Ferrier to telephone Barnsley Football Club, and the final details of the transfer were completed in a telephone kiosk.

GOING DOWN

Pompey's 32-year spell in Division One ended in 1959. They suffered several crushing defeats, and failed to win a League match after beating Burnley 4-2 in November 1958. They went bottom of the table following a 4-4 draw against Tottenham Hotspur at White Hart Lane on 21 February, and only picked up two more points from 13 matches thereafter. Ron Saunders was top scorer with 21 League goals from 35 appearances.

Football League Division One 1958/59

	Pl	W	D	L	F	A	W	D	L	F	A	Pts
1 Wolverhampton W	42	15	3	3	68	19	13	2	6	42	30	61
2 Manchester United	42	14	4	3	58	27	10	3	8	45	39	55
3 Arsenal	42	14	3	4	53	29	7	5	9	35	39	50
4 Bolton Wanderers	42	14	3	4	56	30	6	7	8	23	36	50
5 West Bromwich Albion	42	8	7	6	41	33	10	6	5	47	35	49
6 West Ham United	42	15	3	3	59	29	6	3	12	26	41	48
7 Burnley	42	11	4	6	41	29	8	6	7	40	41	48
8 Blackpool	42	12	7	2	39	13	6	4	11	27	36	47
9 Birmingham City	42	14	1	6	54	35	6	5	10	30	33	46
10 Blackburn Rovers	42	12	3	6	48	28	5	7	9	28	42	44
11 Newcastle United	42	11	3	7	40	29	6	3	11	40	51	41
12 Preston North End	42	9	3	9	40	39	8	4	9	30	38	41
13 Nottingham Forest	42	9	4	8	37	32	8	2	11	34	42	40
14 Chelsea	42	13	2	6	52	37	5	2	14	25	61	40
15 Leeds United	42	8	7	6	28	27	7	2	12	29	47	39
16 Everton	42	11	3	7	39	38	6	1	14	32	49	38
17 Luton Town	42	11	6	4	50	26	1	7	13	18	45	37
18 Tottenham Hotspur	42	10	3	8	56	42	3	7	11	29	53	36
19 Leicester City	42	7	6	8	34	36	4	4	13	33	62	32
20 Manchester City	42	8	7	6	40	32	3	2	16	24	63	31
21 Aston Villa	42	8	5	8	31	33	3	3	15	27	54	30
22 POMPEY	42	5	4	12	38	47	1	5	15	26	65	21

COUPONS APPEAL

In 1945, with clothes rationing in force, the club appealed to supporters for 500 clothing coupons. Enough came in to buy a new strip to begin the 1945/46 campaign, and every supporter who made a donation received a letter of thanks from secretary-manager Jack Tinn.

MONTY'S ORDER, "SIGN REID"

Duggie Reid was one of the club's finest ever players, and they had reason to thank the club president Field Marshal Montgomery for that. Reid served in the army at El Alamein, and took part in many football matches that were witnessed by Monty. He was on the books of Stockport County, but after the war a host of top clubs were looking to acquire his signature. It was because of Montgomery's recommendation that Reid ended up signing for Pompey.

HALF A MATCH, HALF A PITCH

Thick fog caused the Isle of Wight ferries to be suspended on 13 March 1948, but that didn't prevent Mr Gordon Holmes and his young son Colin getting to Fratton Park to watch Pompey play Blackpool. Being told at Sandown Railway Station that all ferries were cancelled, they travelled to Ryde in the hope that the fog may have cleared sufficiently for service to have resumed. The fog was even more dense at Ryde, but they heard a man offering trips to Portsmouth in a small boat and took up his offer, paying five times the amount of the normal fare. They reached Fratton Park at half-time, squeezing in at the back of the Fratton End, but could only see as far as the halfway line. They arrived home at midnight after seeing half a match on half a pitch.

BESIDE THE SEASIDE

The reason Ernie Butler was the Pompey goalkeeper throughout the club's glory years of 1948-1950 was that Portsmouth was by the sea. Attracting the attention of league clubs with his displays for Bath City, he finally had the choice of three clubs, but chose Pompey because he loved the sea air.

A HAPPY EASTER

It was certainly a happy Easter for Pompey in 1957. They entered the holiday programme in 21st place, four points behind Cardiff City with only four matches to play, but gained maximum points from their three games. A Peter Harris goal was enough to beat Cardiff at Fratton Park on Good Friday, and the next day at Fratton, Wolverhampton Wanderers were beaten 1-0 thanks to a goal by Ron Newman. On Easter Monday, Pompey travelled to Ninian Park for the return game with Cardiff, and Peter Harris scored twice in a 2-0 win. This meant that relegation would be decided on the final day of the season, and although Pompey lost 1-0 at home to West Bromwich Albion, Cardiff's 3-2 defeat at home to Manchester United meant the Welshmen were relegated to the Second Division with Charlton Athletic.

FIRST LEAGUE WIN AT ST ANDREW'S

It took Pompey 21 years before they beat Birmingham City at St Andrew's. They first played on the ground on 7 April 1928, and were beaten 2-0. By the time Birmingham were relegated in 1939, Pompey had taken one point off them in 12 visits. After the war, Pompey lost at St Andrew's in one First Division match and two third round FA Cup ties before they claimed their first away victory over Birmingham, winning 3-0 on 8 October 1949.

CHIEF SCOUT AT 28

Andy Awford became the youngest chief scout in Pompey history when on 1 December 2000 he was appointed at the age of 28. Awford, who was only 16 when he made the first of 372 Pompey appearances, had suffered two broken legs during his career and decided to retire from the game.

MANLEY INJURY

In December 1973, worried by the number of goals being conceded, Pompey chairman John Deacon made £200,000 available for the club to sign central defenders Paul Went from Fulham and Malcolm Manley from Leicester City. In the 15th match of their partnership, Manley suffered a serious knee injury during an away game with Notts County, and despite featuring in one more Pompey match, he was forced to retire.

THEY'VE ALL PLAYED IN GOAL

The following goalkeepers have all represented Pompey in league matches: Ned Robson, Tommy Newton, Dan McPhail, Sandy Kane, John Jarvie, Ben Lewis, Jock Gilfillan, Jock McHugh, Cyrille Jolliffe, Bob Muir, Jimmy Strong, Harry Walker, Jim Hall, Ernie Butler, Ron Humpston, Maurice Leather, Charlie Dore, Norman Uprichard, Ted Platt, Mervyn Gill, Alan Barnett, Ray Drinkwater, Fred Brown, Dick Beattie, Bob Gaddes, John Milkins, Peter Shearing, John Armstrong, Ray Potter, Jim Standen, Graham Horn, Ron Tilsed, David Best, Phil Figgins, Grahame Lloyd, Steve Middleton, Alan Knight, Peter Mellor, Andy Gosney, Brian Horne, Mart Poom, Jimmy Glass, Aaron Flahavan, Andy Petterson, Russell Hoult, Chris Tardif, Dave Beasant, Sasa Ilic, Yoshi Kawaguchi, Shaka Hislop, Harald Wapenaar, Pavel Srnicek, Kostas Chalkias, Jamie Ashdown, Sander Westerveld, Dean Kiely, David James, Asmir Begovic, Stephen Henderson, Simon Eastwood, Mikkel Andersen, Alex Cisak, John Sullivan, Phil Smith and Trevor Carson.

ONLY REID

Duggie Reid was the only Pompey player to score a hat-trick in the Football League in the first five seasons after World War II. He hit seven trebles in all, the first in the penultimate game of the 1946/47 season as Pompey beat Chelsea 4-1 at Stamford Bridge. He netted his first treble at Fratton Park in a 4-0 victory over Grimsby Town in November 1947, then scored all three goals in a home win over Charlton Athletic in September 1948. During 1949/50, he recorded three hat-tricks. His first of the season came in a 7-0 thrashing of Everton at Fratton Park in September 1949, and there were three more in a 4-0 win at home to Chelsea in March 1950. His most important hat-trick came on the last day of the 1949/50 campaign, for the League Championship was decided when Pompey beat Aston Villa 5-1 at home. Reid's final hat-trick came in September 1950, against Stoke City who were beaten 5-1 on their visit to Fratton Park.

TOP GOALSCORERS II

Pompey's top league goalscorers from 1946/47 to 1958/59 were:

1946/47	Duggie Reid	29
1947/48	Duggie Reid	14
1948/49	Peter Harris	18
1949/50	Ike Clarke	17
1950/51	Duggie Reid	21
1951/52	Duggie Reid	16
1952/53	Peter Harris	23
1953/54	Peter Harris	20
1954/55	Johnny Gordon	13
1955/56	Peter Harris	23
1956/57	Peter Harris	13
1957/58	Peter Harris	18
1958/59	Ron Saunders	21

SCOULAR MAKES FA CUP HISTORY

In 1946, Jimmy Scoular made history by becoming the first player to play for two different clubs in the same FA Cup competition. He played in Pompey's 1-0 defeat away to Birmingham City in the third round first leg, having appeared for Gosport Borough in a preliminary round. The only other player to later play for two different clubs was Stan Crowther, who was allowed to represent Manchester United in the 1958 FA Cup Final, since United had lost so many players in the Munich air disaster. He had earlier played for Aston Villa.

JIMMY DICKINSON

The name Jimmy Dickinson is the most famous in the history of Portsmouth Football Club. Universally known as Gentleman Jim, he was never spoken to by a referee, let alone booked or sent off in a 20-year career that won him two Football League Championship medals, a Third Division Championship medal and 48 England caps. He was born in Alton, and attended the town's Senior Boys' School. He was spotted playing football in the playground there by teacher Eddie Lever, who would one day be his manager at Fratton Park. In 1943, Lever recommended to Jack Tinn that Dickinson be given a trial, and on 1 May 1943, Dickinson played in a friendly against Reading that Pompey won 4-2. The press reported that he "gave a good account of himself." When League football resumed in 1946, Pompey's first opponents were Blackburn Rovers at Fratton Park, and Dickinson played at right-half in a 3-1 win. He soon switched to left-half, and held the position for the rest of the season, missing just two games. He was ever-present throughout 1947/48, and missed only three matches over the next two seasons, both of which ended in League titles for the club. His contribution to the team's success could have been overlooked compared to the skills of other stars in the side such as Jimmy Scoular, Peter Harris, and Len Phillips, but it was Dickinson who displayed supreme consistency. He was appointed captain in 1953, but the great side was breaking up, and he found himself leading a team that each year took a step closer to Division Two. The club was relegated in 1959, and two years later slipped into the Third Division. Dickinson led the club back to Division Two at the first attempt, and played his 764th and final league match on his 40th birthday at Northampton Town. Pompey drew 1-1 to avoid being relegated back to the Third Division. He took the job as Public Relations Officer at Fratton Park, and was later appointed secretary, but in 1977 became manager of the club. After Pompey drew 1-1 at Barnsley on 30 March 1979, he suffered a major heart attack in the dressing-room and resigned two months later on health grounds. He died on 8 November 1982, aged 57.

PROPERTY DEVELOPERS

On 27 November 2003, the club revealed plans to build hundreds of homes. It was announced that the £90m scheme would pay for the £36m ground to be built alongside it on the existing Fratton Park.

GREAT COMEBACK

One of the most exciting Pompey comebacks took place at Fratton Park on 10 September 1955. Trailing 3-0 to Bolton Wanderers with 13 minutes to go, Pat Neil pulled a goal back, then Peter Harris scored twice to earn the Blues an unlikely point.

FRIEND NOT FOE

Marc-Vivien Foe was on the brink of signing for Pompey when he collapsed and died of a heart attack during Cameroon's match against Colombia in Lyon on 26 June 2003.

UNITED STATES HALL OF FAME

In 1967, former Pompey player Ron Newman moved to the United States of America to play for Atlanta Chiefs in the National Professional Soccer League. He later took over as manager of Dallas Tornado, Fort Lauderdale, San Diego Sockers and Kansas City Wizards and achieved success with all four clubs. In 1992, he was inducted into the United States Soccer Hall of Fame.

THREE OFF

Pompey had three players sent off in a Second Division match against Sheffield United at Bramall Lane on 13 December 1986. Billy Gilbert saw red for dissent, Kevin Dillon was sent off for two bookings, and Mick Tait received his marching orders for an off-the-ball incident involving Blades' Peter Beagrie, who was also ordered off.

POMPEY HUMBLE THE CHAMPS

On 3 September 1955, Pompey produced one of their greatest performances of all time when they defeated reigning League champions Chelsea 5-1 at Stamford Bridge. Peter Harris lobbed in Pompey's first goal on 20 minutes, and a superb shot by Jackie Henderson doubled the lead before Derek Rees slotted home the third in the 42nd minute. Rees made it four after the break, but with seven minutes to go, Chelsea's Seamus O'Connell pulled a goal back. Peter Harris restored Pompey's four-goal advantage, and Pat Neil went close to grabbing a sixth goal.

TOP GOALKEEPERS

The five goalkeepers who have made the most league appearances for Pompey are:

Alan Knight......................683
John Milkins....................344
Jock Gilfillan 330
Ernie Butler 222
Norman Uprichard 162

GOING DOWN II

Two years after suffering relegation from the First Division in 1959, Pompey slipped into Division Three. They failed to win in 14 league and cup matches, from Boxing Day 1960 until Leeds United were beaten 3-1 at Fratton Park on 18 March 1961. Manager Freddie Cox was sacked during the season, and caretaker-manager Bill Thompson made two inspired signings, in the shape of Allan Brown and former Fratton favourite Johnny Gordon, before George Smith took over the reins. The team collected ten points from their last nine games, but a 3-0 defeat away to Middlesbrough consigned them to relegation.

Football League Division Two 1960-61

	Pl	W	D	L	F	A	W	D	L	F	A	Pts
1 Ipswich Town	42	15	3	3	55	24	11	4	6	45	31	59
2 Sheffield United	42	16	2	3	49	22	10	4	7	32	29	58
3 Liverpool	42	14	5	2	49	21	7	5	9	38	37	52
4 Norwich City	42	15	3	3	46	20	5	6	10	24	33	49
5 Middlesbrough	42	13	6	2	44	20	5	6	10	39	54	48
6 Sunderland	42	12	5	4	47	24	5	8	8	28	36	47
7 Swansea Town	42	14	4	3	49	26	6	3	12	28	47	47
8 Southampton	42	12	4	5	57	35	5	6	10	27	46	44
9 Scunthorpe United	42	9	8	4	39	25	4	9	8	30	39	43
10 Charlton Athletic	42	12	3	6	60	42	4	8	9	37	49	43
11 Plymouth Argyle	42	13	4	4	52	32	4	4	13	29	50	42
12 Derby County	42	9	6	6	46	35	6	4	11	34	45	40
13 Luton Town	42	13	5	3	48	27	0	8	13	23	52	39
14 Leeds United	42	7	7	7	41	38	7	3	11	34	45	38
15 Rotherham United	42	9	7	5	37	24	3	6	12	28	40	37
16 Brighton & Hove A.	42	9	6	6	33	26	5	3	13	28	49	37
17 Bristol Rovers	42	13	4	4	52	35	2	3	16	21	57	37
18 Stoke City	42	9	6	6	39	26	3	6	12	12	33	36
19 Leyton Orient	42	10	5	6	31	29	4	3	14	24	49	36
20 Huddersfield Town	42	7	6	8	33	33	6	3	12	29	38	35
21 POMPEY	42	10	6	5	38	27	1	5	15	26	64	33
22 Lincoln City	42	5	4	12	30	43	3	4	14	18	52	24

LEVERETT HOUSE

In 1958, Pompey opened a hostel for young players and named it Leverett House, after Sydney Leverett who had been a director of the club since 1912. The house, approximately two miles from Fratton Park, was on four floors, and housed 15 players plus wardens' accommodation. Duggie Reid and his wife Mary were wardens of the home until it was sold in 1965, when the club made the decision to abolish the youth and reserve set-up.

DUNCAN GILCHRIST

Duncan Gilchrist died after heading a ball in a reserve match at Gosport in March 1924. The coroner's verdict was accidental death, so as Portsmouth Football Club had no legal claim on the Football League Insurance Fund, the League made an *ex gratia* payment of £100 to the directors, with instructions to administer the sum as they thought fit. It was agreed at a board meeting that the money be sent to the player's mother.

THEY COULDN'T BELIEVE IT

Tottenham Hotspur supporters thought the scoreline should have been the opposite way round in January 1937 when they heard that their team had beaten Pompey 5-0 at Fratton Park in the FA Cup third round. Pompey were then seventh in the First Division, while Spurs occupied 11th place in Division Two.

WHAT A GUY

Guy Whittingham scored hat-tricks for Pompey in consecutive FA Cup ties. In the third round in January 1991, he scored three times in a 5-0 victory at non-league Barnet, and bagged four second-half goals in the fourth round as AFC Bournemouth were beaten 5-1.

TWO APPEARANCE RECORDS

Jimmy Dickinson held two appearance records when he retired from the game in 1965. His 764 games were a Football League record, and they were also played for one club. The overall record was beaten in 1975, when Terry Paine turned out for Hereford United in their Third Division home fixture with Peterborough United. John Trollope overtook the one-club record when he played his 765th league game for Swindon Town at home to Carlisle United in October 1980. However, under different circumstances, Dickinson might still have held the one-club appearance record. In his day, international matches often clashed with Football League fixtures, and he played for England on 12 occasions when Pompey would have been glad of his services.

FUNDRAISING FRIENDLY

On 17 August 1982 Pompey and Coventry City drew 1-1 in a friendly at Fratton Park. The match was staged to raise money for the South Atlantic Fund in memory of men whose lives were lost when HMS *Coventry* was sunk during the Falklands crisis. A crowd of 3,066 watched the match and over £5,000 was raised.

BEST 4 X 4

Four players have scored four goals against Pompey in the Football League at Fratton Park.

Harry Kirk
03/03/1924.........Pompey 3 Exeter 4................... Division Three (South)
David Halliday
18/02/1928.........Pompey 3 Sunderland 5 .... Division One
Alec Gardiner
21/02/1934.........Pompey 3 Leicester City 5...... Division One
Bobby Davidson
12/12/1936.........Pompey 1 Arsenal 5 .... Division One

WIN OVER THE BABES

Pompey's last match against the Busby Babes before the Munich air disaster of February 1958 ended in a 3-0 win at Old Trafford. On 19 October 1957, Jackie Henderson gave Pompey an early lead, then two goals in the last three minutes of the first half by Ron Newman and Peter Harris secured a great victory over the reigning League champions. Four of the Manchester United side that day, Mark Jones, Eddie Colman, Billy Whelan, and David Pegg, perished at Munich.

POP GROUP

Two Pompey juniors were part of a Portsmouth pop group at the beginning of the 1960s. Bobby Ridley was a singer, and Bill Williams played the guitar. The group performed regularly at hospitals and youth clubs in the Portsmouth area.

LONG WAIT FOR LIVE MATCH

Pompey were shown live on television for the first time when they faced Liverpool in the FA Cup semi-final at Highbury on 5 April 1992.

FA CUP WINNERS

Listed below are the teams who won the FA Cup after beating Pompey in the competition.

1924.........Newcastle United ....Round 1
1929.........Bolton Wanderers.............Final
1931.........West Bromwich Albion....Round 5
1934.........Manchester City...............Final
1952.........Newcastle United ....Round 6
1967.........Tottenham Hotspur..........Round 4
1968.........West Bromwich Albion....Round 5
1971.........Arsenal..............................Round 4
1991.........Tottenham Hotspur..........Round 5
1992.........Liverpool ....Semi-final
1997.........Chelsea.............................Round 6
2006 ....Liverpool ....Round 4
2010.........Chelsea.............................Final

TINDALL'S VISION

In 1966, Ron Tindall devised a new points plan, and submitted the system to the Football League. The idea was that the team that led at half-time would receive two points, as would the winners of the second period. One point each would be given to sides that drew the first half, second half or overall. He received no reply from the Football League, but the system was used in a Western Australia Summer Night Series in 1978.

KENNEDY FINED

In August 1987, Pompey midfielder Mick Kennedy was fined £5,000 – the heaviest fine in the history of English football to that date. He appeared at Lancaster Gate on a charge of bringing the game into disrepute, following two controversial articles that appeared in *The Sun* newspaper. In the articles, Kennedy claimed that he was the hardest man in soccer and enjoyed hurting opponents. He also boasted he "took no prisoners", and accused top players of being chicken.

FOUR ON HOME DEBUT

On 20 March 1925, Harry Havelock scored four goals on his home debut for Pompey. He had made two appearances in away games before Pompey faced Nottingham Forest in the Second Division at Fratton Park, and he scored a first-half hat-trick, later adding another goal as Pompey won 5-1.

WE ARE THE CHAMPIONS III

Pompey won the Third Division championship in 1961/62 at the first attempt. They remained unbeaten until losing 2-1 away to Notts County in their 13th match, and their experienced side won the league by five points, making sure of the title by beating Watford 2-1 at home on Easter Monday. Skipper Jimmy Dickinson was the only ever-present in the side, and Ron Saunders, who scored 26 League goals, topped the goalscoring charts for the fourth successive season.

Football League Division Three 1961/62

	Pl	W	D	L	F	A	W	D	L	F	A	Pts
1 POMPEY	46	15	6	2	48	23	12	5	6	39	24	65
2 Grimsby Town	46	18	3	2	49	18	10	3	10	31	38	62
3 Bournemouth	46	14	8	1	42	18	7	9	7	27	27	59
4 Queens Park Rangers	46	15	3	5	65	31	9	8	6	46	42	59
5 Peterborough	46	16	0	7	60	38	10	6	7	47	44	58
6 Bristol City	46	15	3	5	56	27	8	5	10	38	45	54
7 Reading	46	14	5	4	46	24	8	4	11	31	42	53
8 Northampton Town	46	12	6	5	52	24	8	5	10	33	33	51
9 Swindon Town	46	11	8	4	48	26	6	7	10	30	45	49
10 Hull City	46	15	2	6	43	20	5	6	12	24	34	48
11 Bradford Park Avenue	46	13	5	5	47	27	7	2	14	33	51	47
12 Port Vale	46	12	4	7	41	23	5	7	11	24	35	45
13 Notts County	46	14	5	4	44	23	3	4	16	23	51	43
14 Coventry City	46	11	6	6	38	26	5	5	13	26	45	43
15 Crystal Palace	46	8	8	7	50	41	6	6	11	33	39	42
16 Southend United	46	10	7	6	31	26	3	9	11	26	43	42
17 Watford	46	10	9	4	37	26	4	4	15	26	48	41
18 Halifax Town	46	9	5	9	34	35	6	5	12	28	49	40
19 Shrewsbury Town	46	8	7	8	46	37	5	5	13	27	47	38
20 Barnsley	46	9	6	8	45	41	4	6	13	26	54	38
21 Torquay United	46	9	4	10	48	44	6	2	15	28	56	36
22 Lincoln City	46	4	10	9	31	43	5	7	11	26	44	35
23 Brentford	46	11	3	9	34	29	2	5	16	19	64	34
24 Newport County	46	6	5	12	29	38	1	3	19	17	64	22

EUROPEAN CHAMPION

Tony Barton is the only former Pompey player to manage a European Cup-winning side. He achieved the feat in 1982, when his Aston Villa side beat Bayern Munich 1-0 in Rotterdam.

POMPEY TRIED FOR SIR ALF

After John Mortimore was suspended as Pompey manager in September 1974, chairman John Deacon offered the job to Sir Alf Ramsey. He had been sacked by England earlier in the year, and told Mr Deacon that he was not yet ready to re-enter football management.

WEMBLEY RECORD

When Wembley Stadium was bulldozed to make way for the new design, former Pompey manager Tony Adams had made the most appearances in the stadium's history. He had played on the famous turf on 60 occasions – 36 for England and 24 for Arsenal.

ALL IN ONE HALF

When Pompey beat Swindon Town 5-0 at Fratton Park on 19 September 1964, all the goals were scored before half-time. On 3 October 1970 Pompey thrashed Watford 5-0 at home with all the goals coming in the second half.

THE POMPEY SWAP SHOP

In September 1966, manager George Smith wrote to clubs asking if they would be interested in doing business with Pompey in the form of player-exchange deals. With the club still owing money to two clubs for players bought months previously, there was no cash to bring in new faces.

ROUND WITH THE HAT

In November 1975, more than a thousand people attended a public meeting at Portsmouth Guildhall, as chairman John Deacon spelled out the financial plight of the club. A collection of over £1,000 was raised.

EARLY TWO-GOAL LEAD

The earliest Pompey have taken a two-goal lead is four minutes. This occurred on 27 October 1962, when Tony Barton shot them ahead in the second minute of their Second Division home clash with Bury. David Dodson followed up with a goal two minutes later. That was the end of Pompey's scoring for the day – they won the match 2-1.

DEATH OF BOB KEARNEY

In February 1931, Portsmouth Football Club were shocked by the death of centre-half Bob Kearney. Pompey were due to play West Bromwich Albion at Fratton Park in the FA Cup fifth round, and Kearney had not missed a match all season, but was one of several players doubtful for the match because of an outbreak of influenza at the club. All the players declared themselves fit to play, but were beaten 1-0 by their Second Division opponents. Far more seriously, Kearney was taken seriously ill after the game, and died a week later aged 27. The club instantly set up an appeal fund for the player's widow and child, and when it closed in April 1931, it had raised almost £1,700.

MOATS AT FRATTON PARK

In 1974, Pompey were the first club to build moats behind both goals following the recommendation of Sports Minister Dennis Howell. This followed a series of pitch invasions throughout the country.

EARLY SENDING-OFF

The second Football League match to be played at Fratton Park produced a sending-off. Harry Higginbotham of Luton Town was ordered off after fouling Pompey's Joe Turner in a Division Three (South) fixture in September 1920, which Pompey won 3-0.

NORTH STAND SEATS

During the 1951 close season, 4,226 seats were installed in the North Stand. Three-quarters of these were available as season-tickets.

DOUBLES

No team did the double over Pompey during the First Division title-winning season of 2002/03, but they achieved it against nine clubs. They were Bradford City, Burnley, Derby County, Gillingham, Grimsby Town, Millwall, Nottingham Forest, Rotherham United and Walsall.

ONLY TWO KEEPERS

No goalkeeper other than Alan Knight and Andy Gosney played in goal for Pompey between August 1981 and August 1993. Knight was chosen as first-choice custodian at the start of the 1981/82 campaign, and Gosney was his deputy for all of those 12 years. Gosney was transferred to Birmingham City in the summer of 1993, and his place was taken by Brian Horne, who made his Pompey debut in a 1-1 draw away to Grimsby Town in August of that year.

WORLD CUP GOALKEEPERS

Two former Pompey goalkeepers took part in the 2006 World Cup finals in Germany, Yoshikatsu Kawaguchi for Japan and Shaka Hislop for Trinidad & Tobago. Hislop, at 37, was the oldest player in the tournament.

FIRST FOUR-FIGURE RECEIPTS

The FA Cup first round tie between Pompey and Manchester United on 12 January 1912 attracted a crowd of 24,329 to Fratton Park, and gate receipts – £1,101/10/0 – reached four figures for the first time. The match ended in a 2-2 draw, and Pompey won the replay 2-1.

BEST SINCE 1956

Pompey finished their first season in the Premiership (2003/04) in 13th, their best position since 1956, when they came 12th in the First Division.

DURABLE BILL

Right-back Bill Probert was the only player to appear in all the club's matches of the Southern League championship-winning season (1919/20) and the first Football League campaign (1920/21).

CAR ACCIDENT LEADS TO SIGNING A LEGEND

Mr Fred Prescott was on holiday in the west of England in 1923 when he met with a car accident. Delayed by this, he went to watch Frome Town in a Somerset League match, and saw Billy Haines score six goals in the home side's 8-0 win. He immediately alerted Pompey manager John McCartney, who, after watching him play only once, offered Haines professional forms. Haines went on to score 119 goals for the club, and was top scorer for five consecutive seasons during the 1920s.

GOING CONTINENTAL

In 1973, the club decided to break from tradition and drop their royal blue colours in favour of a continental-style strip. A competition was held to design the new strip, and the winner was Mr Bob Ingram, who came up with a white shirt with two vertical stripes, blue shorts, and white socks with blue and red tops. Many supporters were unhappy with the idea, and wanted to see a return to the old blue and white. When the club was relegated to the Third Division, some even blamed the new strip. The favoured blue shirts and white shorts were re-introduced for the 1976/77 campaign, but to prove the continental-style strip was not to blame for the club's ill fortune, Pompey were relegated to the Fourth Division the following season.

FIRST SUNDAY MATCH

Pompey's first Sunday match was at home to Orient in the FA Cup fourth round on 27 January 1974. A bumper crowd of 32,838 watched a 0-0 draw.

ALBERT MCCANN

Albert McCann gave sterling service to Pompey from 1962 until 1974. After spells with Coventry City and Luton Town, he came to Hampshire in August 1962, and played at inside-forward for the first five years at Fratton Park. Always hard working, he possessed a fine shot and scored 98 goals for Pompey, including a hat-trick in a 3-3 draw at Bristol City in October 1966. Throughout the 1967/68 campaign, he was employed in a wider role, but still managed to fire in 16 goals, his best ever tally, making him the side's leading scorer for the third successive season. In his later years with the club, he was used more in midfield, and was extremely capable of blotting out a dangerous opponent when handed a marking job. He left Fratton Park in 1974, but is still a regular sight at Pompey's home matches.

STOLEN GLOVES

During Pompey's 1-1 draw against Huddersfield Town at Leeds Road on 9 October 1982, Pompey goalkeeper Alan Knight had gloves worth £100 stolen from his goal.

BRIEF STAY

Lee Chapman was a Pompey player for five weeks. Jim Smith won the race with West Ham to sign Chapman from Leeds United in August 1993, and the striker scored twice in the season's opener – a 3-2 defeat at Oxford United. He was sent off in his first home match, and was clearly not happy at Fratton Park, so Smith alerted his West Ham counterpart Billy Bonds. By mid-September, Chapman had joined the Hammers for £250,000 – the sum Pompey had paid Leeds United.

FIRST GOAL FOR TEN YEARS

Justin Edinburgh was feeling ill before Pompey's First Division match at home to Sheffield United in 2001 but decided to play. In the 40th minute, he scored the only goal of the game – his first for ten years.

FIRST SUBSTITUTE GOALKEEPER

Aaron Flahavan was Pompey's first substitute goalkeeper. Alan Knight was sent off for carrying the ball outside his penalty area in the FA Cup fourth round tie at home to Leicester City in January 1995, and Flahavan took to the field for his first taste of first-team action.

ALAN KNIGHT

Alan Knight holds the Pompey goalkeeper appearance record, and his 683 league appearances make him second only to Jimmy Dickinson. Alan grew up in Balham, south London, and as a youngster trained with Queens Park Rangers. A week's trial at Fratton Park was organised, and when it was over he was offered schoolboy forms, which he signed on his 14th birthday. At 15, he began to play for Pompey Youth in the South East Counties League, and his displays attracted the scouts of big clubs, but Knight promised he would sign apprentice forms on his 16th birthday, and duly did so. Knight made his first-team bow at Rotherham United on the final day of the 1977/78 season, and Pompey, already relegated to Division Four, won 1-0. Coincidentally, it was manager Jimmy Dickinson who handed young Knight his debut. He spent three seasons as understudy to Peter Mellor, and eventually was made first-choice keeper at the start of 1981/82. He spent the next 15 years as the regular Pompey goalkeeper and displayed remarkable consistency. He won a Third Division championship medal in 1982/83, and was part of the side that clinched promotion to Division One in 1986/87. When Pompey began their first season back in the top flight, away to Oxford United on 15 August 1987, Knight made history by being the first Pompey player to appear in all four divisions. In January 1997, he made his 601st League appearance for the club against Grimsby Town, thus breaking Peter Bonetti's record of 600 games for Chelsea. Pompey's first match of the new millennium – a 2-0 defeat away to Norwich City – was Knight's 683rd and last, and he remained at Fratton Park in a coaching capacity until 2005.

FIRST MATCH IN DIVISION ONE

On 27 August 1927, Sunderland hit back from three goals down in front of 35,106 at Roker Park to deny Pompey a victory in their first match in Division One. Freddie Cook gave Pompey a dream start, flashing a shot high into the net on four minutes, and Jerry Mackie pounced to double the advantage. Billy Haines shot through a crowd of players on 24 minutes, but Bobby Marshall pulled a goal back for the home side before half-time. After the break, Dave Halliday scored with a cross-shot, and with Sunderland going all out for the equaliser, Billy Moffat planted the ball into his own net when attempting to clear. The Pompey team was: Dan McPhail, George Clifford, Jock McColgan, Reg Davies, Harry Foxall, Billy Moffat, Fred Forward, Jerry Mackie, Billy Haines, Dave Watson, Freddie Cook.

EARLY FRIENDLY

The earliest Pompey have played a pre-season friendly was in 2002, when they hosted Celtic at Fratton Park on 10 July. A crowd of 11,553 saw Celtic win 3-2, with Richard Hughes and Linvoy Primus scoring for the Blues.

GOING DOWN III

In 1976, Pompey were relegated to the Third Division after spending 14 consecutive seasons in Division Two. In a disappointing campaign the team only managed four home wins all season, the first not coming until January. A great escape looked possible when they won four matches out of six between mid-February and mid-March, but their fate was sealed on 6 April when a last-minute goal by Mick Channon earned Southampton a 1-0 win at Fratton Park. Leading goalscorer for the campaign was Norman Piper with 11.

League Division Two 1975/76

	Pl	W	D	L	F	A	W	D	L	F	A	Pts
1 Sunderland	42	19	2	0	48	10	5	6	10	19	26	56
2 Bristol City	42	11	7	3	34	14	8	8	5	25	21	53
3 West Bromwich Albion	42	10	9	2	29	12	10	4	7	21	21	53
4 Bolton Wanderers	42	12	5	4	36	14	8	7	6	28	24	52
5 Notts County	42	11	6	4	33	13	8	5	8	27	28	49
6 Southampton	42	18	2	1	49	16	3	5	13	17	34	49
7 Luton Town	42	13	6	2	38	15	6	4	11	23	36	48
8 Nottingham Forest	42	13	1	7	34	18	4	11	6	21	22	46
9 Charlton Athletic	42	11	5	5	40	34	4	7	10	21	38	42
10 Blackpool	42	9	9	3	26	22	4	6	11	14	27	42
11 Chelsea	42	7	9	5	25	20	5	7	9	28	34	40
12 Fulham	42	9	8	4	27	14	4	6	11	18	33	40
13 Orient	42	10	6	5	21	12	3	8	10	16	27	40
14 Hull City	42	9	5	7	29	23	5	6	10	16	26	39
15 Blackburn Rovers	42	8	6	7	27	22	4	8	9	18	28	38
16 Plymouth Argyle	42	13	4	4	36	20	0	8	13	12	34	38
17 Oldham Athletic	42	11	8	2	37	24	2	4	15	20	44	38
18 Bristol Rovers	42	7	9	5	20	15	4	7	10	18	35	38
19 Carlisle United	42	9	8	4	29	22	3	5	13	16	37	37
20 Oxford United	42	7	7	7	23	25	4	4	13	16	34	33
21 York City	42	8	3	10	28	34	2	5	14	11	37	28
22 POMPEY	42	4	6	11	15	23	5	1	15	17	38	25

DICKINSON STAYS

Looking for a centre-forward in the autumn of 1947, Pompey manager Bob Jackson was ready to smash Pompey's transfer record by spending £17,000 on Chelsea's Tommy Lawton. Chelsea would only allow Lawton to join Pompey if Jackson was prepared to let Jimmy Dickinson move to Stamford Bridge, so the interest in Lawton was immediately dropped.

PRICELESS FIRST GOAL FOR BENJANI

In January 2006, Harry Redknapp paid £4.5m for striker Benjani Mwaruwari from Auxerre. He failed to score in 14 matches, but broke his duck in his 15th appearance, away to Wigan Athletic. The goal cancelled out Henri Camara's earlier strike, and when Benjani's goalbound header was handled by Gary Teale, Matt Taylor converted the penalty to earn Pompey the win that made them safe from relegation.

FLEWIN SKIPPERED THE CHAMPIONS

Reg Flewin took over as skipper from Guy Wharton early in the 1946/47 campaign, and captained Pompey to their two successive League Championships in 1948/49 and 1949/50. He only missed three games in 1948/49, but was not so lucky the following year. An appendix operation caused him to miss a run of ten matches, and an eye injury meant him sitting out six end-of-season games, but he was able to return to lead the side to a 5-1 victory at home to Aston Villa and so clinch the title for a second time.

LATE END TO SEASON

The 1946/47 campaign suffered numerous postponements owing to atrocious weather conditions, and because of this, the season ended much later than usual. Pompey's final game ended in a 2-1 defeat to Derby County at Fratton Park on 31 May. This was the latest Pompey have ever played a Football League fixture.

NOT EVEN AROUND

Alan Knight's last match for Pompey was a 2-0 defeat at Norwich City on 3 January 2000. In the side that day was Jason Crowe, who hadn't been born when Knight made his league debut at Rotherham United on 29 April 1978.

THREE AT THE WRONG END

Noel Blake scored three own goals during the 1984/85 season. The goals assisted Wimbledon, Blackburn Rovers and Brighton and Hove Albion.

THE FIRST FA CUP SUBSTITUTE

Alex Wilson was Pompey's first substitute in the FA Cup competition. In the third round tie against Hull City at Boothferry Park on 28 January 1967, he replaced Albert McCann, and was called upon again in the replay at Fratton Park, when Bobby Kellard was carried off after only 15 minutes.

ANTI-CLIMAX

After a 28-year absence, Pompey were finally promoted to the First Division on 5 May 1987, less than 48 hours short of the 60th anniversary of their elevation to the top flight in 1927. However, promotion was something of an anti-climax, as Pompey were not involved in a match. Oldham Athletic had a chance of sneaking into the promotion frame, but their 2-0 defeat away to Shrewsbury Town meant Pompey had reached Division One. There was still a chance that Pompey could finish as champions, but on the last day of the season, leaders Derby County beat Plymouth Argyle 4-2 at the Baseball Ground while Pompey slumped to a 2-1 defeat at home to Sheffield United.

TWO OFF IN SEASON OPENER

Pompey's 1996/97 season got off to a bad start. Beaten 3-1 at Bradford City, they also had Andy Awford and Aaron Flahavan sent off.

ALAIN PERRIN

Frenchman Alain Perrin was Pompey's first foreign manager. He began his coaching career with AS Nancy in 1983, as junior to Arsène Wenger. His first management appointment was with non-league Troyes AC, and he led the club to three promotions in six years and qualification for the UEFA Cup. He was sacked by the French club in January 2004, and then had a short spell with Al-Ain in the United Arab Emirates before taking over at Fratton Park in April 2005 from Velimir Zajec, who had been in temporary charge since the resignation of Harry Redknapp. Perrin's first match at the helm brought a 4-2 victory over Charlton Athletic at Fratton Park, and two weeks later Pompey thrashed Southampton at home 4-1. But only three months into the new season, Perrin was sacked. He had been in charge for just 20 League matches, and his record was four wins, six draws and ten defeats.

POMPEY COLOURS

Pompey's first colours were salmon-pink shirts and white shorts, but they changed to white shirts and dark blue shorts in 1909. It was not until 1912 that they introduced the famous blue shirts and white shorts.

SIX OR MORE

Pompey have scored six or more in a match 16 times since World War II:

```
14/04/1947 .... Division One ............. Pompey 6  Middlesbrough 1
25/09/1947 .... Division One ............. Pompey 6  Sheffield United 0
08/01/1949 .... FA Cup third round .. Pompey 7  Stockport County 0
10/09/1949 ..... Division One ............. Pompey 7  Everton 0
03/02/1951 ..... Division One ............. Pompey 6  Everton 3
09/10/1954 ..... Division One ............. Pompey 6  Sheffield United 2
04/12/1954 ..... Division One ............. Pompey 6  West Bromwich Albion 1
19/12/1959 ..... Division Two ............. Pompey 6  Middlesbrough 3
23/10/1971 ..... Division Two ............. Pompey 6  Fulham 3
25/08/1979 ..... Division Four ............ Pompey 6  Scunthorpe United 1
29/12/1979 ..... Division Four ............ Pompey 6  Northampton Town 1
14/03/1992 ..... Division Two ............. Pompey 6  Millwall 1
08/02/2003 .... Division One ............. Pompey 6  Derby County 2
08/11/2003 .... Premiership ............... Pompey 6  Leeds United 1
29/09/2007 ..... Premiership ............... Pompey 7  Reading 4
```

PETER HARRIS AUCTION

More than £14,000 was raised at an auction in Nottingham in November 2002, when a host of items belonging to Peter Harris went on sale. The pair of boots Harris wore when he scored all five goals against Aston Villa in September 1958 went for £700, and a photograph of the 1948/49 League Championship winning team, signed by Field Marshal Montgomery of Alamein, was sold for £3,100.

LAST DAY ESCAPE III

3 May 1998, Division One, Bradford City 1 Pompey 3

Pompey's fate went to the last game for the second time in three years, and they nearly fell behind after 12 minutes when Nigel Pepper smacked a shot against the Pompey bar. Craig Ramage prodded the rebound against the post. News came through that Manchester City had scored at Stoke, and temporarily Pompey were in the bottom three, but Sammy Igoe forced Gary Walsh into a sliced clearance, and rolled the loose ball into the path of John Durnin to give Pompey the lead. Aaron Flahavan made two fine saves early in the second half before Igoe made it 2-0 with a firm finish. John Durnin then nodded in a third. Ramage netted a late consolation goal for the home side. **Pompey:** Aaron Flahavan, Robbie Pethick, Matthew Robinson, David Hillier, Dave Waterman, Andy Awford, Michalis Vlachos, Sammy Igoe, Mathias Svensson, John Durnin, Andy Thomson.

TOP GOALSCORERS IV

Pompey's top league goalscorers between 1976/77 and 1987/88 were:

1976/77	David Kemp............16	1982/83	Alan Biley...............23
1977/78	David Kemp............16	1983/84	Mark Hateley..........22
1978/79	Colin Garwood 15	1984/85	Neil Webb...............16
1979/80	Colin Garwood 17	1985/86	Nicky Morgan 14
1980/81	David Gregory........13	1986/87	Mick Quinn............22
1981/82	Billy Rafferty..........17	1987/88	Kevin Dillon 9

SPECIAL FRIENDLIES

The 1973/74 campaign was Pompey's 75th anniversary, and to mark the occasion, friendlies were played against Arsenal and Manchester United. A disappointing crowd of 8,850 saw Pompey beat Arsenal 2-1, but 17,228 watched a 1-1 draw when Manchester United were the visitors.

QUIET PURSUITS

Jimmy Scoular, Alex Mackie, and Bobby Kellard were three of the toughest competitors to wear the Pompey shirt, and yet off the field they involved themselves in gentle pastimes. Scoular was a keen bowls player, Mackie enjoyed fishing, and Kellard liked nothing better than to paint in watercolours.

THE POMPEY CHIMES

The Pompey Chimes is football's oldest anthem, and could never be forgotten by anyone who has heard a massed Fratton choir in full voice. "Play up Pompey – Pompey Play Up" is derived from the hour chime of the Portsmouth Guildhall clock. "Play up" was a catchphrase in the early 1900s, and it was at this time the Chimes were first heard at Fratton Park.

AWAY VICTORIES

Pompey gained 11 away victories as they stormed to the First Division title in 2002/03. They had only won ten matches on their travels over the previous four seasons.

BERESFORD INJURED ON DEBUT

John Beresford made his debut in a 2-2 draw at home to Watford on 27 March 1989, following a £300,000 move from Barnsley. He broke an ankle in the game and didn't feature any more that season.

100% FA CUP RECORD

Pompey have met four non-league teams in the FA Cup, and have won on each occasion.

15/01/1972	Third round	Boston United 0 Pompey 1
11/12/1976	Second round	Pompey 2 Minehead 1
26/11/1977	Second round	Pompey 3 Bideford Town 1
05/01/1991	Third round	Barnet 0 Pompey 5

GEORGE SMITH

George Smith managed Pompey from 1961 to 1970. He played for Brentford and Queens Park Rangers, and his coaching career began with Ipswich Town, before becoming manager of Eastbourne United. From 1952-54 he was the first professional manager of the England youth team. In 1956 he joined Sheffield United as coach, before taking charge of Sutton United, and then Crystal Palace. When he became manager of Pompey in 1961, the team were already heading for the Third Division, but the following season he took them straight back up as champions. He turned Pompey into pioneers by introducing a one-team scheme in the cause of economy, scrapping the reserve and youth policy and working with a basic squad of players. He was unable to take the club into the First Division – the highest position the team reached under his command was fifth in Division Two in 1967/68. He took the title General Manager in 1967, but stayed in charge of the team until 1970 – when Ron Tindall arrived. Smith, whose reign was often turbulent, made a rather muted departure in April 1971. He retired to Bodmin, Cornwall, where he died aged 68 in November 1983.

THE 1967/68 SEASON

Since Pompey were relegated from the First Division in 1959, they had not threatened a return until the 1967/68 campaign. They started well, going unbeaten until their tenth match, when they lost 4-1 away to Charlton Athletic. They went top of the table on 4 November, following a 3-0 home victory over Hull City, and moved three points clear of second-placed Blackpool when they defeated the Seasiders 3-1 at Fratton Park before a crowd of 35,038 on 2 December. The FA Cup also brought in big crowds to Fratton Park, with 44,050 attending the 1-0 win over Fulham in a fourth round replay, and 42,642 turning up for the fifth round tie against West Bromwich Albion, who beat Pompey 2-1. A week earlier, Pompey had lost their unbeaten home record, going down 2-1 to Birmingham City, and also lost Ray Pointer, who broke a leg. This seemed to knock the stuffing out of the side, and promotion slipped away, with the team eventually finishing in fifth position.

GOING DOWN IV

Five years after John Deacon took control of Portsmouth Football Club with the promise of great things, the club were relegated to the Fourth Division. During the 1977/78 season, Pompey suffered humiliating home defeats against Tranmere Rovers and Plymouth Argyle, and relegation was confirmed when they lost 2-0 at home to Oxford United on 4 April.

Football League Division Three 1977/78

	Pl	W	D	L	F	A	W	D	L	F	A	Pts
1 Wrexham	46	14	8	1	48	19	9	7	7	30	26	61
2 Cambridge United	46	19	3	1	49	11	4	9	10	23	40	58
3 Preston North End	46	16	5	2	48	19	4	11	8	15	19	56
4 Peterborough United	46	15	7	1	32	11	5	9	9	15	22	56
5 Chester City	46	14	8	1	41	24	5	8	10	18	32	54
6 Walsall	46	12	8	3	35	17	6	9	8	26	33	53
7 Gillingham	46	11	10	2	36	21	4	10	9	31	39	50
8 Colchester	46	10	11	2	36	16	5	7	11	19	28	48
9 Chesterfield	46	14	6	3	40	16	3	8	12	18	33	48
10 Swindon	46	12	7	4	40	22	4	9	10	27	38	48
11 Shrewsbury	46	11	7	5	42	23	5	8	10	21	34	47
12 Tranmere	46	13	7	3	39	19	3	8	12	18	33	47
13 Carlisle	46	10	9	4	28	26	2	14	7	27	33	47
14 Sheffield Wednesday	46	13	7	3	34	14	2	9	12	22	38	46
15 Bury	46	7	13	3	35	22	6	6	11	28	34	45
16 Lincoln City	46	10	8	5	30	26	5	7	11	18	35	45
17 Exeter City	46	11	8	4	38	18	4	6	13	19	41	44
18 Oxford United	46	11	10	2	33	21	2	4	17	26	46	40
19 Plymouth Argyle	46	7	8	8	26	28	4	9	10	28	40	39
20 Rotherham United	46	11	5	7	28	19	2	8	13	25	49	39
21 Port Vale	46	7	11	5	40	23	1	9	13	18	44	36
22 Bradford City	46	11	6	6	28	29	1	4	18	16	57	34
23 Hereford United	46	9	9	5	31	22	0	5	18	6	38	32
24 POMPEY	46	4	11	8	21	38	3	6	14	10	37	31

MANNION'S HAT-TRICKS

Middlesbrough and England inside-forward Wilf Mannion scored hat-tricks against Pompey at Ayresome Park before and after World War II. On 29 March 1939, his treble helped his side to an 8-2 victory, and on 23 November 1946 he grabbed another in a 3-3 draw. Mannion had a further reason to remember Pompey with fondness: he made his debut against them as a 17-year-old in a 0-0 draw at Ayresome Park on 26 January 1938.

ONLY FISH IN THE SEA

In 1965, in an effort to cut costs and because of the concern that so few young players were coming up through the ranks and making their mark in Pompey's first team, the club made the drastic decision of abandoning their youth and reserve teams and decided to concentrate solely on an 18-man squad. Manager George Smith made the statement that there were "only fish in the sea around Portsmouth". Ironically, one young player allowed to leave Fratton Park was Mick Mills, who went on to win 42 caps for England, and also captained his country on a few occasions.

VERSATILE FROGGATT

There are hardly two more contrasting positions than outside-left and centre-half, yet Jack Froggatt played for England in both. He won the first two of his 13 caps in the outside-left position, then appeared nine times at centre-half before returning to the wing.

THE RESERVES WON TOO!

Whilst Pompey were outplaying Wolves at Wembley to win the FA Cup in 1939, Pompey Reserves beat Tottenham Hotspur's second string 3-0 at White Hart Lane thanks to a second-half hat-trick by Jimmy Beattie. Appearing in the Pompey team were Reg Flewin, Phil Rookes, and Bill Hindmarsh, three men who would contribute greatly to the club's double League Championship success a decade later.

TOP FIVE HOME ATTENDANCES

26/02/1949	Derby County, FA Cup sixth round	51,385
01/10/1949	Wolverhampton Wanderers, Division One	50,248
15/02/1950	Manchester United, FA Cup fifth round replay	49,962
24/03/1951	Tottenham Hotspur, Division One	49,716
12/02/1949	Newport County, FA Cup fifth round	48,581

NEW SONG

In 1973, Pompey supporters were invited to enter a competition to write a new song for the club. The winner was Mr W M Benfield, who wrote the following words to the tune *Camptown Races*:

Who's the team that plays the best? Pompey! Pompey!
Who's the team to beat the rest? Pompey all the way,
Pompey all the way, Pompey all the way,
We'll cheer our team 'cause they're supreme,
Pompey all the way.

28-YEAR WAIT

Pompey supporters who hoped for a swift return to the First Division after the club was relegated in 1959 would have been very disappointed. It was 28 years before Fratton Park staged Division One football again, and Oxford United and Wimbledon, both non-league clubs at the time Pompey dropped into the Second Division, reached the top flight before Pompey completed their climb back in 1987.

SIX EVER-PRESENTS

Six members of the Pompey side that achieved promotion to the First Division in 1927 played in every match throughout the campaign. They were: George Clifford, Reg Davies, Harry Foxall, Billy Moffat, Billy Haines, and Freddie Cook.

POMPEY'S FIRST MATCH

Pompey's first competitive match was played at Chatham in the Southern League on 2 September 1899. They won the match 1-0, with the goal being credited to Nobby Clarke, although the ball struck a defender before entering the net.

SUBSTITUTE BARTLETT

Two players with the surname Bartlett have appeared in Pompey's league side, but neither started a match. Gordon Bartlett made two appearances as substitute during the 1974/75 season, and Kevin Bartlett (no relation) came off the bench three times in the 1980/81 campaign.

THE POMPEY

The Pompey Shop that stands outside Fratton Park on the corner of Frogmore Road and Carisbrooke Road was for many years a public house called 'The Pompey'. The change from pub to club shop was made in 1988.

BUYING A GOALKEEPER

When Pompey paid £200,000 to Swiss club FC Wil for Mart Poom in 1995, it was the first time in 21 years that the club paid a transfer fee for a goalkeeper. David Best was the last keeper bought by the club, from Ipswich Town for £22,500 in February 1974.

PAUL WELD

At the end of 2011 Portsmouth Football Club bade farewell to its longest serving employee Paul Weld who retired after 38 years with the club. He joined Pompey's administration staff in 1973 having spent two years in the Football Association's accounts department. He was promoted to club secretary in 1989 and held the position until his retirement, working under nineteen different managers. Looking back over his many years at Fratton Park he said, "I have worked with some great people and some not so great but life has never been dull at this football club."

THEY LET THEM GO

Two players who hold all-time goalscoring records for league clubs began their careers with Pompey. Ray Crawford, a Pompey player in the late 1950s, scored 203 league goals in two spells with Ipswich Town, and John Atyeo, who played twice as an amateur during the 1950/51 season, struck 214 times as well as breaking the league appearance record with 597 for Bristol City.

LAST-DAY SURVIVAL

Pompey saved themselves from relegation on the last day of the season three times in six years. In 1996, a Deon Burton goal was enough to earn Pompey, then managed by Terry Fenwick, an away win at Huddersfield Town, and two years later a brace by John Durnin and another from Sammy Igoe gave Alan Ball's team a 3-1 win against Bradford City at Valley Parade. By 2001, Graham Rix was in charge, and a 3-0 win at home to Barnsley, thanks to goals by Lee Bradbury, Gary O'Neil and Kevin Harper, kept them afloat.

BOBBY STOKES

Portsmouth-born Bobby Stokes scored the only goal in the 1976 FA Cup Final as Southampton beat Manchester United at Wembley, but he could well have moved to Fratton Park earlier in the season. It was all set for Pompey's Paul Went to sign for Saints in December 1975, with Stokes coming to Fratton Park as part of the package, but the deal fell through at the last hurdle. Stokes eventually signed for Pompey in August 1977. He died tragically in May 1995, aged 44.

JACK'S FIRST MATCH

Leeds United and England legend Jack Charlton led Middlesbrough to the Second Division championship in 1973/74, his first season as a manager. His first match in charge was against Pompey at Fratton Park on the opening day of the campaign. Boro won 1-0.

SCOULAR WINS THE CUP

Jimmy Scoular was the only member of Pompey's double championship side to win a major honour with another club. He skippered Newcastle United to FA Cup triumph over Manchester City at Wembley in 1955.

GRAHAM IN TWO SWAP DEALS

George Graham left Fratton Park as he arrived – in a straight swap deal. In November 1974, he signed from Manchester United, with Ron Davies moving to Old Trafford, and two years later he was transferred to Crystal Palace in a swap for David Kemp.

HANDSOME GEORGE

In 1968, Pompey full-back George Ley was voted the most handsome footballer in a poll run by the *Football League Review*, a magazine given free with a matchday programme. With one day to go before the final count, Ley and George Best were joint top with 40,179 votes each, and on the last day, three more votes came through the door, all for the Pompey player.

DOWN AND BACK

Peter Ellis was the only player to make Pompey's round trip from the Second Division to the Fourth and back again. Making his league debut in Division Two as an 18-year-old in 1974, he suffered two relegations in 1976 and 1978, but played his part in the Pompey revival that saw them return to Division Three in 1980 and the Second Division in 1983. He stayed with the club for one season in Division Two before joining Southend United.

JIMMY'S RETIREMENT GIFT

Jimmy Dickinson played his 764th and final league match at Northampton on his 40th birthday on 24 April 1965. After the match the Northampton directors presented him with a retirement present – a pair of slippers.

IN THE BASEMENT

Pompey spent two seasons in the Fourth Division. They were relegated to the basement of the Football League in 1978 and, after looking certainties for instant promotion in the first half of the season, they finished in seventh place. The following season they won promotion on the final day, winning 2-0 at Northampton and going up on goal difference.

KEEP IT IN THE FAMILY

In the late 1960s, six former Pompey players held full-time jobs at Fratton Park. Jimmy Dickinson was employed as Public Relations Officer and later secretary – and manager in the 1970s – while his former team-mate of the 1940s and 1950s, Duggie Reid, was the groundsman. Gordon Neave, a former reserve half-back, was head trainer, with Bobby Campbell as his assistant. The others were chief scout Tony Barton, and John McClelland, who worked at the ground as a maintenance man.

FOUR FOR MIDDLETON

Harry Middleton is the only Pompey player to have scored four goals in a League Cup tie. He achieved the feat on 1 November 1961, in a 4-2 second-round replay win at Derby County.

SENIOR SERVICE

Trevor Senior, who scored more than 150 goals in two spells at Reading, began his league career with Pompey. He scored just two goals while at Fratton Park – both against Reading.

EIGHT CONSECUTIVE CLEAN SHEETS

Pompey's longest run of matches without conceding a goal is eight. They began the 1922/23 season with a goalless draw at home to Bristol Rovers, and goalkeeper Tommy Newton was not beaten until the ninth match of the campaign, when Jack Fowler netted at Fratton Park for Plymouth Argyle. The visitors won the match 2-1.

POMPEY'S FIRST CONTINENTAL

Dan Ekner from Sweden was Pompey's first continental player. He came to Portsmouth in 1949 to take up a business studies course, and played five matches as an amateur during Pompey's second League title campaign.

YOUNGEST CAPTAINS

The youngest player to captain Pompey in a senior game was Kit Symons, who was aged 19 when he skippered them in a Zenith Data Systems Cup match against Plymouth Argyle at Home Park. Pompey lost 1-0. The youngest club captain was Paul Cahill, who was aged 21 when he led them throughout the 1976/77 campaign.

JACK TINN

Jack Tinn, at 20 years, is Pompey's longest-serving manager. He didn't play football seriously, but his ability to spot a player with potential was second to none. After working as a senior clerk for the South Shields County Court, he took over as manager of South Shields in 1919. Following Pompey's promotion to Division One in 1927, he succeeded John McCartney, and quickly went about building a side to make an impact in the top league. He acquired the likes of Jack Smith from his old club South Shields, along with Jimmy Nichol, Johnny Weddle, and Jock Gilfillan, and the team reached the FA Cup Final in 1929, only to be beaten 2-0 by Bolton Wanderers. The team was ever improving, and finished fourth in the First Division in 1930/31, even leading the table briefly in September 1932. The club reached Wembley again in 1934, but were beaten on this occasion 2-1 by Manchester City. Tinn gradually rebuilt the side, and they went top of the League in September 1936, remaining there for four months before finally slipping to ninth. It was third time lucky for Pompey when they beat Wolverhampton Wanderers 4-1 in the 1939 FA Cup Final, which is remembered for Jack Tinn's lucky spats. League football was suspended for seven years due to World War II, so what heights Tinn's young team would have reached will never be known. Tinn resigned in 1947 after managing the club throughout the first post-war Football League season, but left a legacy in the shape of players he signed during the war – the likes of Jimmy Dickinson, Peter Harris, Duggie Reid, Jack Froggatt, Len Phillips, and Jimmy Scoular, all of whom would play a major part in Pompey's success story of the late 1940s and early 1950s.

THEOFANIS GEKAS

While it is almost certain that Jimmy Dickinson's record of 764 League appearances for Pompey will never be surpassed it is just as likely that another club appearance "record" – held by Theofanis Gekas – will stand for ever. The Greek striker played a whole one minute of senior football for the club during a loan spell in 2009. He was signed from German club Bayer Leverkusen, in February, by Tony Adams in a loan deal until the end of the season with a view to a permanent move. However, Adams was sacked soon afterwards and the player failed to impress caretaker boss Paul Hart. Gekas eventually made an appearance, replacing Jermaine Pennant in the last minute of Pompey's 2-2 home draw with West Bromwich Albion on 11 April. He returned to Bayer Leverkusen shortly afterwards.

FIRST OFF

The first Pompey player ever to be sent off while playing for the club was Roderick Walker. He received his marching orders in a 2-1 home defeat to Bristol Rovers on 7 January 1905.

EITHER SIDE OF THE WAR

Seven players have represented Pompey before and after World War II. A record of their league appearances and goals is set out below.

	Pre-war		Post-war		Total	
	Apps	Gls	Apps	Gls	Apps	Gls
Bert Barlow	14	5	91	27	105	32
Reg Flewin	1	0	152	0	153	0
Jimmy McAlinden	20	4	33	5	53	9
Cliff Parker	173	50	69	7	242	57
Phil Rookes	5	0	109	0	114	0
Harry Walker	38	0	11	0	49	0
Guy Wharton	66	2	18	1	84	3

PROMOTION – EVENTUALLY

A win at Fratton Park against bottom club Sheffield Wednesday on 12 April 2003 would have clinched promotion to the Premiership. Lee Bradbury's early goal looked to be enough, but 14 minutes from time Ashley Westwood equalised for the Owls. Then, in the second minute of injury time, Michael Reddy slotted home the winning goal, so promotion celebrations were put on hold for three days until a Svetoslav Todorov goal earned Pompey that priceless win at home to Burnley.

MOST CONSECUTIVE LEAGUE APPEARANCES

The longest run of consecutive league appearances by a Pompey player is 185 by Jimmy Dickinson. The run began on 4 February 1961 in a 2-0 defeat at Plymouth Argyle in Division Two, and ended on 19 April 1965 as Pompey defeated Norwich City 4-0 at home in another Second Division fixture. This was Dickinson's final match at Fratton Park before his retirement.

GUTHRIE REUNITED WITH CUP MEDAL

Jimmy Guthrie, who captained Pompey to their 1939 FA Cup Final triumph, was without his winners' medal for 33 years. In 1940, he lent the medal to a sick friend, but never went back to retrieve it, and as time went by they lost touch. For many years the medal was in the possession of Mrs Netta Tilbury, daughter of former Pompey captain and chairman Bob Blyth, who tried in vain to trace Guthrie. However, in 1973, he attended a reunion of former Pompey players, and was presented with the medal in front of some of his former team-mates.

GOING UP

The 1979/80 season saw Pompey climb out of Division Four on goal difference. Promotion looked a certainty early in the season, as the team won ten out of the first 11 games, and continued to win in style, scoring 61 league goals before the turn of the year. They stuttered after Christmas, but a good run of results put them in with a chance as they travelled to Northampton Town on the final day, and a 2-0 Pompey victory, coupled with Bradford City's defeat at Peterborough, put them up on goal difference.

Football League Division Four 1979/80

	Pl	W	D	L	F	A	W	D	L	F	A	Pts
1 Huddersfield Town	46	16	5	2	61	18	11	7	5	40	30	66
2 Walsall	46	12	9	2	43	23	11	9	3	32	24	64
3 Newport County	46	16	5	2	47	22	11	2	10	36	28	61
4 POMPEY	46	15	5	3	62	23	9	7	7	29	26	60
5 Bradford City	46	14	6	3	44	14	10	6	7	33	36	60
6 Wigan Athletic	46	13	5	5	42	26	8	8	7	34	35	55
7 Lincoln City	46	14	8	1	43	12	4	9	10	21	30	53
8 Peterborough	46	14	3	6	39	22	7	7	9	19	25	52
9 Torquay United	46	13	7	3	47	25	2	10	11	23	44	47
10 Aldershot	46	10	7	6	35	23	6	6	11	27	30	45
11 Bournemouth	46	8	9	6	32	25	6	9	9	20	26	44
12 Doncaster Rovers	46	11	6	6	37	27	5	8	11	25	36	44
13 Northampton Town	46	14	5	4	33	16	2	7	14	18	50	44
14 Scunthorpe United	46	11	9	3	37	23	3	6	14	21	52	43
15 Tranmere Rovers	46	10	4	9	32	24	4	9	10	18	32	41
16 Stockport County	46	9	7	7	30	31	5	5	13	18	41	40
17 York City	46	9	6	8	35	35	5	5	13	30	48	39
18 Halifax Town	46	11	9	3	29	20	2	4	17	17	52	39
19 Hartlepool	46	10	7	6	36	28	4	3	16	23	36	38
20 Port Vale	46	8	6	9	34	24	4	6	13	22	46	36
21 Hereford United	46	8	7	8	22	21	3	7	13	16	31	36
22 Darlington	46	7	11	5	33	26	2	6	15	17	48	35
23 Crewe Alexandra	46	10	6	7	25	27	1	7	15	10	41	35
24 Rochdale	46	6	7	10	20	28	1	6	16	13	51	27

NUMBERED SHIRTS

The first time Pompey wore numbered shirts was on 25 March 1939, when they beat Huddersfield Town 2-1 at Highbury in the FA Cup semi-final. The numbering of shirts became official at the beginning of the 1939/40 season, and Pompey wore shirts with numbers for the first time at Fratton Park on 26 August 1939 in a 2-1 win against Blackburn Rovers.

NEARLY A HAT-TRICK FOR GARWOOD

Kevin Dillon is the only player to have scored a hat-trick of penalties for Pompey, but Colin Garwood almost beat him to the record. In a Fourth Division fixture with York City at Fratton Park in September 1979, he converted two penalties as Pompey defeated their opponents 5-2. With six minutes to go, he had the chance to make it a trio of spot-kicks, but visiting goalkeeper Joe Neenan produced a spectacular save to deny him his treble.

MICK BAXTER – A TRAGEDY

Mick Baxter was Alan Ball's first signing when he took over as manager in 1984, but tragically he never played a first-team game. Signed from Middlesbrough to shore up a defence that had conceded 64 goals from 42 league matches the previous season, he played in one pre-season friendly, but complained of feeling unwell during a training session. It was discovered he was suffering from Hodgkin's Disease, and although he remained on the Fratton payroll for some time, his football career had come to an end. He died in 1989, aged 32.

LET'S SHAKE ON IT

On Christmas Day 1957, Pompey's Cyril Rutter ran the length of the field to shake the hand of Chelsea centre-half John Mortimore for scoring an own goal. Rutter had scored in his own net minutes earlier.

DICKINSON REMEMBERED

On 19 July 2006, Alton Town Council honoured the memory of Jimmy Dickinson by unveiling a plaque on the wall of 13 Bow Street, the cottage where he lived as a boy. Dickinson's widow Ann attended the ceremony, along with the couple's son Andrew, daughter-in-law Michelle, and grandsons Edward (9) and Alexander (5), as well as representatives from Portsmouth Football Club.

CHAMPIONSHIP MANAGERS

Ron Saunders and George Graham are the only two former Pompey players to have managed League Championship-winning sides. Saunders achieved the honour with Aston Villa in 1981, and Graham led Arsenal to two titles in 1989 and 1991.

HONOURS WON BY POMPEY

FA Cup 1939, 2008
FA Cup Finalists 1929, 1934, 2010
FA Charity Shield (shared) 1949-50
Western League Champions 1901, 1902, 1903
Southern League Champions..1902, 1920
Southern League Runners-up 1912
Football League Division One Champions 1948/49, 1949/50, 2002/03
Football League Division Two Runners-up................... 1926/27, 1986/87
Football League Division Three Champions 1961/62, 1982/83
Football League Division Three (South) Champions................... 1923/24
Hants Charity Cup Winners..1906, 1907
South Western League Champions 1916
South Hants War League Champions 1918
Pickford Cup Winners 1914, 1915, 1921, 1924, 1926, 1928, 1931-36
Hants Benevolent Cup Winners 1911
Hospital Cup Winners 1924-27, 1929, 1930, 1933-35
Hants Professional Cup Winners..1935, 1982
Hants Professional Cup Runners-up 1983
Hants Combination Cup Winners... 1933, 1941
Hampshire Football Association Benevolent Fund Cup......(shared) 1909
London Combination Winners (reserves)..1936
London Midweek League Champions (reserves) . 1974, 1977, 1983, 1984
London Midweek League Cup Winners (reserves)............................1984
Hants League Champions (reserves)........................ 1903, 1904, 1939-40
Hants League Southern Division Champions (reserves)....................1911
Southern Charity Cup Winners..1903
Southern Charity Cup Runners-up...1909
South Western Combination Champions..1916
Southern Professional Floodlight Cup Winners 1958
Southern Floodlit Combination Cup Winners...................................1958

JOHN MCCARTNEY

John McCartney was Pompey's first manager in the Football League. He arrived immediately after Pompey had won the Southern League championship in 1920, and promised First Division football in six years. It actually took seven but it was still a great achievement. McCartney had played for Manchester United (in the days when they were known as Newton Heath), Luton Town, and Barnsley, with whom he sustained a knee injury and was forced to retire. He spent three seasons as secretary-manager of the Yorkshire club and then took charge at St Mirren for six years. At Fratton Park, he soon introduced what he referred to as "the Pompey style", where teamwork rather than individual brilliance was encouraged. The club won the Division Three (South) championship in 1924, and three years later Pompey were promoted to the First Division. With his dream fulfilled, Mr McCartney resigned on health grounds, and died in 1933.

BOBBY MOORE NEARLY JOINED POMPEY

England's 1966 World Cup-winning captain Bobby Moore was very close to becoming a Pompey player. In 1974, chairman John Deacon was first in the race – long before West Ham officially announced they were to part with their skipper and a fee of £25,000 was agreed. Moore seemed certain to sign, but then Fulham stepped in, and he moved to Craven Cottage.

BARNARD DENIED

Pompey midfielder Leigh Barnard was denied a spectacular first league goal by referee Alan Gunn. In a Fourth Division clash with Crewe Alexandra at Fratton Park in September 1978, Barnard let fly from 25 yards and his shot flew into the top corner and bounced out. As the Pompey players congratulated him, Crewe carried on with the play. Mr Gunn thought Barnard's shot had hit the crossbar.

SPECTACULAR OWN GOAL

In 1976, Pompey tried young centre forward Steve Foster at centre-half in a reserve match as "an experiment". So good were his early displays in the position that he was soon promoted to first-team duty for a Third Division clash at home to Bury. He gave a faultless performance... except that he made a spectacular dive to head the ball clear, and only succeeded in powering it into the top corner past his own goalkeeper.

FASTEST DEBUT GOAL

The fastest goal by a player making his Pompey debut was scored by David Dodson. Three days after signing from Swansea in December 1961, he played at outside-left in a Second Division home fixture against Swindon Town, and headed Pompey into the lead after 19 seconds. The match ended 2-2.

FIRST PREMIERSHIP MATCH

Pompey's first Premiership fixture was at home to Aston Villa on 16 August 2003, and they won the match 2-1. Teddy Sheringham gave Pompey the lead three minutes before half-time, and Patrik Berger added a second on 63 minutes. Gareth Barry pulled a goal back with a disputed penalty six minutes from time, but Pompey held out for a deserved win. The Pompey team was as follows: Shaka Hislop, Boris Zivkovic, Hayden Foxe, Dejan Stefanovic, Arjan De Zeeuw, Steve Stone, Amdy Faye (Sebastien Schemmel), Nigel Quashie, Patrik Berger, Teddy Sheringham, Yakubu Ayegbeni (Vincent Pericard).

NEW STAND

In October 1997, Pompey opened a new stand behind the Fratton goal, known as the KJC Stand. The cost was £2.5m, and the 4,500 seats raised Fratton Park's capacity to 19,000.

UP FOR THE CUP II

FA Cup Final 1934
v Manchester City, 28 April 1934
Wembley Stadium. Attendance 93,258

Five years and one day after losing to Bolton Wanderers, Pompey returned to Wembley to face Manchester City in the FA Cup Final. They took the lead through Sep Rutherford after 27 minutes, but the match turned when centre-half Jimmy Allen was carried off with concussion. Fred Tilson equalised for City, and although Allen returned, he was still dazed, and could do nothing to stop Tilson grabbing the winner for City. **Pompey:** Jock Gilfillan, Alex Mackie, Willie Smith, Jimmy Nichol, Jimmy Allen, Dave Thackeray, Fred Worrall, Jack Smith, Johnny Weddle, Jimmy Easson, Freddie Cook.

LUCKY FIRST FOR HARRIS

Peter Harris is Pompey's record league goalscorer, but he was fortunate with his first goal for the club. Playing in only his second match, against Aldershot in a Wartime League South fixture in 1944, he aimed for the far corner, but the ball sliced off his boot and crept inside the near post.

KELLARD SETS RECORDS

Pompey collected their then-record transfer fee in June 1968, when Bobby Kellard was sold to Bristol City for £35,000, and they paid their then-record fee when they brought him back to Fratton Park from Crystal Palace for £42,000 in December 1972.

TWO FRATTON DEBUTS

Former England captain Gerry Francis made his Football League debut for Queens Park Rangers at Fratton Park in September 1969. He also made his debut for England under-23s at the ground, against Denmark in 1973.

HARRIS KEPT POMPEY UP

A header by Harry Harris on 23 April 1960 kept Pompey in Division Two. He cancelled out a goal by Hull City's Chris Morris in the penultimate match of the season at Fratton Park, and the 1-1 draw meant Pompey stayed up and the Tigers went down.

GREAT START

When Pompey beat Millwall 1-0 at Fratton Park on 14 September 2002, it meant they had made their best start to a season. Seven wins and a draw from eight matches eclipsed the start of 1922/23 and 1948/49. They followed the win over the Lions with a 4-1 victory at home to Wimbledon, but suffered their first defeat of the campaign the following week, losing 1-0 away to Norwich City.

THREE DEBUT SCORERS

On the opening day of the 1982/83 campaign, Pompey beat Sheffield United 4-1, and three Pompey players scored on their debuts. Alan Biley equalised in the first half, and after the break Ernie Howe put Pompey in front, with Neil Webb adding a third. The fourth goal was scored by old-stager Mick Tait.

FATHER CHRISTMAS

In December 1984, Pompey beat Oxford United 2-1 at Fratton Park in a top-of-the-table clash. With time running out and Pompey 1-0 down, a fan dressed as Father Christmas ran onto the pitch, and in the time added on for this incident, Alan Biley headed two goals for the Blues. The victory put Pompey in second place, with Oxford dropping to fourth.

LET'S START WITH A HAT-TRICK

Two Pompey players have scored a hat-trick on the opening day of the season. On 18 August 1962, David Dodson scored three times in a 4-1 home win over Walsall in Division Two, and Guy Whittingham grabbed a hat-trick on 15 August 1992, in a 3-3 draw in a First Division fixture at Bristol City.

STIRRING THE BLOOD

A free day for the players was introduced by George Smith soon after his appointment as manager in 1961. It was designed to enable the individual to develop and improve his own skill, and to practise the aspect of his play that he felt needed extra attention. Thursday was the day for 'stirring the blood', the day the players were extended to the peak of their fitness.

LET'S SWITCH GROUNDS

Requesting to play a home FA Cup tie on the opponent's ground is not a new idea. In 1904, Chesterfield were drawn to play Pompey at their Saltergate home, but chose to play the tie at Fratton Park. The match finished 0-0, and Pompey won the replay 2-0 at Fratton Park four days later.

POMPEY SET GROUND RECORD

Before Scunthorpe United moved to Glanford Park in 1988, their home was the Old Showground. The visit of Pompey in the FA Cup fourth round on 30 January 1954 set a ground record of 23,935 that was never beaten. The match finished 1-1, and Scunthorpe then forced a 2-2 draw at Fratton Park, but Pompey won 4-0 at Highbury in the second replay.

GUNNERS HELD

Arsenal went the entire 2003/04 season without being defeated in the Premiership and beat every team in the division at least once – except Pompey and Manchester United. Pompey could take some pride from the fact that both of their matches against the Gunners – at Highbury and Fratton Park – ended in 1-1 draws.

POMPEY SPOILT THE PARTY

Already certain of winning the 1931/32 First Division title, it was known before kick-off that Everton were to be presented with the Football League Championship trophy immediately after their final match of the season at home to Pompey. But instead of the Toffees finishing the season on a high note, they were beaten 1-0 by Pompey; the goalscorer was Jimmy Easson with a first-half header.

FIRST EVER-PRESENT

The first Pompey player to feature in every match in an entire season was goalkeeper Tom Cope, who played in all 42 Southern League matches and four FA Cup games throughout the entire 1909/10 campaign. Cope almost matched his own record the next season: he missed just one match during the following campaign, but the club finished bottom of the Southern League Division One and were relegated.

FIRST £1M SALE

The first player to leave Pompey for £1m was Mark Hateley in June 1984, when he signed for AC Milan. He had impressed Pompey a year earlier when he played in an England under-21 international at Fratton Park, and they paid Coventry City £190,000 to bring him to the south coast. He played 38 matches in the Second Division side, and topped the goalscoring charts with 22 league goals. After making four appearances for the full England side at the end of the season, it was inevitable that he would join a major club.

SMITH WAS PLAYER-MANAGER

Jim Smith was player-manager of non-league Boston United when Pompey beat them 1-0 in an FA Cup third round tie in January 1972. It was Smith who headed only partially clear after a free kick, and Nick Jennings was on hand to curl in the winner.

A POINT LOST

Pompey found points hard to come by throughout the 1975/76 season, and with a minute to go at Notts County, they thought they had done enough to earn one. But Paul Went was adjudged to have fouled Les Bradd in the penalty area, and John Scanlon buried the spot-kick. There was hardly time to re-start... but Eric Probert still found time to add another goal for Notts County.

IGOE THE SUPER SUB

Sammy Igoe has appeared more times as a substitute for Pompey than any other player. He made his league debut when he came off the bench during the final match of the 1994/95 season, when Pompey drew 1-1 with Oldham Athletic at Fratton Park. His last substitute appearance came on 1 March 2000, in a 2-1 defeat at home to Tranmere Rovers, shortly before his transfer to Reading. This was the 68th time Igoe had played as a substitute.

JUBILEE LIFT-OFF

Pompey's Golden Jubilee season opened with them fighting back from being 2-0 down to draw 2-2 away to Preston North End. Willie Dougal put the home side in front on the stroke of half-time and Tom Finney placed a penalty-kick past Ernie Butler on 53 minutes after he had been tripped by Jimmy Scoular. Duggie Reid headed a goal back from Jack Froggatt's centre before Bert Barlow hit the equaliser on 74 minutes. The Pompey team was: Ernie Butler, Phil Rookes, Harry Ferrier, Jimmy Scoular, Reg Flewin, Jimmy Dickinson, Peter Harris, Duggie Reid, Jack Froggatt, Len Phillips, Bert Barlow. On the same afternoon a crowd of 8,600 saw Pompey Reserves thrash Bristol Rovers 5-0 in the London Combination at Fratton Park. The team was: Charlie Dore, Jasper Yeuell, Ian Drummond, Gordon Neave, Gerry Bowler, Bill Thompson, Tommy Brown, Lindy Delapenha, Albert Juliussen, Johnny Beale, Cliff Parker and the goalscorers were Delapenha (2), Juliussen, Beale and Thompson.

GOING UP II

Pompey ended the 1982/83 season as champions of Division Three after spending seven years in football's lower reaches. They won nine consecutive home matches, and also won a club record seven successive victories. Promotion was clinched as Pompey beat Southend United 2-0 at Fratton Park on 7 May 1983, and the title was won a week later at Plymouth, where an Alan Biley goal was enough to secure victory.

Football League Division Three 1982/83

	Pl	W	D	L	F	A	W	D	L	F	A	Pts
1 POMPEY	46	16	4	3	43	19	11	6	6	31	22	91
2 Cardiff City	46	17	5	1	45	14	8	6	9	31	36	86
3 Huddersfield Town	46	15	8	0	56	18	8	5	10	28	31	82
4 Newport County	46	13	7	3	40	20	10	2	11	36	34	78
5 Oxford United	46	12	9	2	41	23	10	3	10	30	30	78
6 Lincoln City	46	17	1	5	55	22	6	6	11	22	29	76
7 Bristol Rovers	46	16	4	3	55	21	6	5	12	29	37	75
8 Plymouth Argyle	46	15	2	6	37	23	4	6	13	24	43	65
9 Brentford	46	14	4	5	50	28	4	6	13	38	49	64
10 Walsall	46	14	5	4	38	19	3	8	12	26	44	64
11 Sheffield United	46	16	3	4	44	20	3	4	16	18	44	64
12 Bradford City	46	11	7	5	41	27	5	6	12	27	42	61
13 Gillingham	46	12	4	7	37	29	4	9	10	21	30	61
14 Bournemouth	46	11	7	5	35	20	5	6	12	24	48	61
15 Southend United	46	10	8	5	41	28	5	6	12	25	37	59
16 Preston North End	46	11	10	2	35	17	4	3	16	25	52	58
17 Millwall	46	12	7	4	41	24	2	6	15	23	53	55
18 Wigan Athletic	46	10	4	9	35	33	5	5	13	25	39	54
19 Exeter City	46	12	4	7	49	43	2	8	13	32	61	54
20 Orient	46	10	6	7	44	38	5	3	15	20	50	54
21 Reading	46	10	8	5	37	28	1	9	12	27	51	53
22 Wrexham	46	11	6	6	40	26	3	2	13	16	50	51
23 Doncaster	46	6	8	9	38	44	3	9	17	19	53	38
24 Chesterfield	46	6	6	11	28	28	2	7	14	15	40	37

FOUR OR MORE GOALS IN A MATCH

Players who have scored hat-tricks for Pompey are too many to mention, but below is a list of players to have scored four or more goals in a competitive game since Pompey entered the Football League in 1920:

5.... Alf Strange
20/01/1923 5-1 v Gillingham   Division Three (South)
5.... Peter Harris
03/09/1958 5-2 v Aston Villa   Division One
4.... Harry Havelock
20/03/1926 5-1 v Nottingham Forest   Division Two
4.... Billy Haines
07/05/1927 5-1 v Preston North End   Division Two
4.... Peter Harris
09/10/1954 6-2 v Sheffield United   Division One
4.... Harry Middleton
01/11/1961 4-2 v Derby County   LC 2
4.... Ray Hiron
12/04/1969 5-2 v Norwich City   Division Two
4.... Guy Whittingham
26/01/1991 5-1 v Bournemouth   FAC 4
4.... Guy Whittingham
26/12/1992 4-1 v Bristol Rovers   Division One
4.... Yakubu Ayegbeni
15/05/2004 5-1 v Middlesbrough   Premiership

TOP FA CUP GOALSCORER

Peter Harris holds the record for scoring the most goals for Pompey in the FA Cup. He hit 15 goals during a career that spanned 13 years – 1946 to 1959 – his first in the competition coming in a 4-1 win at home to Brighton & Hove Albion in January 1948. His best effort in one season was five in 1948/49, which included a hat-trick at Fratton Park when Pompey thrashed Stockport County 7-0.

LUCKY THIRTEEN

Pompey made it lucky 13 at Selhurst Park on 18 January 1997, when they finally beat Crystal Palace. Since winning 2-0 against Palace, thanks to goals by Ray Hiron and Albert McCann in December 1966, it took Pompey another 31 years and 13 attempts before they repeated the feat. Pompey looked to be heading for another defeat when Robert Quinn put the Eagles ahead on the half-hour mark, but Lee Bradbury equalised and Andy Thomson struck the winner.

TEN MEN HIT BACK

Ten-man Pompey pulled off a remarkable victory at Huddersfield Town on 15 March 1997. David Hillier was sent off midway through the first half and when Marcus Stewart broke the deadlock, things looked grim for Pompey. However three goals in a four-minute spell during the second half handed Pompey three points. Sammy Igoe levelled for the Blues, then Paul Hall scored twice to complete an amazing comeback and 3-1 victory.

MOST GOALS IN A SEASON

The following Pompey players have top scored for another club:

David Crown	Southend United 1985/86	 24
Ralph Hunt	Norwich City 1955/56	 31
Brian Yeo	Gillingham 1973/74	 31

HARRY HARRIS

Harry Harris served Pompey from 1958 to 1971, playing in three divisions as an inside-forward, midfield player and central defender. He began his league career with Newport County, and left the Welsh club for Pompey in July 1958 for a fee of £8,000, plus £2,000 when he had completed 15 appearances. His first season at Fratton Park ended with Pompey losing their First Division status after 32 years, but Harris always played with 100% commitment, and scored 13 goals. He continued to hustle and bustle in Division Two, and his goal against Hull City on the penultimate day of the 1959/60 campaign earned the point that saved the club from a second successive relegation. He later settled into the centre of defence, and was ever-present throughout the 1964/65 campaign. When Jimmy Dickinson retired at the end of the season, Harris took over the club captaincy. In 1970, he rejoined Newport County on loan, making 17 appearances for the Welshmen, but made a sentimental farewell to Hampshire on 1 May 1971, the final day of the 1970/71 season, when, at the age of 37, he captained Pompey in their 2-1 defeat by Second Division champions Leicester City.

FAMILY DAY

Following the success of Ladies' Day at Fratton Park, Jimmy Dickinson, in his role as Public Relations Officer, organised a Family Day in 1966. The club's gymnasium was turned into a children's crèche so that couples could leave the children in the care of Mrs Ann Dickinson and her team of helpers. The Royal Navy supplied the equipment for the children. The day was such a success that the crèche continued for some years.

BEATING THE CHAMPIONS

When Pompey beat Manchester United 1-0 at Fratton Park on 17 April 2004, it was the first occasion they had beaten the reigning Football League champions – coincidentally Manchester United – since 19 October 1957.

19 October 1957 – Manchester United: Ray Wood, Bill Foulkes, Mark Jones, Eddie Colman, Jackie Blanchflower, Wilf McGuinness, Johnny Berry, Liam Whelan, Alex Dawson, Dennis Viollet, David Pegg. **Pompey:** Norman Uprichard, Phil Gunter, Alex Wilson, Bill Albury, Cyril Rutter, Jimmy Dickinson, Peter Harris, Johnny Gordon, Derek Dougan, Jackie Henderson, Ron Newman.

17 April 2004 – Pompey: Shaka Hislop, Linvoy Primus, Arjan De Zeeuw, Dejan Stefanovic, Matt Taylor, Alexei Smertin, Amdy Faye, Steve Stone, Eyal Berkovic (Nigel Quashie), Lomana LuaLua (Teddy Sheringham), Yakubu. **United:** Roy Carroll, Gary Neville, Wes Brown, Mikael Silvestre, John O'Shea (Darren Fletcher), Paul Scholes, Eric Djemba-Djemba (Ronaldo), Nicky Butt (David Bellion), Ole Gunnar Solskjaer, Ryan Giggs, Louis Saha.

Here are the other games in which Pompey got the better of the champions:

17/12/1927	Newcastle United, away	3-1
05/01/1929	Everton, home	3-0
18/04/1934	Arsenal, home	1-0
19/10/1935	Arsenal, home	2-1
22/02/1936	Arsenal, away	3-2
13/03/1937	Sunderland, home	3-2
13/09/1947	Liverpool, home	1-0
31/01/1948	Liverpool, away	3-0
27/11/1948	Arsenal, home	4-1
24/11/1951	Tottenham Hotspur, home	2-0
06/09/1952	Manchester United, home	2-0
03/09/1955	Chelsea, away	5-1

LAST 40,000 GATE

The last time Fratton Park housed a 40,000-plus gate for a League match was on 23 August 1958, when West Ham United were the visitors on the opening day of the season. The crowd of 40,470 saw the Hammers celebrate their return to the First Division after a period of 26 years by beating Pompey 2-1. Vic Keeble and Johnny Dick gave the Londoners a 2-0 lead before Peter Harris pulled a goal back for Pompey.

TWO JOHN MCLAUGHLINS

Two men with the name John McLaughlin have played for Pompey. The first was a midfield player who played five games on loan from Liverpool during the 1975/76 season. The second John McLaughlin was from Swindon Town, and he made 179 league and cup appearances – all in the right-back position – between 1979 and 1984.

SHEARER BREAKS TOON RECORD

Alan Shearer broke Newcastle United's all-time goalscoring record in a Premiership fixture against Pompey at St James' Park on 4 February 2006. He scored the Magpies' second goal in the 64th minute of their 2-0 win.

O'NEIL'S THE YOUNGEST

Gary O'Neil became the youngest player to play for Pompey when he appeared as substitute in a First Division match against Barnsley on 29 January 2000. He was aged 16 years 256 days, beating the record previously held by Andy Awford, who was 16 years 275 days when he made his debut away to Crystal Palace on 15 April 1989.

FRATTON FACELIFT

Almost immediately after Jim Gregory took charge of the club in 1988, work began to revamp Fratton Park. The top tier of the Fratton Stand came down, and the cladding on the North and South stands was replaced, while a new boardroom and dressing rooms were constructed. The contractors faced a tight deadline, having to complete the work by the start of the season, and they almost managed it. There was still work to be done on the South Stand when Leicester City visited Fratton Park on 29 August, so only part of the stand was open to the public.

BAD BAIRD

Ian Baird is the only player to be sent off at Fratton Park both for and against Pompey. He was ordered off against Charlton Athletic in September 1987 soon after his transfer from Leeds United, and in September 1988, while playing for Leeds in his second spell with them, he was once again sent to the dressing-room.

MOST GOALS CONCEDED

The most goals Pompey have conceded in one season is 112 in 1958/59. Not surprisingly, the season ended in relegation from the First Division.

GOING UP III

Pompey finally returned to the First Division in 1987 after 28 years. They were unbeaten at home until 20 April when Plymouth Argyle won 1-0. Alan Knight and Kenny Swain were the only two ever-presents, and Mick Quinn was the leading goalscorer with 22 league goals. The average home league attendance was 13,401.

Football League Division Two 1986/87

	Pl	W	D	L	F	A	W	D	L	F	A	Pts
1 Derby County	42	14	6	1	42	18	11	3	7	22	20	84
2 POMPEY	42	17	2	2	37	11	6	7	8	16	17	78
3 Oldham Athletic	42	13	6	2	36	16	9	3	9	29	28	75
4 Leeds United	42	15	4	2	43	16	4	7	10	15	28	68
5 Ipswich Town	42	12	6	3	29	10	5	7	9	30	33	64
6 Crystal Palace	42	12	4	5	35	20	7	5	13	16	33	62
7 Plymouth Argyle	42	12	6	3	40	23	4	7	10	22	34	61
8 Stoke City	42	11	5	5	40	21	5	5	11	23	32	58
9 Sheffield United	42	10	8	3	31	19	5	5	11	19	30	58
10 Bradford City	42	10	5	6	36	27	5	5	11	26	35	55
11 Barnsley	42	8	7	6	26	23	6	6	9	23	29	55
12 Blackburn Rovers	42	11	4	6	30	22	4	6	11	15	33	55
13 Reading	42	11	4	6	33	23	3	7	11	19	36	53
14 Hull City	42	10	6	5	25	22	3	8	10	16	33	53
15 West Bromwich Albion	42	8	6	7	29	22	5	6	10	22	27	51
16 Millwall	42	10	5	6	27	16	4	4	13	12	29	51
17 Huddersfield Town	42	9	6	6	38	30	4	6	11	16	31	51
18 Shrewsbury Town	42	11	3	7	24	14	4	3	14	17	39	51
19 Birmingham City	42	8	9	4	27	21	3	8	10	20	38	50
20 Sunderland	42	8	6	7	25	23	4	6	11	24	36	48
21 Grimsby Town	42	5	8	8	18	21	5	6	10	21	38	44
22 Brighton & Hove A	42	7	6	8	22	20	2	6	13	15	34	39

WARTIME SCORELINES

Pompey's biggest victory during World War 2 was 16-1 at home to Clapton Orient on 28 February 1943. Andy Black scored eight of the goals. Other big victories during the war were:

25/01/1941 .... Pompey 10 Bournemouth 2
08/03/1941 .... Pompey 9 Luton Town 2
10/05/1941 .... Pompey 10 Aldershot 2
21/03/1942 .... Pompey 9 Fulham 1
26/12/1945 .... Pompey 9 Crystal Palace 1

DEBUT HAT-TRICK

No Pompey man has managed to score a hat-trick on his debut, but an opposing player achieved the feat. On 25 March 1967, 19-year-old Colin Viljoen scored three times for Ipswich Town in their 4-2 win over Pompey in a Second Division clash at Portman Road.

JOE FAGAN GUESTED FOR POMPEY

Joe Fagan, who managed Liverpool from 1983 to 1985, once guested for Pompey during World War II. While on Manchester City's books, he played at centre-half in the game against Clapton Orient at Brisbane Road in a League South fixture that Pompey lost 3-2.

GORDON – THE FIRST PRODIGAL SON

Johnny Gordon was the first Pompey player to return to the club after being transferred. He left for Birmingham City for £15,000 in September 1958 after making 220 appearances for Pompey. He scored 40 goals in 115 appearances for Birmingham City, and when Pompey made it clear in March 1961 they wanted him to return, he turned down offers from Stoke City and Blackpool to come back to Fratton Park. The team were on the brink of relegation to Division Three, but the following year he helped them to the Third Division title in his first full season back with his local club. He clocked up 266 appearances in his second spell with the club, and decided to quit the professional game when he was released in 1967 at the age of 35.

FIRST INTERNATIONALS

The match between Ireland and England in Dublin on 17 March 1900 included Pompey's first internationals. Danny Cunliffe turned out at inside-right for England, and Matt Reilly kept goal for Ireland, who won 2-0.

PARKER MAKES 'EM

Veteran outside-left Cliff Parker was recalled to the Pompey side for the FA Cup fourth round tie against Grimsby Town at Fratton Park in 1950. Pompey won 5-0 and Parker set up four of the goals.

DEATH OF 'BEDDY'

One of Pompey's earliest star players died under tragic circumstances. Centre-forward Frank Bedingfield, affectionately known as Beddy, had been under medical treatment prior to Pompey's FA Cup third round tie at Reading in February 1902, but that didn't stop him from declaring himself fit to play. He collapsed in the dressing-room after scoring the only goal in the match, and consumption was diagnosed. A public fund raised £500 to send him to South Africa in the hope that he would recover, but tragically he died there in 1904 at the age of 27.

FA CUP WIN AT LAST

When Pompey defeated London Caledonians 5-1 in the FA Cup first round in December 1923, it was the first time they'd won a match in the competition since Bristol Rovers were beaten 2-1 in January 1912.

WHEN POMPEY OUT-SANG THE KOP

Around 12,000 Pompey fans travelled to Anfield on 28 October 1980 to watch the team take on Liverpool in the fourth round of the Football League Cup. They out-sang the famous Liverpool Kop choir throughout the match as Pompey, then a Third Division side, produced a memorable performance. Kenny Dalglish gave Liverpool the lead on 22 minutes, but Alan Kennedy then put through his own goal 14 minutes later for the equaliser. David Johnson gave Liverpool a 2-1 half-time lead and Pompey spent all the second half going for an equaliser, only for Johnson to score Liverpool's third with just ten minutes to play. Graeme Souness volleyed home the fourth in the last minute.

POMPEY'S FIRST MATCH IN EUROPE

Pompey's first European match took place in November 1992. Over 250 fans travelled to Italy to see the 3-0 Anglo-Italian Cup defeat to Bari. The San Nicola Stadium held 60,000 but there were only 837 at the game.

HAVING A LAUGH

Pompey manager Jack Tinn was eager that his players be relaxed before the 1939 FA Cup Final with Wolverhampton Wanderers, so he invited comedian Albert Burden to entertain the players in the dressing-room.

GOING DOWN IV

Pompey's first campaign back in the First Division, in 1987/88, ended in relegation. Only one point from the first four matches, including a 6-0 thrashing at Arsenal, was not the best start, and by Christmas, a return to the Second Division looked inevitable. A five-match unbeaten run, beginning with a 2-0 win over Southampton at The Dell, lifted them up the table, but after losing 2-0 at home to Liverpool at the end of February, they slipped back into the relegation mire, and their fate was finally sealed away at Coventry City where a disputed penalty, converted by Brian Kilcline, consigned them to the drop.

Football League Division One 1987/88

	Pl	W	D	L	F	A	W	D	L	F	A	Pts
1 Liverpool	40	15	5	0	49	9	11	7	2	38	15	90
2 Manchester United	40	14	5	1	41	17	9	7	4	30	21	81
3 Nottingham Forest	40	11	7	2	40	17	9	6	5	27	22	73
4 Everton	40	14	4	2	34	11	5	9	6	19	16	70
5 Queens Park Rangers	40	12	4	4	30	14	7	6	7	18	24	67
6 Arsenal	40	11	4	5	35	16	7	8	5	23	23	66
7 Wimbledon	40	8	9	3	32	20	6	6	8	26	27	57
8 Newcastle United	40	9	6	5	32	23	5	8	7	23	30	56
9 Luton Town	40	11	6	3	40	21	3	5	12	17	37	53
10 Coventry City	40	6	8	6	23	25	7	6	7	23	28	53
11 Sheffield Wednesday	40	10	2	8	27	30	5	6	9	25	36	53
12 Southampton	40	6	8	6	27	26	6	6	8	22	27	50
13 Tottenham Hotspur	40	9	5	6	26	23	3	6	11	12	25	47
14 Norwich City	40	7	5	8	26	26	5	4	11	14	26	45
15 Derby County	40	6	7	7	18	17	4	6	10	17	28	43
16 West Ham United	40	6	9	5	23	21	3	6	11	17	31	42
17 Charlton Athletic	40	7	7	6	23	21	2	8	10	15	31	42
18 Chelsea	40	7	11	2	24	17	2	4	14	26	51	42
19 POMPEY	40	4	8	8	21	27	3	6	11	15	39	35
20 Watford	40	4	5	11	15	24	3	6	11	12	27	32
21 Oxford United	40	5	7	8	24	34	1	6	13	20	46	31

MR PORTSMOUTH FOOTBALL CLUB

Pompey fanatic John Anthony Westwood is one of the club's best known supporters. In 1989 he changed his name to John Anthony Portsmouth Football Club Westwood.

SQUAD NUMBER RETIRED

Before the start of the 2001/02 season, Aaron Flahavan was given number one as his squad number. After he was killed in a car accident a week before the season began, the club retired the squad number in his memory.

TOP-FLIGHT LOWEST

The smallest number to attend Fratton Park for a post-war top-flight game is 12,391. This was for the visit of Luton Town on 10 October 1987. Two goals by Kevin Dillon – one a penalty – and a header by Paul Mariner helped Alan Ball's side to a 3-1 victory.

POMPEY'S SCHOOLBOY

Pat Neil played nine matches in Pompey's First Division side in 1956 while he was still at school. Aged 17, he was a student at Portsmouth Northern Grammar School, and with no reserve-team experience was drafted into the first team for the season's opening fixture at Huddersfield Town. He played a further eight games, scoring three goals, before being given a well-deserved rest and put in the reserve side.

CUP SHOCK

Pompey produced an FA Cup shock on 15 February 1997, when they beat Premiership Leeds United 3-2 at Elland Road in the fifth round. Alan McLoughlin put Pompey ahead, Lee Bowyer equalised, and Matt Svensson and Lee Bradbury wrapped it up for Pompey. Bowyer struck a second Leeds goal in the dying seconds.

FLOODLIGHT BREAKTHROUGH

Pompey made history on 7 January 1956 when they played a third round FA Cup tie under floodlights at Fratton Park, beating Grimsby Town 3-1. Four other ties were played under lights that day – the first time the FA had permitted artificial lights at that stage of the competition. A few weeks later, on 22 February, Pompey were the first club to stage a league match under floodlights, when Newcastle United came to Fratton Park and won 2-0.

SEMI-FINAL HEARTACHE

The most shattering blow during Pompey's League Championship-winning season of 1948/49 was undoubtedly the FA Cup semi-final defeat by Leicester City at Highbury. Pompey were almost home and dry as champions, and they only had to beat Leicester City – a struggling Second Division club – to reach Wembley, and possibly be the first club of the 20th century to win the League and Cup double. Pompey started the game well, but fell behind to a Don Revie goal after 15 minutes. Peter Harris levelled for Pompey, but Ken Chisholm netted a second goal for Leicester before half-time. It was clearly not Pompey's day – Harris missed a sitter from six yards, and the match was wrapped up for Leicester when Revie scored a third.

WEAKENED SIDE WINS 5-1

Pompey fielded a much-weakened side, making seven changes, for a League Cup second round tie away to Brighton and Hove Albion in September 1962, but won 5-1. The team was: John Milkins, Phil Gunter, Alfie Noakes, Bobby Campbell, Brian Snowdon, Harry Harris, Tony Barton, Keith Blackburn, Ron Saunders, Roy Smith, David Dodson. The Pompey goalscorers were Ron Saunders (3), and Roy Smith (2).

MOST CONSECUTIVE INTERNATIONALS

The most consecutive international appearances made by a Pompey player is 25 by Jimmy Dickinson. He began the run by playing in a 1-1 draw in Cardiff against Wales on 20 October 1951, and appeared in his 25th consecutive international match when England were beaten 4-2 by Uruguay in the 1954 World Cup.

TREBS' EARLY GAMES

Record signing Mike Trebilcock made his Pompey debut away to Rotherham United in February 1968. Albert McCann followed up to score after Trebilcock's shot hit the crossbar. Three minutes into his home debut, Trebilcock scored against Derby County in a 3-2 victory.

FIRST WIN AT MOLINEUX

Molineux has not been the happiest of venues for Pompey, but they enjoyed their first visit there in February 1925. They beat Wolverhampton Wanderers 5-0, with Billy Haines scoring a hat-trick in the last six minutes. This created an away record for the club, and the five-goal margin has still never been bettered in an away fixture.

MCLOUGHLIN THE IRISH HERO

Alan McLoughlin scored the goal that put the Republic of Ireland in the 1994 World Cup finals. Six minutes after coming on as substitute against Northern Ireland at Windsor Park, with the Republic 1-0 down, he sent a curling shot into the net to send his national side to the USA.

STARTING EARLY

John Milkins was always going to be a goalkeeper. When he was five years old, his father put up two posts and a rope crossbar on a plot of land next to the family home in Dagenham, Essex.

THREE ON ONE DAY

In January 2006, Pompey signed three players from one club on the same day. Pedro Mendes, Sean Davis, and Noe Pamarot joined from Tottenham Hotspur for a combined fee of £7.5m.

POMPEY'S WAR HERO

Tommy Rowe, who died on 8 May 2006 aged 92, was the last surviving member of Pompey's 1939 FA Cup-winning team. He played in the final at centre-half, a position he had made his own since September 1937. When war broke out in 1939, Rowe volunteered to join the Portsmouth City Police, and two years later, became a Royal Air Force bomber pilot. In 1943, he was awarded the Distinguished Flying Cross, and in March 1944, on his 40th mission over Germany, his plane was shot down. He parachuted to relative safety north of Frankfurt, but was a prisoner of war until hostilities ceased. He returned to captain Dorchester, and became their manager in 1953 after a fractured skull ended his playing days.

GAYDAMAK CHEERS PUPILS

A Portsmouth school party were turned away from the Czech Republic v Ghana game in the 2006 World Cup because they fell victim to a ticket scam. When Pompey's joint-owner Sacha Gaydamak heard of their plight, he arranged for tickets to be made available for a new match and paid for their flights to Germany.

FA CUP SUPER SUB

Nicky Morgan was the first Pompey substitute to score a goal in the FA Cup. His effort gave Pompey a 2-1 win at home to Grimsby Town in the third round in January 1984.

RECORD FEE FOR DALE

In July 1951, Pompey paid Chesterfield a £20,000 fee for outside-left Gordon Dale – a record at the time for both clubs. Dale only played in eight matches during his first season at the club because of a series of niggling injuries. It was not until the 1954/55 campaign that he played in more than half the team's league fixtures. During his time at Fratton Park he gave both pleasure and frustration, for he had an extremely individualistic style which supporters either loved or hated. He appeared to adopt a lazy approach, but this was his most dangerous weapon – he would suddenly burst into action, use great ball control, produce a body swerve, and deliver a telling cross. On his day, he was as good as any player in his position in the country, but he couldn't always produce this magical form, and spent a lot of time in the reserves. His presence would put hundreds, if not thousands, on the reserve attendances. In October 1957, he was transferred to Exeter City.

HALL'S LAST MATCH

On 21 March 1959, Pompey drew 1-1 at home to Birmingham City – but the visitors' defender Jeff Hall was unknowingly playing his last match. Three days later, Hall was taken critically ill, and died on Saturday 4 April. A minute's silence for the player was held at Fratton Park that afternoon before the First Division match between Pompey and Preston North End.

HIGHEST SOUTHERN LEAGUE ATTENDANCE

The highest attendance at Fratton Park for a Southern League game was the 24,606 people who attended on 3 April 1920. The match with Cardiff City ended in a goalless draw.

FIRST LEAGUE CUP TIE

Pompey won their first League Cup tie 2-0 at home to Coventry City on 2 November 1960. The new competition provided some teething problems, as Coventry wanted the match played on a Monday or Tuesday, while Pompey insisted it must be on a Wednesday, as that was early closing day in the city. It was up to clubs to agree between themselves, but in this case the Football League Management Committee intervened, and came down in favour of the home team. A crowd of 5,523 attended the game, and Tony Priscott scored the first goal after three minutes. Ron Saunders netted Pompey's second goal. The Pompey team was: Dick Beattie, Cyril Rutter, Jimmy Dickinson, Ron Howells, Phil Gunter, Harry Harris, Tony Priscott, Ron Saunders, Jimmy White, Sammy Chapman, Ron Newman.

LAST DAY ESCAPE IV

6 May 2001, Division One, Pompey 3 Barnsley 0

Pompey escaped relegation to Division Two on the last day of the season with an easy victory over Barnsley before a crowd of 17,064. Kevin Miller made a superb save from Lee Bradbury before the striker hammered a close-range shot into the roof of the net on 17 minutes to put Pompey ahead. Steve Lovell should have doubled the lead, but after rounding Miller, he shot wide of the far post. In the 62nd minute, Gary O'Neill grabbed his first senior goal, tapping in a cross from Kevin Harper. Harper then sealed the win, crashing Lovell's cross into the top corner. There was an anxious wait after the final whistle, as fans listened to their radios for results of other matches involved in the relegation issue, but Fratton Park erupted as soon as it was known that Pompey were safe. **Pompey**: Aaron Flahavan, Scott Hiley, Jamie Vincent, Linvoy Primus, Carl Tiler, Gary O'Neil, Garry Brady, Lee Sharpe, Kevin Harper, Steve Lovell, Lee Bradbury.

PROUD CUP DISPLAYS

The 1975/76 season saw Pompey finish bottom in Division Two. Their league form was appalling, but they fared well against First Division sides in both cup competitions. They held Leicester City to a 1-1 draw in the first leg of a second round League Cup tie, only to lose to a single goal in the last minute of extra time in the second leg at Filbert Street. In the FA Cup, they beat Birmingham City 1-0 in a third round replay at St Andrew's after drawing 1-1 at Fratton Park.

PEACEFUL PROTEST

In December 1998, Pompey fans invaded the Fratton Park pitch during the interval of the match with Grimsby Town to protest against chairman Martin Gregory in front of the Sky TV cameras. Grimsby won the match 1-0.

POMPEY'S FIRST LEAGUE MATCH

Pompey won their first Football League match 3-0 at home to Swansea Town in Division Three (South). Frank Stringfellow was captain, in the absence of A.E. Knight. Billy James, Stringfellow and Billy Reid got the goals. **Pompey**: Ned Robson, Bill Probert, Joe Potts, Shirley Abbott, Jack Harwood, Joe Turner, Ernie Thompson, Frank Stringfellow, Billy Reid, Billy James, Willie Beedie.

TOO BULKY

In 2007 Pompey defender Hermann Hreidarsson was named Iceland's Player of the Year. His prize for winning the award was an encyclopaedia of Icelandic grammar but it was too bulky for him to bring back to England.

ALL IN THE RESERVES

Following a bad display against Carlisle United at Fratton Park in a Third Division fixture – Pompey lost 2-1 – manager Frank Burrows put the entire first team in the reserves. Whatever the idea was, it failed, because they could only draw 0-0 against an Exeter City reserve side that included five apprentices. The Pompey team was: Alan Knight, John McLaughlin, Steve Bryant, Bobby Doyle, Steve Aizlewood (Peter Ellis), Andy Rollings, Jeff Hemmerman, Steve Berry, Billy Rafferty, Alex Cropley (Alan Rogers), David Crown.

GREAVES RECORD BROKEN

Alan Shearer, at 17 years 220 days, now holds the record as the youngest player to score a hat-trick in the top flight. It was previously set by Jimmy Greaves, who scored three times for Chelsea in their 7-4 victory over Pompey at Stamford Bridge on Christmas Day 1957. He was then 17 years 308 days.

TOP OF THE PREMIERSHIP

Pompey went top of the table in August 2003, only three matches after reaching the Premiership. A year to the day since beating Grimsby Town 1-0 to go top of Division One, a win over Bolton Wanderers at Fratton Park would have put Pompey fourth, but a four-goal victory was required to take them to top spot. Goalless at half-time, Steve Stone opened the scoring before Teddy Sheringham's thundering header rounded off a magnificent move. With two minutes to go, Sheringham scored again, and suddenly Pompey were in touching distance of going top of the pile for the first time since January 1952. In the last minute, substitute Vincent Pericard was brought down in the box, and Sheringham completed his hat-trick from the spot.

FIRST HAT-TRICK IN DIVISION ONE

Jack Smith was the first Pompey player to score a hat-trick in the First Division. He achieved the feat on 18 February 1928 against Sunderland at Fratton Park. However, he was not the highest scoring player on the field that day. David Halliday scored four goals for Sunderland, who won 5-3.

ST JOHN PLAYED FOR SCOTLAND

Ian St John is the only Pompey manager to have played international football for a country other than England. He won 21 Scotland caps and scored nine goals between 1959 and 1965, while his assistant manager at Fratton Park, Billy Hunter, represented the Scots on three occasions.

UP FOR THE CUP III

FA Cup Final
v Wolverhampton Wanderers. 29 April 1939
Wembley Stadium. Attendance 99,570

Pompey won the FA Cup by beating favourites Wolves 4-1 at Wembley. Nearly all the play took place in the Wolves half in the first ten minutes and Pompey had a strong appeal for a penalty turned down. After 20 minutes, Pompey's Harry Walker turned a left-foot drive from Dickie Dorsett round the post but this was Wolves' only goalscoring effort up to that time. In the 31st minute Jock Anderson beat Stan Cullis to the ball and nodded it to Bert Barlow who beat Bob Scott with a fine shot. A minute before the interval Pompey skipper Jimmy Guthrie lobbed the ball into the centre and Anderson curled a shot just out of Scott's reach. Within a minute of the second half, Cliff Parker turned the ball back to Barlow who drove in a terrific shot. Scott dived full length to save but Parker followed up to score. Wolves hit back and after two fierce raids Dorsett reduced the deficit with a shot from close range. Fred Worrall set up Pompey's fourth goal for Parker to head home in the 72nd minute. After the match, Guthrie received the Cup from King George VI. The team travelled back to Portsmouth the same evening and on their arrival in the city, were met by thousands of jubilant fans. **Pompey**: Harry Walker, Lew Morgan, Bill Rochford, Jimmy Guthrie, Tommy Rowe, Guy Wharton, Fred Worrall, Jimmy McAlinden, Jock Anderson, Bert Barlow, Cliff Parker.

POMPEY FINED

In February 2002, Pompey were fined £10,000 for receiving 15 bookings in less than a month.

TWELVE POINT LEAD

On 24 March 1962, Pompey opened up a 12-point lead over second-placed Bournemouth at the top of the Third Division. It was just as well, as they only managed to pick up one point in the next five matches. Promotion was assured on Easter Monday, when Ron Saunders scored twice at Fratton Park in a 2-1 win over Watford.

GREGORY FINED AND BANNED

Former Pompey manager John Gregory was fined £7,500, as well as receiving a five-match touchline ban, for abusing the referee in a First Division game at Fratton Park while manager of Derby County in February 2003. His old club beat the Rams 6-2.

ALF STRANGE

Alf Strange was the first of only two players – Peter Harris being the other – to score five goals in a match for Pompey. He had not been a great success at centre-forward prior to his fantastic five-goal feat in January 1923, and the majority of supporters wanted him to be dropped for the visit of Gillingham in a Third Division (South) fixture. However, Strange responded by scoring a first-half hat-trick, and then added two more goals after the half-time interval. In November 1925, he was transferred to Port Vale, and it was at Vale Park that a switch of positions dramatically changed his career. He moved to right-half, and was soon snapped up by Sheffield Wednesday. He won two League Championships, in 1929 and 1930, while at Hillsborough, and was capped 20 times for England.

FIRST GOAL CONCEDED

When Bobby Barclay put Huddersfield Town ahead against Pompey in the 1939 FA Cup semi-final at Highbury, it was the first goal Pompey had conceded in that year's competition.

GORDON'S HAT-TRICK

Johnny Gordon scored over 100 goals in two spells with Pompey, but only managed one hat-trick. It came against Sheffield Wednesday at Hillsborough on 24 October 1953, and helped Pompey to a 4-4 draw. His first goal brought Pompey level at 2-2, and then, with his side 4-2 behind, he struck twice in the last 15 minutes.

RELIEF ON CENTENARY DAY

Pompey met Birmingham City on 4 April 1998 in Division One, 100 years all but one day since the formation of the club. Many former players were invited, and the match was a vital one, since Pompey were on the brink of relegation to the Second Division. A defeat looked certain when Dele Adebola gave the visitors an 87th-minute 1-0 lead, but Pompey defender Andy Thomson popped up in the last minute to stab home the equaliser.

TOP OF THE TABLE

Pompey went top of the First Division in September 1936 following a 2-1 win at home to Manchester City. They held the position for two months, dropping to second after a 4-0 defeat by Everton at Goodison Park on 21 November. A 1-1 draw at home to Bolton Wanderers put them back on top, but another 4-0 reverse, at Brentford the following week, saw them slip to third. They finished the season in ninth place, and didn't reach top spot again until 4 September 1948, when a Peter Harris goal earned a 1-0 victory away to Stoke City.

CLIFF PARKER

Cliff Parker starred for Pompey either side of the war. He joined Pompey from Doncaster Rovers in December 1933 and, once established in the Pompey line-up, he hardly missed a game until the outbreak of war. He was a wonderful crosser of the ball, and it was said he was capable of dropping a ball on a sixpence. A gentleman off the field, he was totally fearless on it and was often in trouble of his own making. This may be why international honours passed him by. His greatest moment came in 1939, when he scored twice at Wembley as Pompey beat Wolverhampton Wanderers 4-1 in the FA Cup Final. He was still a fixture in the side during the first post-war season of 1946/47, and he made a valuable contribution to the double League Championship success of 1948/49 and 1949/50, continuing to be a member of the playing staff until 1953, when he was appointed chief scout. In May 1954, he became assistant trainer and continued in the role until 1957.

GREGORY OUT PROTEST

About 20 Pompey supporters demonstrated outside Martin Gregory's home in December 1998, the last month of the club's centenary year. The protestors took with them a letter from the Independent Supporters' Club to Gregory. It criticised the handling of the latest financial crisis and urged him to leave. One banner said, "Proud Pompey, 100 years old and dying courtesy of Mr Gregory."

CHERRETT'S DEBUT GOAL

Percy Cherrett was transferred from Pompey to Plymouth Argyle on 28 August 1923, and scored on his debut against his old team-mates in a Third Division (South) fixture at Home Park.

LONG-AWAITED VICTORIES

Below is a list of teams over whom an away win is long overdue (as at 31st December 2014) – along with the result and date of Pompey's last away victory over those clubs.

05/11/1955 ...... 3-1 v Sheffield United .... Division One
17/09/1955 ...... 3-1 v Arsenal .... Division One
03/09/1955 ...... 5-1 v Chelsea .... Division One
02/09/1961 ...... 1-0 v Queens Park Rangers......... Division Three

TIP FOR THE TELEGRAM BOY

In 1949, 15-year-old John Wearne delivered a telegram telling Jack Froggatt he had been picked for England. The surprised Froggatt gave the boy two shillings (10p).

UP TO THE PREMIERSHIP

Pompey won the First Division title in 2002/03. They began with a 2-0 home win over Nottingham Forest, went top on 26 August following a 1-0 victory at Grimsby Town, and never looked back. Skippered by Paul Merson, the team broke three club records and equalled another. They scored 97 goals, collected 98 points, and won 29 matches. They also equalled the club record of 11 away victories. Promotion was secured with a 1-0 victory at home to Burnley, and they made certain of the title by beating Rotherham United 3-2 at Fratton Park.

Football League Division One 2002/03

	Pl	W	D	L	F	A	W	D	L	F	A	Pts
1 POMPEY	46	17	3	3	52	22	12	8	3	45	23	98
2 Leicester City	46	16	5	2	40	12	10	9	4	33	28	92
3 Sheffield United	46	13	7	3	38	23	10	4	9	34	29	80
4 Reading	46	13	3	7	33	21	12	1	10	28	25	79
5 Wolverhampton W.	46	9	10	4	40	19	11	6	6	41	25	76
6 Nottingham F.	46	14	7	2	57	23	6	7	10	25	27	74
7 Ipswich Town	46	10	5	8	49	31	9	8	6	31	25	70
8 Norwich City	46	14	4	5	36	17	5	8	10	24	32	69
9 Millwall	46	11	6	6	34	32	8	3	12	25	37	66
10 Wimbledon	46	12	5	6	39	28	6	6	11	37	45	65
11 Gillingham	46	10	6	7	33	31	6	8	9	23	34	62
12 Preston North End	46	11	7	5	44	29	5	6	12	24	41	61
13 Watford	46	11	5	7	33	26	6	4	13	21	44	60
14 Crystal Palace	46	8	10	5	29	17	6	7	10	30	35	59
15 Rotherham United	46	8	9	6	27	25	7	5	11	35	37	59
16 Burnley	46	10	4	9	35	44	5	6	12	30	45	55
17 Walsall	46	10	3	10	34	34	5	6	12	23	35	54
18 Derby County	46	9	5	9	33	32	6	2	15	22	42	52
19 Bradford City	46	7	8	8	27	35	7	2	14	24	38	52
20 Coventry City	46	6	6	11	23	31	6	8	9	23	31	50
21 Stoke City	46	9	6	8	25	25	3	8	12	20	25	50
22 Sheffield Wednesday	46	7	7	9	29	25	3	9	11	27	48	46
23 Brighton	46	7	6	10	29	31	4	6	13	20	36	45
24 Grimsby Town	46	5	6	12	26	39	4	6	13	22	46	39